Human Development

This new edition of *Human Development* has been thoroughly revised and updated to incorporate recent developments in the field. New material is introduced on the development of a sense of self, the social self and moral development.

Beginning with a discussion of birth and childhood, the reader is led through each of the crucial stages in human development, through adolescence, parenthood, mid-life and old age to dying, grief and mourning. A range of theoretical perspectives are represented, including psychoanalysis and developmental psychology. Throughout, the authors manage to combine scientific objectivity with a sensitive and sympathetic approach to the subject.

This comprehensive introduction will prove invaluable to students of the helping professions.

Eric Rayner is a retired psychoanalyst, formerly in private practice, and a training analyst at the British Institute of Psychoanalysis.

Angela Joyce is an adult and child psychoanalyst and a parent–infant psychotherapist at the Anna Freud Centre.

James Rose is a psychoanalyst in private practice and is a senior psychotherapist at the Brandon Centre for Counselling and Psychotherapy for Young People, Kentish Town, London.

Mary Twyman is a psychoanalyst in private practice.

Christopher Clulow is Director of the Tavistock Centre for Couple Relationships.

Human Development

An introduction to the
psychodynamics of growth,
maturity and ageing

Fourth Edition

Eric Rayner, Angela Joyce,
James Rose, Mary Twyman &
Christopher Clulow

 Routledge
Taylor & Francis Group

LONDON AND NEW YORK

First published 1971 by Unwin Hyman Ltd

Fourth Edition published 2005 by Routledge
27 Church Road, Hove, East Sussex, BN3 2FA

Simultaneously published in the USA and Canada
by Routledge
711 Third Avenue, New York NY 10017

Routledge is an imprint of the Taylor & Francis Group, an Informa business

Typeset in Times by Garfield Morgan, Rhayader, Powys

British Library Cataloguing in Publication Data
A catalogue record for this book is available from the British Library

Library of Congress Cataloging in Publication Data
Human development: an introduction to the psychodynamics of growth,
maturity, and ageing / Eric Rayner ... [et al.].– 4th ed.
    p. cm.
  Includes bibliographical references and index.
  ISBN 1-58391-111-8 (hardcover) – ISBN 1-58391-112-X (pbk.)
1. Developmental psychology. I. Rayner, Eric.
  BF713.R38 2005
  155–dc22
                                                        2005004179

ISBN 978-1-58391-111-2 (hbk)
ISBN 978-1-58391-112-9 (pbk)

Contents

Acknowledgements

It is more than thirty years since I began writing the first edition of this book. Since then, so many people have helped and taught me that I cannot do them individual justice. The list of their names would be a life story in itself. This 4th edition is in fact an example of the Life Process. As I have grown older I have asked younger people to join me in writing this edition. This has meant that all our contributions had to be brought together in a form required by modern information technology. Jim Rose performed this feat, and we all thank him. Alison Vaspe has edited my own text and I owe her my thanks.

I hope these younger people will take the book over completely in the future and make it their own. All of us writers thank our patients, colleagues, friends, and especially our families. They are the necessary elements of our lives.

Finally, in bringing this 4th edition into the world, I must mention my wife, Dilys Daws, who has been the essential midwife, getting us to push at the appropriate times.

Eric Rayner

Preamble

Throughout the book, for the sake of simplicity, a single person, child or adult will be referred to as 'he' or 'him', no matter which sex they are. We apologise for continuing this traditional usage but no-one has yet invented a pronoun, in English at least, that refers to a person of either sex equally; to replace 'he' by 'she' would be equally discriminatory. Likewise, when men and women are referred to collectively, they will be called 'man' or 'men'.

Furthermore, since the legalization of partnership in marriage is no longer sacred for many people, the terms 'male partner' and 'female partner' should be used instead of 'husband' and 'wife'. However, this terminology is clumsy and long-winded. So 'husband' and 'wife' will be used for partners in stable, long-term relationships, whether legally tied or not.

Chapter 1

Introduction

Eric Rayner

This book aims at being a primer for those needing to learn about the emotional and intellectual complexities that can come into people's lives. It is mainly designed for students of the helping professions; but anyone – from parents to young people still at school – might find it worth reading. It is a simple exercise in combining cool scientific objectivity with the warmth of thoughtful sympathy for people. Its main point of view is that we humans get on best together when enjoying understanding each other; and that one way to start is to be interested in a person's background.

Our enjoyment of looking back to the start of a person's life – in biography – is probably as old as mankind's speech itself. After many millennia of vocal communication came the written word, and then the publication of histories of people. For instance, about 2400 years ago, Xenophon, a Greek soldier and historian, wrote one of our first known biographies about the childhood and youth of Cyrus the Great, king of Persia, a renowned religious conciliator. The title of the book was 'Cyropaedoeia' – 'The Education of Cyrus'.

However, focus upon a person's *individuality* only fully arrived, in the Western world at least, about 2000 years after Xenophon. It seems to have come especially with the Renaissance, centred in Italy. For instance, about 500 years ago, Michelangelo wrote unequivocally what he thought about his own early development. He said 'Whatever little talent I may have, I owe to the cool winds of Arezzo, the milk of my wet-nurse and the hands of her husband'. In fact, Michelangelo's parents had placed him in foster-care near Arezzo for the first 10 years or so of his life, with a wet-nurse and her husband who was a stonemason.

Why are we so interested in our experiences of childhood? The answer is that *developmental history* is crucial because we humans have brains of great complexity and capacity, and these give us uniquely huge and flexible *memories*. We are great learners from experience. With regard to reference books, Beckett (1981) is useful for general physiology and Pally (2000) is about the mind and brain. Hindle and Smith (1991); Rutter (1993); Sroufe (1996) and Sugarman (1986) are about personality development – all tending to concentrate on childhood. In the Tavistock Clinic series 'Understanding your Child' (published in 2004/5), each book deals with one year of age. A baby's brain starts with controlling simple muscular movements but, using its memory, it rapidly combines and coordinates activities in increasingly complex ways. Later capacities often depend upon earlier experiences. This means that it takes a long time to develop skills to maturity. But we can then often be wide-ranging, adaptable, socially *cooperative*, sympathetic, thence frequently idiosyncratic – even *original* and creative.

Of these characteristics, *sympathy* and *cooperativeness* are perhaps our most precious gifts – and the most frequently abused. Each person has a chance to end up with their own particular *style of thinking and feeling* – their own *character* or personality in other words. But we can be very vulnerable on the way. Humans usually flourish if *kindly* treated and looked after with *fondness*, especially when young and dependent. Learning is fastest then, but little children can be catastrophically and lastingly disturbed, not only by the loss of a loved one, but also by their carers' unfairness, neglect, unpredictability, madness or cruelty.

Sympathy and science

Like other animals, we humans are by nature greedy and competitive; and unlike most other animals, we often find pleasure in killing others of our own species. Violence comes easily to us, but we are also group-living creatures, often crowding in families into villages, towns, suburbs and cities. Here, sympathy and friendliness, like that of Michelangelo's foster parents, are vital for our survival. These crucial sociable and moral emotions have often been profoundly strengthened by religious traditions – which have, however, also often fostered violent prejudices and murderousness on a great scale.

At the same time humans, like all animals, have to feed to live. We must exploit the environment, and this needs an understanding of the elemental systems surrounding us. Nowadays, knowledge of the physical world is the domain of physics and biology. These are our most crucial sciences – and behind them stands the supreme theoretical discipline of mathematics.

Our desire for systemization probably came with the emergence of these *empirical sciences*, with their emphasis upon the collection of *data*. However, while the history of knowledge and reflective wisdom, or philosophy, is a long one, the desire to understand each other's minds systematically has grown only within the last century or so. One stream of thought here began, largely in France, over a century ago with an interest in collecting data about *intellectual* functions; this then led particularly to intelligence testing. Here was one root of *psychology*; another root, also emerging in France, was psychiatry and the investigation of mental illnesses.

Sigmund Freud in Vienna was stirred by this work and, towards the end of the nineteenth century, began to develop his crucial ideas about *emotional development*, *conflict* and *mental pathology*. Freud himself was not particularly interested in spending time on the systematic collection of empirical data to verify his ideas. He was discovering new ways of knowing about *how* people's minds worked. He called this psychoanalysis, and that was enough for one lifetime.

From this, a new dimension to *human morality* has probably arisen. For instance, the great moral command 'love little children' has been explicit for at least 2000 years, since the time of Christ. This command is still profoundly necessary, but it is no longer sufficient. We now know that love alone can choke a child unless his or her *developmental needs* are also recognized. The same applies throughout life. This is another way of saying that, to know as fully as possible about a person, you first need *sympathy* for them, and then also *objectivity* about them. For this, knowledge of their background is necessary – where and how they grew up – then, lastly, how they might have been affected by it.

Scientific thinking about the physical world holds its information together using consistent logical and mathematical rules. Thinking about emotions and sympathy is more elusive: our knowledge here comes through awareness of *feelings* about self and others. A combination of intellectual discrimination about another person's thinking, together with emotional sympathy about self and others, is usually called *empathy*. It involves mental acts of identifying with, or feeling the same as another person, while also knowing about our differences from them.

We know now that empathy, crucial to humans living together, begins to take shape in the first days, weeks and months after birth. From the beginning, a mother and baby can be seen *attuning* to each other. They copy each other's movements and expressions with mutual relaxed smiles, and later with laughing delight. Daniel Stern, an American psychiatrist, researcher and scholar, wrote about this attunement and how it is an essential precursor of speech and language generally (Stern, 1985). It is now recognized as vital to early mother–infant *bonding* and *attachment*, a subject introduced and systematically written about by an English psychiatrist, psychoanalyst and scholar, John Bowlby (1969, 1973, 1980), more than 30 years before Stern's classic book. There is now widespread scholarly interest in the vital importance of human attachment (Fonagy, 2001; Karen, 1994; Marrone, 1998).

At the same time, pain, indignation, anxiety and misery can easily be communicated – as when we wince on seeing someone getting hurt, or when a baby breaks into tears on hearing another baby cry, or when we find ourselves sobbing at someone else's tragedy (Klein, 1987).

Summarizing so far: sympathetic sensitivity and scientific objectivity need to be combined to create useful systematic thought about the experiences of people. This sort of thinking is needed over wide abstract vistas, as when thinking socially about cultures; and also in narrow focus, as when making sense of a particular family. Most intimately, sympathy is essential when trying to comprehend the predicaments of a single other person. This is the book's main interest.

Sympathetic understanding has obviously gone on for millennia in everyday *gossip*, and in religion. But the development over these last two centuries of socially minded humanitarian ideas, and more systematic attempts to help others by understanding, have resulted in a multitude of innovations: in casework and counselling, in psychotherapy, psychoanalysis, group therapy, encounter groups, family and marital therapy, and in many other meditative methods.

This book does not go into detail about these therapies. It is essentially concerned with some of the crucial experiences of people as they grow up, take on responsibilities and find new satisfactions, until old age and death. It focuses upon individual 'single-selves'; and then sees how people may *develop new structures* of thought, feeling and action (Piaget, 1999) as they go through life. Psychological development seems often to have some rudiment of *inventiveness* or *creativity* in it – but this can often be stunted or distorted. A vital new region of knowledge (Beckett, 1981; Pally, 2000) is now showing us that learning things actually changes the structured patterning of the brain and its neural pathways.

It seems that cultural practices, let alone our personal relationships, need to be deeply attuned to individuals. If this does not happen, ordinary people can easily become playthings for the dreams of ruthlessly grandiose people holding political power. Only individuals suffer or are happy – never social systems.

Biological evolution

Understanding individual experiences probably becomes clearer if set in a wider background of biological evolution. Digesting food from the environment and excreting into it, each organism changes its chemical constituents, but, as a living *dynamic system*, it nonetheless keeps its own *characteristic form* until it dies. Some would describe this as having a *spirit* of its own. What is more, living things tend to perpetuate their own species, often to their own detriment and even death. It seems that many living organisms have inbuilt propensities to preserve their own species' gene pool rather than themselves.

With the evolution of living things over millions of years, the variety of some species' exchanges with the environment has developed profoundly. Vertebrates, for instance, can hunt, feed, rest and escape in complex ways that are impossible in simpler living beings. This flexibility is most striking with mammals: their combination of large brains and long infancy, during which time they learn fast, has enabled them to develop a range of activities that far exceeds that of lower animals. Their brains are central control systems. Their neural complexity allows innate reflex patterns to be modified and combined in nigh infinite ways, yet still have coherence for the animal as a whole.

Primates function at a more complex level of central control than any other mammal. Hundreds of thousands of years ago the early ancestors of us human beings seem to have been meat-eating, group-living, nearly erect, large-brained primates. They were hunters and gatherers, intelligent about the environment, guileful with prey and wary of threats (Dunbar, 1996).

As they lived in groups, humans must have evolved into being *sensitively sympathetic* – that is, *friendly* and *cooperative* with each other. Those who survived must usually have done so because they could easily attune and submit to *group decisions* while still keeping their individual skills, self-determination – and pride. Man's huge brain, with its vast memory, also makes possible *reflective* thinking and *self-consciousness*. This is vital for human cooperativeness, and essential when living packed together in mutual dependence.

Attending to an individual

As we are group-living creatures, the need to help other people in difficulty must arise. Friendly *concern* – by pals, parents, teachers, colleagues, managers, counsellors, social workers and therapists – must come to the fore. Systematic conceptual abstraction and generalization – needed for theorizing by mathematicians, philosophers and research scientists – need to step into the background. However, we shall think abstractly a great deal about feelings and emotional characteristics.

'Being personally helpful' is a keynote of this book. We five writers are specialized workers with individuals. Angela Joyce and Mary Twyman were originally social workers, while Jim Rose and I were psychologists. Chris Clulow started out as a probation officer before specializing in couple work. Our underlying viewpoint will be psychoanalytic, although observations from other disciplines will continually be drawn upon. The book is thus largely based upon knowledge gleaned from intimate, detailed, emotional–verbal understanding; from therapy, casework and friendships with individual people.

As we have seen, Freud found a starting point for his own systematic thinking from the French psychiatrists – and psychoanalysis was born. Since those days, thinkers from across the world have modified his ideas. There is no need to go into these theories now, but it is important to be clear that this book is, in one way at least, like psychoanalysis. Both are concerned with an *open-minded, relaxed way of paying attention to another person*; then feeling along with them and thinking about what they are saying, doing, feeling and thinking.

Let us imagine an everyday example of a similar kind of relaxed attention, but of a non-professional kind. Say, we are having a cup of tea at the home of an old schoolfriend who is now a young mother. As she is cutting up some food and putting it into a pan, she comments with a note of exasperation in her voice, 'Must get this damn stuff done before Jo wakes up. It won't be done in time if I have to go off to collect the others from school first, and Bill always says he's hungry when he gets home'. The baby stirs upstairs; the young woman looks drawn and purses her lips. She says nothing, then the cloud seems to lift from her face and she says, 'Do you remember that first evening of the sixth form play, oh, that applause! I'll never forget it. We were somebody then. But that old cow of a drama teacher – all she would do was tell us when we had fluffed our lines.'

We have here noticed the mother's movements about the kitchen, the expressions on her face and so on. We have also empathized with her. We sympathetically *felt along with* her hurry, her weariness, her affection and sense of duty – and her anger. We *identified* ourselves with her. We also noted her shifting away from the present, probably in relief, to an enjoyable memory of the past.

We might go on to wonder whether her gloom was transient – or was she getting more chronically depressed? We noted that her memory of the past was a moment of rest, perhaps even flight, from her present exhaustion and frustration. We could guess that, taken up by her family, she doesn't feel she is anybody of public or professional note at present and yearns for some recognition and applause again. We might then say sympathetically, 'Must be rotten feeling nothing but a slave to them all'. She might reply, 'Oh yes of course – but there's nothing like seeing them growing up and being happy – and Bill is a dear – and knows he's got an easier job in his office than I have here!' In which case we would probably sigh with relief for her. On the other hand she might say, 'Oh no, the children are such lovely darlings and Bill is a wonderful man'. In this case we might wonder whether she is really angry and depressed but *denying* it – switching into adoring or idealizing the family and nothing else. This would mean that she was unaware of, or unconsciously avoiding – *defending against* in other words – some important, probably negative, emotional aspects of her life.

This thinking about the *emotional patterns* of individual people – with as few preconceptions as possible – is at the core of the psychoanalytic disciplines. However, we have found it crucial to use other viewpoints as well. For instance, knowing about the social and cultural background of a person is essential; so is a grasp of the nature of intellectual thought, and feelings, which are rooted in body functions. This book must also rest on *cognitive psychology* and *physiology* – particularly about the brain. We will not have room to go into these vital subjects but it is essential to get some understanding of them through other reading (Beckett, 1981; Pally, 2000; Sroufe, 1996; Sugarman, 1986).

Equally, we will be centrally concerned with feeling and emotion, but these are meaningless without recognizing *intellectual development* as well. Starting particularly with the great pioneer Jean Piaget (1929, 1935, 1951, 1953, 1999), it has been research psychologists who have contributed most in this region.

Another frame of reference will also be used repeatedly. An individual's predicaments naturally occur within a family and social network. This is the province of sociologists and anthropologists, so the book owes a special debt to them too. A prime inspiration for this book was undoubtedly Erik Erikson (1963, 1995) – one of the first to bring psychoanalysis and anthropology together. From about 50 years ago, he was a great model of humane depth and broad-mindedness.

Finally, it must also be recognized that educationists actually devote their lives to people's development. We writers of this book, frankly, work on the fringes of many disciplines.

Life situations and the developmental point of view

Returning to the brief description of a young mother. Notice how we tried to 'get inside' her. She is thinking about herself with others. We know that she is married, her husband goes to work and she presumably does not earn money at present, she has at least three children to bring up, two of school age and one a baby. She has a lot of things to coordinate at once without much outside help. She seems burdened by it all and can get angry. She tussles with desires and aspirations within her, seeking to satisfy both herself and those around her. Her mind aims towards goals, and tussles with conflicting issues standing in her way.

This thinking about people as *striving towards goals* is called a psycho*dynamic* conception of the mind. It is about problem solving in its broadest sense as part of ordinary life. In fact, a core viewpoint in this book is that all psychological growth or development involves informal *problem solving* of a sort.

It is, perhaps, curiosity about such everyday 'problematic matters' – muddles, conflicts, failures and despair, as well as achievements, joy and happiness – that makes *gossip* so important

(Dunbar, 1996). Gossip is the most common way of gleaning, enjoying and passing on vital information about the fate and ways of the people we know. We group-living humans cannot do without it; even when malign, it can still be useful. Although everyone normally picks up knowledge of friends' lives in this gossipy way, professionals need to be more self-critical, searching and systematic about their clients' or patients' situations. Attention must be focused both on their inner worlds and environmental structures, together with their interactions with others, and particularly on things that have gone wrong or right for them.

Some people go wrong repeatedly; they may never seem to manage, they may be deemed backward – of 'low intelligence'. They may behave in strangely mechanical ways and be diagnosed as autistic. They may become dramatically anxious and prone to fall into an agitated chaos of feelings and ideas – and be called *phobic*, in an *anxiety state*, or *hysterical*. On the other hand, they may grind along repeating worries in a machine-like way and be diagnosed as *obsessive*. They may disintegrate in their thought, hopping from one bit of an idea to another – and be diagnosed as *borderline*. On the other hand, they may believe in a dreamy world, thinking it to be real – and be called *schizophrenic*. They may be grudging and chronically suspicious of those around them and said to be *paranoid*. Or they may slip into a slow, black, self-accusing despair – then be thought of as *melancholic* or severely *depressive*. Another person could slip into ruthless lying, cheating or theft. They are then likely to be called *delinquent*, if they are still young; or, if older, they are often referred to as *psychopathic*. Finally, if they commit crimes, get caught by the police and taken to court, they are classified as criminal.

These mental disturbances will probably be mentioned in the book but they are not its focus. The central aim is more elementary – it is to build a basic foundation from which one can set about seeing how individuals get into the awful muddles and troubles that they do. Hopefully, it will provide an essential, everyday backcloth to stir up thought and feeling about people's experiences. It outlines some of the main situations that face people in life, and how they may, or may not, solve them as they grow up, age and die.

In other words, we are viewing life as '*task-ridden*'. Here, one puzzle or demand after another turns up and has to be tackled – or is avoided – leading to its own consequences. Each developmental level provides a new pattern of problems to solve and achievements to enjoy. With this in mind, the book is laid out roughly in age phases from birth to death, giving some of the common experiences and describing the new mental patterns that emerge with each phase; this is followed by how the patterns can continue and affect things later. Having these lifespan conceptions in the background of one's mind can help an ordinarily thoughtful person, especially a professional, to be ready to understand, and perhaps help, someone who is stumbling in their way of doing things.

The chapters about the earlier phases of life will introduce concepts important at later ages. This is the essence of thinking *developmentally*. It is then often possible to detect that, however mature a person may be, there are still primitive ideas and feelings active within them. These may be working valuably together with more mature levels, or they may be virulently disowned, or they can be quietly invasive, disturbing or deleterious. Our task is not so much to focus upon such disturbances, as to begin charting their background psychodynamics.

Here is an example coming from my own experience. When I was preparing this chapter, I had a stirring dream. Quite simple, but seeming to have echoes in many places, the dream was of an idea of *revolution*. It was awesome but not violent – no-one was being killed or hurt – but it was a revolution nonetheless. Next morning I told my wife the dream – and she interpreted it for me! She thought it must be about the meaning to me of this book: for surely every developmental phase and leap must involve at least some *revolt*, some revolution, against habits from the past. So, to grow up happily, it looks as if we might need to have some revolutions going on all the time within us. They would then be like very small-scale Industrial Revolutions, Scientific Revolutions and other bloodless coups – disturbing but creative!

Things to do when reading this book

Since concepts introduced early in the book are used later, it is best to start at the beginning and go on from there step by step. Remember, what is written down is not gospel and is certainly limited in its data and vision. Think of it as asking pertinent questions to argue with, criticize and laugh about – think for yourself. It is a warm-up for reading and thinking about more detailed books.

At the same time, if you have the opportunity, talk and argue with friends and teachers. It is a good idea, if possible, to observe, play with, or talk to those at the age you are studying. People usually like talking about themselves – so long as the listener is neither scornful nor punitively moralistic.

Remember that this is *not* a book focussing particularly on pathology, abnormality or handicap. If you are a worker in the helping professions, many of your clients or patients will be much more disturbed or disadvantaged than the people quoted here. You will be disappointed if you read the book for direct help in coping with the dire problems you may have to face every day. However, remember that sick mental processes can only be well understood by contrast with healthy thought. Such comparisons can help gather ideas together to extend and enhance ordinary discourse between people. Remember that the ability to be happy being ordinary is a gift, often possessed even by outstanding people – but it eludes those who are self-centred or arrogant.

There is perhaps another general value in the book. Problems can lead to *creativity*. Everybody is faced with problems each waking day; most are small and easily solved, and other people may help. Failure probably always heralds an emotional disturbance, small or large; and finding a solution is always something of a creative achievement, however ordinary. Then, when a creative achievement has settled in memory for further use, the mind has managed an *integration* into something *more complex*. Development will then have truly taken place.

However, the converse also readily occurs: ideas, resolutions and intentions are *discarded* every day – sometimes for no good reason, sometimes leading to more trouble, but often for very good reasons such as mental overload, or because an idea is misleading, or because it really has no further use. There is no such noun as 'discardation' for this act of throwing away. It is the opposite of development, but it can be complementary, and it can help it along. The nearest we have in the dictionary is 'dereliction', meaning 'to make derelict'. So, perhaps this book could be best entitled 'Human Development and Dereliction'!

Further reading

Dunbar, R. (1996) *Grooming, Gossip and the Evolution of Language*. London: Faber & Faber. About the links between man and other primates in their ways of communication. A delight to read.

Fonagy, P. (2001) *Attachment Theory and Psychoanalysis*. New York: The Other Press. Beautifully clear; may become a classic text.

Marrone, M. (1998) *Attachment and Interaction*. London: Jessica Kingsley. A good read for those not familiar with the subject.

Pally, R. (2000) *The Mind–Brain Relationship*. London: Karnac. A beautifully simple exposition on a very complex subject.

Sroufe, L.A. et al. (1996) *Child Development, its Nature and Course*. New York: Basic Books. An encyclopaedic book about child development; but clear and enjoyable; packed with information and references; in softback, so, easy to handle and not expensive.

Waddell, M. (1998) *Inside Lives: Psychoanalysis and the Growth of the Personality*. London: Duckworth.

Chapter 2

Being pregnant

Mary Twyman

The nature of becoming pregnant is a physical, physiological act resulting in the conception of a child. But it is, of course, also an event of emotional significance. Whether the pregnancy is wished for or not, whether it arises out of a loving act of sexual intercourse, or a casual 'accidental' encounter, something happens which is momentous for all the three people concerned. For the woman and the fetus, from the very instant of conception a physiological relationship begins. While the woman may not be fully conscious that this relationship has begun, many women sense very quickly that they have conceived after a particular intercourse. Intuitively they are aware that something is different this time, there may be some slight physical sensations of discomfort, but more often there is a secret sense of profound change; someone else is coming into being. Immediately cell division and differentiation begin, the exchanges of substances between the mother's system and the baby's are underway. The pattern of dependence, of interdependence and the preparation for independent life, as yet very far ahead, is being laid down in the formation of the baby's biological structure, and also in the foundations of the baby's psychological being.

Looking back to the pregnant woman as a girl, it is noticeable how often the games and play scenarios of little girls involve secrets. Something is devised among a group of girls, maybe some gossip, but then comes the elaborate hierarchy of who is to be told, who is to be kept out, what is to be shared with whom, how far and when. We might make the observation that this form of play presages the way in which women experience and handle 'the news' of a pregnancy. While there is a strong pull to share the news, first with a partner, then perhaps with the woman's parents, particularly her mother, then her partner's parents, then perhaps siblings and friends, there may also be an urge to keep the secret, at least for a time. There are a number of factors that come into this. One may be the sheer sense of wonderment at the achievement of a desired, perhaps long-awaited pregnancy. Another may be the wish of the couple to keep the news to themselves, to enjoy the secret and the sense of achievement for a while before making the announcement to the wider world of family and friends. It may be that the couple need a while to begin the adjustment to the new roles that are now to be stepped into. How am I going to be as a mother? How and what sort of a father will I become? How are we as a couple going to make the transition to parenthood? Perhaps some of the early secrecy has the function of preserving a space for the parents-to-be in the first stages of their psychological accommodation to their new roles. As the increasingly complex development of the fetus proceeds, so the mother's body adapts, and simultaneously both parents begin to try out in their minds scenarios, a sort of rehearsal, of what it might be like to be a parent. While much of this may be conscious thought, speculating and imagining, much more will be taking place at an unconscious level and belong to the internal world of both the mother and the father. Their experiences of their own childhoods with their parents and how these are represented in their internal worlds will play a crucial part here.

Where there are difficulties in conception, the new technologies now available to parents can make an enormous contribution where formerly the sadness of childlessness was inevitable. Here, both partners who embark on these treatments have to be prepared to tolerate intrusive medical procedures, which to some extent bypass the autonomy and the spontaneity of their ordinary sexual lives. That so many couples are prepared to undergo such interventions, sometimes repeatedly if there are failures, testifies to the urgency of their wish to become parents. When the outcome is a viable pregnancy followed by the birth of a healthy baby, especially valued after the ordeals of repeated cycles of treatment, there can be no question but that there is much for the parents and their families to celebrate.

Failures, and repeated failures, are hard. Strain will be put upon the couple's relationship, for this kind of failure is hard to share without some, maybe hidden, sense of blame being present. Repeated, increasingly frantic, efforts to become pregnant can distort the pattern of intimacy between the couple. There can develop a determination to achieve the desired result at all costs. These costs may be damagingly high in emotional terms. Too much disappointment can be corrosive to the relationship, and perhaps one partner needs to be realistic enough and brave enough to say at some point, 'We have tried. Now let us stop and mourn what we cannot have.' Forgoing what emerges as unattainable can constitute a mature acceptance that life is not always controllable, and that it is unrealistic and probably omnipotent of us to behave as though it could be. However, the techniques now available to couples with fertility problems provide a valuable service and the gratitude of those helped by such treatments is understandably deep. It is clear that current generations benefit enormously from these techniques compared with previous generations, where childlessness was an often silently evident but privately lamented deprivation for the couple concerned. With successful treatment there remains the possibility of multiple births as an outcome, a serious factor that both members of the couple are bound to consider in their decision to proceed with treatment. While all couples starting a family need the support of the wider family, if it exists, and of friends, it may be that those undergoing treatment for infertility especially need the support of the human network around them to carry them through their momentous experiences.

Treatment for infertility represents perhaps the ultimate extent of the way in which pregnancy has become medicalized in Western culture. While the safety and health of the mother and child must be the primary focus of medical care, mothers-to-be seem to be increasingly uneasy at what can feel like a conveyor-belt experience in the face of frequently over-stretched maternity services. The relationship between the woman and her carers is an important one and probably charged with feelings that have their origins in earlier stages of the woman's development. A woman who has been busily active in the world, working at her career, for instance, taking roles of responsibility in whatever enterprise she was engaged with, will find herself feeling dependent in a way that recalls the dependency of childhood. She is facing the unknown in many ways and her fears may be hard for her to acknowledge and articulate. One of the things that safe and reliable contraception has afforded women in the last 40 years is the knowledge that they have control of their reproductive processes. While to some extent this is truer than for previous generations, when for many women fear of repeated pregnancies was what defined their lives, the control is not absolute. But to the extent that it exists, it can foster the belief that control of one's body is the norm. For most women, a first pregnancy represents a high experience of learning, of discovery of the gradual unfolding potentialities in her body as it fulfils its reproductive destiny. When a woman is looked after by professionals who recognize and respect this process she can be helped in the preparation for the birth and for motherhood in a way that is enhancing for the development of her confidence and ability to care for herself and her baby. It has always appeared strange to me that, given the average hospital delivery, many women will find themselves attended by staff who are strangers to them, and among these will be junior staff, often adolescent girls, who have not themselves had the experience of pregnancy. One of the drawbacks of the medicalization of pregnancy and childbirth is this curious alienation from the woman's familiar setting and relationships. A mother finding herself without the support of known carers at the time of delivery is faced with a particularly anxiety-inducing situation. The presence of the woman's partner at the delivery, now much more usual, is a recognition of the woman's need for the familiar, close contact while she is engaged in labour. In terms of organization, the development of midwife-led teams in small units represents an effort to regain something of the closer, more intimate setting for giving birth that has been lost through the over-institutionalized medical establishment. This would seem also to give cognizance to the psychological importance of the woman's experience as a determinant of the foundation of a good start for mother and baby.

Just as the woman is entering unknown territory in her pregnancy, her partner also approaches new experiences. What pregnancy and approaching parenthood mean to each of them will have similarities but also differences. For him, fatherhood will bring, amongst other things, a revisiting of his relationship with his own parents, particularly his father. As the woman is appraising her own mother – how far will she model herself as a mother on her mother – so the father-to-be will be measuring himself in terms of how he sees his father. What traits does he identify with, what traits does he want to avoid? While some of this will be consciously thought about, much will be going on unconsciously, a sort of re-positioning of himself as a man in the light of approaching responsibilities as a father. A foretaste of these will be the particular demands made upon him by the changes that he perceives in his partner. She will need his support and reassurance in ways that may not have been apparent before. How far does he comprehend the mood changes, for instance, or her increasing tiredness and especially her withdrawal of a certain interest in him as she makes emotional space for the child she carries. A father-to-be commented to his wife who was lying resting on the sofa in the late stages of pregnancy, 'Why aren't you reading or doing something? You are usually occupied.' Indeed, she had been active, busy and especially intellectually engaged, but at this stage she was quietly preoccupied, hardly really 'thinking about' the baby, but orientated towards what was going on inside her, setting aside in a way that felt natural to her, her previous interests. He was puzzled and somewhat alarmed. Was she losing her intellectual capacities, was she going to become just a mindless mum? What she was giving evidence of was what the psychoanalyst and paediatrician D.W. Winnicott has termed 'primary maternal preoccupations' (Winnicott, 1956). This state he describes as occurring in the late stages of pregnancy and continuing through the early months of the baby's life, when the foundations of secure mental health are laid down within the context of the mother's natural deep identification with her infant and his needs, and her adaptation to such needs while her baby is in a state of total dependence on her.

Sexual activity may decrease during pregnancy, but not necessarily so. Sometimes there are fantasies that intercourse may harm the baby or cause miscarriage in early pregnancy, but many couples find a particularly harmonious kind of love-making comes about as the pregnancy proceeds, as though there is something extra to celebrate in their proud achievement of the pregnancy. The man's pride in making his partner pregnant will be manifest in this, as well perhaps as an assertion of his primary place in her life just at the point when a third person, the baby, is present, but not yet emergent. It is also important to acknowledge the partner's possible antagonism, alongside his pride and expectation, towards the soon-to-be-present interloper.

Two anecdotes illustrate the ambivalence that fathers-to-be feel in relation to the coming arrival of a first-born. Mr A. arrived home from work to find the cat, of which he was quite fond, sleeping comfortably in the chair he usually sat in on coming home from work. This usually affectionate man angrily swept the cat off the chair and plonked himself firmly in his usual chair, saying to his wife, 'He needn't think he's taking over!' Both of them recognized that this outburst was a displacement, an acceptable tirade against the cat, expressing his sense that the coming baby might represent a serious rival and usurper of the man's prime place in the home. Mr B. was on an expedition with his wife to buy the usual equipment that couples acquire before the baby arrives. He found himself in the middle of the department store in a highly irritated state saying to himself, 'What on earth are we getting all this paraphernalia for – it's only a baby, why does it need so much stuff?' This was a realization on his part that among his responsibilities as a father was the sharing of his resources with the coming child, resources both material and emotional. It is not without significance that Mr B. was a first-born child and his parents subsequently had twins shortly after his second birthday. Mr B. had learnt about sharing resources at a very early age and rather dramatically; and it seems likely that the imminent arrival of his own child triggered some emotional responses that had their origin in his early, completely forgotten, responses to the births of his twin siblings.

The relationship between the woman and her mother takes on a central significance when a pregnancy is declared. The declaration itself marks a particular milestone for the woman. It is as if she is saying, 'Look, Mother, I too can do what you have done.' So many elements may be included in this statement. First, the woman seems to identify with her mother. In a woman's development the fluctuations in identification with her mother are many and complex but it is perhaps with her first pregnancy that something like a resolution begins to come about. What a woman often struggles with in her development is how much and to what extent she wants to be like her mother. Mother has this capacity to have babies for which she may be envied; she has prime access to father and for a little girl she is a formidable rival. Feelings surrounding these situations are marked by conflict, for mother is also the source of care, comfort and love, and is depended upon. The pattern of pulling away from mother to increasing independence alternates with a pull towards mother, something we might call a regressive pull, and the girl in her growing-up is usually oscillating between these two directional pulls in her emotional life. What a pregnancy represents is an attainment of the status, the power and the emotional significance for the woman of what previously had been the sole prerogative of her mother. She joins the society of mature women, the matriarchy. But the attainment of such status and power may bring with it anxiety as well as satisfaction. There may be a sense of triumphing over the maternal figure, especially if feelings of rivalry, whether acknowledged or not, have predominated. How things go with the pregnant woman and her mother will depend on how the relationship has fared throughout the woman's life, and the degree to which she has resolved some of the conflicts referred to, especially the mixture of loving and hostile feelings.

Many women resolve to be very different in how they take on the mothering role from their remembrance of how their mothers were. And yet so often the interested observer can discern in how they manage their child, the routines they espouse in their domestic arrangements, distinct traits and attitudes which derive from maternal patterns. It is as though in mothering, many women discover a better internal mother than they thought they had, and they are inclined to let her come into her own and be acknowledged in how they express themselves in their new maternal role.

A pregnancy also brings into focus for a woman and for her partner the interface between what is personal and what belongs to the wider social and cultural milieu in which they live. To some extent this is a given, to some extent it involves choice. While many people are born, grow up, marry, have children, live, work and die in what we might refer to as a stable culture, many do not. Increasing migration, chosen or enforced by adverse political and economic circumstances, means that more people are finding themselves faced with major adaptations personally, in their partnerships and in the establishing of a family.

The pregnant woman will carry within her those cultural norms that are characteristic of her family, her class, her culture and her country. While in her adult development these may have been modified and in many ways she may have transcended them, they may resurface at the time of pregnancy. It is a sort of 'going home' to what is known, what is thought to be appropriate, at a time when the new and the unfamiliar in approaching maternity challenges the adult acquired characteristics. The cultures that she and her partner carry within them may differ – they almost certainly will. However much or little they differ, it may well be that in their life as a couple they have wrestled with these differences and come to some, albeit uneasy, accommodation or at least have been able to agree to differ. But with a pregnancy, for each of them the 'going home' may represent something to which they are especially attached and which they may feel to be non-negotiable. There may be passionate feelings about 'how we always do it in our family'. The pregnancy and the imminent arrival of the next generation may give rise to the emergence of ideas and traditions, which to the holder are completely and obviously right but which to the partner may seem arbitrary in the extreme. For example, 'In our family the first boy is always named after great-grandfather X'. Or, 'In my family, Aunt J always makes the christening cake'. Minor differences and the insistence on their being observed can promote painful conflict, such as the question of circumcision of a male child of a couple, only one of whom is Jewish. How money is used, religious observance, child-rearing practices, the degree of influence/support expected of grandparents are among the familiar areas where differences and their consequences present themselves to be struggled over in the time before the child is born.

Later pregnancy, from the start of the second trimester, brings for the mother increasingly important changes, especially in the experience of the baby's movement within her. The newcomer is evidently present and movements confirm that growth and development are proceeding. Present-day parents also have the availability of ultrasound scanning and will have a clearer visual image of their child in the womb than was available to parents before such technology was available. At these later stages in pregnancy the mother will find her enjoyment of her state enhanced if she can allow herself to give way to her inclination to slow down, to acknowledge her decrease in appetite for the affairs of the wider world and to concentrate on herself and her baby, a sort of nesting impulse. With this shift of focus there comes something of a sense of the loss of the woman's organized self; there is a deconstruction of the former organization of the personality, a perfectly normal one in most cases, but one that can present conflict if the woman is still occupying a role, say at work, where her adult organized self is still required to function. The intensity of this conflict and the anxiety accompanying it can lead a woman to plan a return to work soon after the birth of her child, not so much from a need financial or otherwise, but as a planned retrieval of her adult organized self which she feels will be permanently lost to her unless she makes strenuous efforts to reinstate it. The greater loss, to herself and to her baby, is not to allow this gradual natural state of unintegration to develop and to give herself up to the richness of a new dimension in her experience of herself. She may find herself having imaginary conversations with her baby as he becomes more real to her physically and as a person who is already a significant figure in her inner life. Her curiosity about who this is inside flourishes, and her dreams and fantasies grow more abundant. Gradually, she and her baby wind themselves more closely into each other's lives. While there is curiosity about her baby, there is also curiosity about herself, again accompanied by anxiety. As mothers often say, no amount of preparation can really convey what it is like to be the person on whom this wholly dependent baby relies for his survival. Yet in the later stages of pregnancy the foundations for the emergence of herself as a mother are being laid. The unintegration mentioned above and the preoccupation with the baby contain those elements which will help her to adapt and muster the sheer stamina, physical as well as emotional, demanded of her in her new role. Where it is difficult for a woman to allow this stage to emerge, there are serious implications for herself and her baby. There may be a precipitate return to work after the birth and a too early rupturing of the bond of attachment between herself and her baby. Many mothers try to defend themselves from the sheer impact of a neonate's absolute dependency on them by assuming that any competent caregiver can be substituted for the mother. Since this is often regarded as sensible, if it allows the mother to return to work, it is hard to put the opposing view. Basically, the baby is attuned to mother and she has the responsibility and the privilege of being the primary figure in the baby's life. This is the baby's first and most vital relationship; he will certainly be deeply attached to mother, and the best thing that can happen to the baby is that mother falls deeply in love with him and wants to be there in her primary role from the early months on a more or less continuous basis. This does not mean that no-one else should handle the baby, give a bottle, change a nappy, push the pushchair around the block for an hour, but that the main feeding, handling and ordinary relating should centre around the mother–baby dyad. What help and support is available needs to be geared to allowing the mother the maximum containment for her to fulfil this primary role.

There is something in our culture that militates against recognition of this primary role. Self-esteem in women and in men is so often linked to achievement in career, in activity, in effectiveness, in earning money in the outside world. This is seen to be evident, observable and thus valued. What is less valued, less recognized, is the continuous steadfast capacity for concern for the physical and emotional well-being of an infant, and the contribution that it makes to child and adult mental health. This is the unseen work of parents and the health of individuals and of society relies on this unsung contribution. Young mothers and fathers need the acknowledgement, perhaps especially from their own parents, that they are doing a good job, and a valuable one, in their struggles to raise their children.

The late stage of pregnancy is marked by a growing sense of excitement and anticipation. Heavier now, and slow-moving, the woman is waiting, wanting the baby to put in an appearance. There will have been the practical preparations and most parents now attend antenatal classes in preparation for labour. The familiar figure of her partner will be a reassuring presence, especially if she is to be delivered in hospital. Arrangements for help, from family or friends, for the early days after delivery will need to be put in place. The mother-to-be can be easier in her mind if these supports are assured. In the face of much that is unknown, and most immediately, the labour itself, it is important that surrounding structures properly in place can take away some of the inevitable anxiety. Now it is simply a matter of waiting for a new phase in the life of mother, father and baby to begin.

Further reading

Baradon, T., Broughton, C., Gibbs, I., James, J., Joyce, A. and Woodhead, J. (2005) *The Practice of Parent–Infant Psychotherapy: Claiming the Baby*. London: Routledge.

Birksted Breen, D. (1975) *The Birth of the First Child*. London: Tavistock.

Raphael-Leff, J. (1993) *Pregnancy – the Inside Story*. London: Karnac.

Raphael-Leff, J. (1996) *Psychological Processes of Childbearing*. London: Chapman and Hall.

Stern, D.N. (1985) *The Interpersonal World of the Infant*. New York: Basic Books.

Chapter 3

The first six months: the baby getting started

Angela Joyce

The disruption of birth

For babies, birth means a fundamental change in their whole psychological organization, predicated initially on the bodily changes wrought by the caesura of birth. *In utero* they were supplied with all the necessities for growth and survival through the placenta and umbilical cord. Now all that has changed: they breathe through their lungs, they will very soon feed by sucking, and excrete through bowels and bladder. None of the reflex patterns organizing these functions can have been fully exercised before. The kind of birth a baby and mother experience has an impact on what happens next, and can help set up a good or less good bonding process.

The following is a close observation of what a newborn typically can do if given the opportunity. If, immediately after birth, the baby is dried but not washed, and placed on the mother's abdomen, within the first 90 minutes he will find the mother's breast and begin to suck.

Ten minutes after birth this baby was placed between his mother's breasts. After a few minutes he begins to manoeuvre, moving with small push-ups, first toward his mother's left breast. He frequently stops to rest and suck on his fist and fingers. With push-ups he moves towards the right breast at 30 minutes. Mother and infant gaze at each other. Familiar with the taste and smell of amniotic fluid, he continues to suck on his unwashed hand and soon he moves to a similar smell emanating from the unwashed breast. The baby begins to mouth the nipple, probably raising the mother's oxytocin levels. The baby readies himself for a good placement on the areola, opening his mouth widely, sucking on the breast while the mother and infant look at each other at around 50 minutes. (Klaus & Klaus, 1998)

The mother needs to get the feel of her baby outside her after the 9 months of growing inside. For the baby, it will be his first sight and smell of anything. The *bonding* and *attachment* between newborns and their parents will be the most important foundation for the baby's subsequent development, and the way he is supported in this process is crucial. It only became common practice for fathers to be present at the birth of their child in the second half of the twentieth century. Now it is also usual to give the baby quite quickly to the mother. Newborn babies feel safe if kept close to their mother's body and this facilitates the transition from life in the womb to that outside. Full-term babies seldom cry in the first 90 minutes after birth if they are skin-to-skin with the mother, on her belly or chest. If, however, they are wrapped up and placed in a cradle beside the mother's bed, they will cry about 20 to 40 seconds every 5 minute-period for the next 90 minutes. The newborn is perceptive enough to discern the difference! (Klaus & Klaus, 1998; Klaus et al., 1995).

The story of development should lead to this new baby eventually becoming a person in his own right, thinking, feeling and being himself. The process through which this happens is central to the ultimate outcome – the person is the product of his genetic endowment (*potential*) meeting the environment, embodied in the social and emotional relationships created in the family. For most children, their caregivers will be their natural parents but we realize that for some, other caregivers are very important. In this account we will usually refer to mothers and fathers, whilst acknowledging that others are involved in the child's life.

How does the baby become a person? How does the potential that each of us is born with become the unique individual adult? And how does this happen so that the person lives in a creative and authentic way? At the beginning of life the baby is absolutely dependent upon the mother and father, not only for food and sustenance, but also for the *emotional input* that will provide the core of the baby's experience of himself in the world. This emotional input is centrally important from the very beginning of life.

As a prototype for the setting that would provide a *good enough beginning*, the psychoanalyst and paediatrician D.W. Winnicott described an imaginary first encounter between the new baby and his mother in the first feed in the following way: inside the baby a feeling of tension begins to develop, perhaps hunger pangs, but whatever it is it creates an expectancy of something that the baby is prepared to find, something, somewhere, not knowing what it is. At the right moment then, the mother makes her breast available and the baby sucks. The mother has enabled her baby to have the experience of '*creating*' his own world out of his own inner experience of need. Winnicott called this '*the illusion of omnipotence*'. This is remarkably similar to the observation by Klaus and Klaus quoted above. We can see how utterly dependent this is on the sensitivity of the mother and those who take care of her (Winnicott, 1988):

> It is all one thing, the mother's care of her baby, and the periodic feeding develops as if it were a means of communication between the two – a song without words.

Camilla was born after a long and complicated delivery, with the cord around her neck, which caused a great deal of anxiety in the medical staff caring for her and her mother. She was put to her mother's breast very soon afterwards but seemed not to be interested and she then went to sleep. After many hours of uninterrupted sleep the nursing staff again became anxious and insisted on waking her in case she became dehydrated. Camilla was reluctant to wake up and when put to the breast protested with loud cries. She would not take the nipple and a 'battle' ensued, with Camilla eventually being fed sugar water from a bottle. Subsequently it proved impossible to get Camilla to feed from the breast, although for many weeks her mother was able to express her milk and feed it to her daughter by bottle.

In this example, Camilla's mother was able to recover from a very difficult start and a satisfactory feeding routine was established, albeit with some considerable disappointment because she had enjoyed breastfeeding her first child and was looking forward to doing so again with her new baby.

Even if feeding is by bottle from the start, the attuning of the baby and mother to each other is very important. A baby will have learnt something of his mother's movements and rhythms, like the sound of her voice, while *in utero*. Shortly we will look at the various capacities the baby brings that prime him to relate to the world, and most especially his mother, right from the start of life. But for the moment we will consider the setting within which this readiness to relate emerges.

The personal setting

The early days and weeks after the baby's birth will be taken up with everyone in the family settling down together. Older siblings and father all have to find their place in the new order of things consequent upon the new arrival, but the centre of this will be the mother–infant pair. What greatly enhances this process is the particular state of mind that Winnicott called '*primary maternal preoccupation*' (Winnicott, 1956). This has nothing to do with a mother's intelligence but a heightened sensitivity that gathers in the last weeks of pregnancy and lasts in its acute form into the first months after the baby's birth. It relies on the mother's capacity to identify with her baby and enables her to adapt to the baby's absolute dependency in the first weeks and months of life. 'Primary maternal preoccupation' is a central characteristic of the *ordinary devoted mother* and provides the basis for her imaginative elaboration in her mind, of the experience of her baby being cared for. The mother who is in this state of mind is much more likely to be in tune with her baby's various states of feeling. She will be able gradually, through this imaginative (largely unconscious) identification, to intuit the different meanings of her baby's cries for instance, and respond in ways that enable the baby to experience his feelings as his own and within manageable bounds (more of that later). W. Bion (1967), a psychoanalyst in the Kleinian tradition, described the mother's '*reverie*' through which she receives the baby's communications and understands them, enabling her to respond in calming, soothing, reassuring ways, giving the baby the experience of his distressing feelings being 'contained'.

The father's place has traditionally been to support and protect his partner and baby. With the social changes of the late twentieth century, fathers have been given a more active role directly in relation to the child, and psychoanalytic thinking has not been very slow in catching up with this. Whilst Winnicott emphasized the dyad between mother and baby protected by the father, more recently others have looked at the *triad of mother, father and baby*, right at the beginning of life. A study by von Klitzing and his colleagues in Switzerland (1999) concluded that babies were much more likely to relate equally to both parents, if both were present at 4 months, if the mother had been able to integrate the idea of the transition from being a couple to being a threesome during her pregnancy. Another way of thinking about this is the idea of '*the father in the mother's mind*', that is, that the mother has a representation of 'father' in her mind which allows space for the father of her baby.

Mother and baby (and father) being sociable together

What of the baby in this setting? It used to be thought that babies did very little for the first several months of their lives, but we know now that babies are actively engaged from the beginning. They are specifically motivated '*to communicate intricately with the expressive forms and rhythms of interest and feeling displayed by other humans*' (Trevarthan & Aitken, 2001). It is the case that the early weeks are largely about settling in together, with the baby gradually adopting routines of feeding and sleeping which make his life and those of his parents more predictable: the baby contributes actively to this settling-in process.

Babies are born with awareness specifically receptive to feeling states in other people. From about 2 months of age is the most intensely social period of infancy, when the infant simply wants to relate to the other and in turn to be related to. There is no topic other than the interaction itself. It can be increasingly observed as the sleepy baby of the first weeks gives way to a more wakeful one. But even before this, babies can frequently be observed looking intently into the face of the other. The following is taken from the observation of a 3-day-old baby boy, Corey:

Corey was getting slightly restless; his mother thought he might be hungry and, picking him up, said so to him. She prepared herself to feed him and offered him her breast. He hesitated and instead of taking the nipple he looked at her face. His eyes lightened as he gazed into her eyes. She responded, echoing his brightened eyes in her own. They held each other's gaze for about 20 seconds and Corey broke the spell by looking away, at the breast and beginning his feed.

From about 2 to 3 months of age, the mother's emotionally expressive face is the most powerful visual stimulus for the baby and he tracks her, searching out connection. This is the time of *mutual gazing*, soon including smiling and cooing with signs of turn taking, and often the baby deciding when to initiate or bring to an end a particular sequence. Mothers (and fathers) naturally adjust their voices to a higher pitch with a rhythm at approximately adagio (walking pace in music) termed '*motherese*' (Trevarthan & Aitken, 2001).

As the baby develops, a typical interaction might follow a sequence such as that described above but more elaborate as the baby's range of capacities increases: the baby looks at the mother's face intently, concentrating on her eyes; he smiles, and mother responds by lightening her eyes and gently vocalizing baby talk; the baby in turn makes cooing vocalizations and conspicuous hand movements, ceasing to smile when expressing a sound; mother follows by imitating baby with sound and movement; the baby listens intently and, when mother is silent, takes up the cue, making his own sounds. This may go on for many seconds, and frequently it is the baby who brings it to an end, turning away or closing his eyes, turning back when he is ready to recommence.

Babies are particularly sensitive to the emotional tone of these interactions and prefer the positive affect that is clear in the above example. This is because a preponderance of positive emotions between baby and mother is optimal for the baby's development at all levels, even for the brain. A sensitive, attuned mother resonates with her baby's states, altering her contribution to enhance and maintain his positive feelings, and to modify any feelings of distress. As a result, the mother–baby pair is more likely to increase their feeling of engagement together. Thus we can see how the two-way exchange of emotional expression is mutual, despite the great differences in maturity between the participants (Schore, 2001).

Even at this early stage, we can see from the above examples that speech is also important. Trevarthan sees it as *intersubjective* at a fundamental level. The mother's speech affirms and responds to the infant's eagerness to become involved in *'proto-conversation'*, a non-verbal form of discourse. Speech engages attention, communicates feelings, and facilitates social interaction as well as ultimately facilitating language acquisition. It is typical of this intensely mutually reciprocal state of *'primary intersubjectivity'*.

Other researchers have corroborated the finely tuned mutuality of the interchanges between baby and mother in the first months of life, stressing other aspects as well as speech. Beatrice Beebe and her colleagues have examined in frame-by-frame analysis, video footage of interactions between mother–infant couples. They have shown how babies and mothers interact with each other in *mutually synchronous ways*, like a mutual dance. These 'dance' sequences can lead to babies being able to experience states of feeling that are manageable but, in less favourable circumstances, go out of control and lead to distress (Beebe et al., 1997).

The idiosyncratic style of each baby and mother has already been stressed. Some babies are born very active, others placid, others sensitive; likewise mothers differ in their characteristics, not only from one mother to another but also from culture to culture. Although it is seems intuitively right to assume that frequent mismatches between mother and baby should hardly occur, research suggests that this is the rule rather than the exception. In securely attached babies, 50 per cent of attempts at contact (visual and others) between mothers and infants fail to be registered by the intended recipient (Tronick, 1989). What seems to be crucial, however, is the way in which these mismatches or mis-attunements are repaired. If a mother cannot attune to her baby's rhythm then, as a result, the baby will become distressed. This in turn stresses his mother, usually upsetting him more, so that a vicious circle is likely. Although babies are usually more robust than inexperienced mothers fear, and 'forgiveness' comes quickly when a contented rhythm is re-established, nevertheless a mother needs all her vitality, ingenuity and patience to melt such vicious circles. We can see that for this to happen a mother needs to become loose and attuned in a relaxed sort of way to her baby's rhythm and pattern. This is why relaxing and regressing into maternal preoccupation is so important. A mother with only half her mind on her baby, or over-quick and incisive in her movements, is likely to find it more difficult to provide that smooth synchrony and moderate stimulation when he is awake and minimal stimulation when asleep, which are necessary for an infant's growth. It must not be forgotten that the mother–child relationship is a two-way process. From birth, some babies are in need of very much more adaptation than others and can put more strain on a particular mother especially if they seem temperamentally very different.

Nevertheless, it is under relaxed conditions that the mother–child conversations of feeding, cuddling, talking, smiling, and playing generally seem to come most easily. Under such conditions, a mother seems to experience her baby paradoxically as separate from her and yet at one with her. 'Separate and yet as one' is naturally beautiful to watch. It is most obvious in mothering but also in fathering and in later life between lovers and very good friends; its beauty is also evident in anyone playing or working with consummate skill. This vital state of being together and yet separate is what we mean by loving. It is wonderful to experience and is vital for growth. Recent research in neuroscience has located this deeply emotional relating in the right hemisphere of the brain, which is growing exponentially in the first 2 years of life. At a neurological level we can think of mother and baby, in their finely tuned mutual dance, connecting with each other's 'right brain' and in doing so, enhancing the development of that part of the baby's brain that is especially concerned with social and emotional functioning. Impairments in this area have lifelong effects (Schore, 2001).

It must be becoming clear that, because of their absolute dependency at the beginning, only very few people can have the time to attune really harmoniously with a particular baby. What is more, if mothers themselves are to relax with their babies, they need helpers to continue to be vigilant for them. This is where the baby–mother–father triad can be a most enjoyable and economical unit. A husband or partner who is lovingly attuned to both the mother and baby can move easily between looking after her and helping her out with attending to their child. A partner is the most likely person to fulfil the needs of a vigilant helper, because not only are partners hopefully close but so also are father and baby. Mothers who have unsupportive partners, and who are isolated in other ways, are much more likely to become depressed, which leaves them and their babies extremely vulnerable.

The necessity for an infant to have only one 'mother', feeding her child herself, with attendant father, has often been questioned. In many parts of the world different childcare arrangements prevail, and increasingly in Western industrialized nations the nuclear family is declining as divorce rates rise and many children are brought up in single parent families. In 1992 in Great Britain, 23 per cent of families were headed by a single mother. Many mothers now return to work in their infants' early months, although research in the USA has revealed the detrimental effects that more than 20 hours per week of other-than-mother child care has upon the long-term development of children if it is begun in the first year of life and continues to school age (Belsky, 1999). Successful adoption makes it plain that breast-feeding is not essential. And the participation of nannies, or other members of an extended family, is common throughout the world without apparently catastrophic effects (Clarke & Clarke, 1975). Traditionally, in many societies, mothers have been assisted in the care of their babis by 'allo-mothers' (Blaffer Hrdy, 1999). What is crucial from the baby's point of view is that he has the opportunity for reliable, consistent and continuous relating to a relatively small group of carers who are absolutely committed to knowing him in a loving way. A chaotic whirl of unfamiliar helpers is known to be extremely distressing (Bowlby, 1958, 1969; Spitz, 1965). The grave long-term effects of this will be discussed in the next chapter.

What can a baby do in the early weeks?

As we have said, it used to be assumed that babies did very little except use rudimentary reflexes in sleep and when feeding in the early weeks. There is no doubt that sleep usually initially fills much of the time, but gradually the sleepy baby wakes up. At birth the human brain is remarkably unfinished in its development: more than 75 per cent of the neuronal connections in the brain develop after birth in the first year, in direct relationship with the external environment, and the emotional tone of this environment is as crucial as other aspects of stimulation. Connections amongst neurons (*synapses*) are established when stimuli act upon them. If the synapses are repeatedly used in the infant's day-to-day life they are reinforced and become part of the permanent structure. If they are not used they are shed (*neural Darwinism*). In influencing the reinforcement or pruning of the neural pathways, early experiences have decisive impact on the architecture of the brain and ultimately on the nature and extent of adult capacities (Schore, 1994).

Despite the immaturity of babies' brains, it does seem that the competencies they possess are immensely impressive and support the view that they are primed from the beginning to establish special relationships with those who make up their close social world (Murray & Andrews, 2000). As a consequence of the new investigative techniques, such as video recording and the imaginative use of what babies can do, e.g. sucking and looking, developmental psychologists have been able to demonstrate an impressive array of capabilities in very young infants.

As long ago as the late 1950s infant researcher and psychoanalyst Peter Wolff (1959) documented six different states of arousal in newborns. He was able to show that the seemingly unrelated behaviours of grimaces, twitching, sucking, etc. are not random but can be categorized into these six different states of *quiet sleep, active sleep, drowsiness, quiet alert, active alert* and *crying*. Each state has specific behavioural characteristics and reflects quite different ways of being or acting in the world. In the quiet alert state, for example, the baby is wide awake, attentive with eyes wide open, and taking in the world. The baby gazes directly at the mother's or father's face, and can even imitate another person's facial expression! In the active alert state the baby moves his limbs in discontinuous but rhythmical bursts. Even in sleep there are different states of arousal as the baby goes from quiet to active phases. Drowsiness is the state between waking and sleeping. Crying denotes the baby's distress and is the most potent form of communication available to the infant before language is acquired. These all have adaptive purposes, alerting the caregiver to be interested in the infant and promoting their interaction. It is the quiet alert state that experimental developmental psychologists capitalize on to assess what the very young infant is capable of doing.

Young babies are soon capable of a rough localization of sound and respond differently to its variations. Their startle reflex to sudden stimulation has been known for a long time (*the Moro reflex*). Relatively recently discovered, however, is that the whole body, and face and mouth in particular, responds in minute but quite specific ways, to different patterns. There is evidence that babies *mimic* their parents' facial expressions within minutes of birth. This is matched by mimicry of other body movements (Meltzoff & Moore, 1977). These observations make it clear that the rudiments of echoing another person's pattern of muscular activity, by movements of similar muscles, probably have an innate basis. The clarity of this mimicry seems to get confused later in infancy, presumably through babies' proneness to adapt to many external stimuli at once. What is more, the mimicry is only brought out in the first place by an adult who fits into the baby's arousal pattern. The person most likely to fit like this is, of course, the baby's mother, and sometimes the father if he is taking an active and frequent interest in his child. It is clear that babies and their primary caregivers develop a synchrony with each other from the earliest moments (Murray & Andrews, 2000).

- Smell: within the first hours, babies can discriminate between and show preference for the smell of their mother's milk over that of others. This is thought to be related to the connection between the smell of amniotic fluid and breast milk.
- Hearing: by the beginning of the third trimester of pregnancy the fetus responds in the womb to sounds from outside. Hearing is already functioning and so, when born, babies are able to recognize their mother's voice. A newborn prefers a woman's voice over a man's and it takes a bit of time for the father's voice to be preferred over that of another male (De Casper, quoted in Klaus, Kennel & Klaus, 1995). Experiments involving mothers reading Dr Seuss books whilst in the latter stages of pregnancy and then post-natally have also shown that babies remember what they have heard in the womb.
- Vision: at the beginning, babies can focus at approximately 20 cm (8 inches), just the distance to see the mother's face when cradled in her arms. Babies learn very quickly to recognize their mother's face and within a day or two will spend longer looking at her face than at that of another woman. When an object is brought within the visual range of young infants when they are in the quiet alert state, they will follow intently with their eyes, especially scanning the outline. The same is so of the way babies look at human faces, scanning the outline then moving to the eyes and mouth. In fact, babies prefer to look at the human face:

> In the quiet alert state as the eyes become bright and widely open, infants often stop moving or sucking and become very still. These short periods of rapt visual attention occurring shortly after birth and throughout the early period, draw newborns into eye to eye contact, a vital

element of human interaction. In this mutual gaze the first dialogue begins; parents and children seem magnetically drawn into communication. (Klaus et al., 1995)

At a few weeks, babies will stop crying at the sight of the mother's face, but not at others. One of the beginnings of the sense of *distance* is manifest within a month. Thus a 'defensive' gesture is made with the head and face when an object comes within about 30 cm (12 inches). Objects at a greater distance do not evoke this gesture even though they are bigger and make a larger retinal image.

• Touch: the skin is the largest sense organ of the body. Most babies like to be held, cuddled, stroked and rocked gently. The hands and mouth are the most sensitive areas, and babies are frequently seen sucking their thumbs or fingers. In fact, partly because of their propensity to use their mouths to explore the world, as well as being a major source of pleasure for babies, psychoanalysts refer to the early period of extra-uterine life as the oral phase; more of that later.

Hand–mouth–eye coordination grows apace and the reaching gestures with the hands observable as early as 14 days become the coordinated hand movements of the 3-month-old. Even before this we can see the beginnings of manipulative play, twisting, turning and moving things with the hands that are also looked at, taken into the mouth, chewed at and smelled (Hoffer, 1947).

Amodal perception

One of the amazing discoveries of the 1970s was that babies' senses are already connected up with each other so that they can transfer perceptual experience from one sensory modality to another. Psychologists Meltzoff and Moore (1977) demonstrated experimentally that babies, having had a dummy placed in their mouths without having caught sight of it, then given two objects, one the same texture as the dummy and the other different, will choose to look more at the matching surface. According to Daniel Stern (1985), infants appear to experience the world as a *perceptual unity* from which they can *abstract qualities* and *represent them mentally*. This enables them to form and act upon abstract representations from the earliest days of life. They appear not to be particular objects but qualities of shapes, intensities, and temporal patterns, the more global qualities of experience. Stern sees this as contributing to an *'emergent sense of self'* in the earliest weeks of life.

Non-differentiation of self and object

It used to be thought that young babies could not discriminate between themselves and others; that it took many months of being in an un-differentiated state with the world, then called *'normal autism'*, before they *'hatched'* into psychological life (Mahler, Pine & Bergmann, 1975). This was partly based on the then existing knowledge about what babies could do, the state of their central nervous systems and their apparent perceptual capacities. As we have just seen, developmental research has revealed the extent of babies' capacities to discriminate almost from the very beginning, and Margaret Mahler withdrew the term 'normal autism' in the early 1980s.

However, this idea of the infant's non-differentiation from the world has been a powerful source of understanding for later phenomena evidenced in clinical practice but also captured by poets and novelists, of *fantasies of merger*, that are so common. Margaret Mahler and her colleagues described these early months as being a time when mother and baby were in a *'symbiotic merger'*, i.e. that there was little, if any, sense between mother and baby of them being separate and different individuals. One of Mahler's collaborators, Fred Pine, has struggled to accommodate the new knowledge about infants with the need to trace the seemingly universal experience of merger fantasies later in childhood and adulthood. He has come up with the idea of *'significant moments'*, which may be relatively short but occur at a time in development when they are far more significant than the amount of time would suggest. Pine has taken the fact that these early months of life are when babies have the most access to their mother's body; they are held, carried, rocked, fed. At significant moments the hungry baby is nursing at the breast, possibly elaborating the phantasy of eating up mummy and the milk. (*Phantasy* is the unconscious imaginative elaboration of bodily processes in the context of the environmental provision. It is different from *fantasy*, which is used to denote a conscious thinking activity of the verbal mind.)

The sight of a satiated baby falling asleep at the mother's breast recalls parallel experiences of falling into a pillow, or a lover's body, in later life. At these moments, cognitive functioning is least articulated and one can infer the subjective experience of '*merging*' with the other so that there is a minimal sense of difference between the two. Pine also cites other prototypic moments, of mutual gaze, echoing of cooing voices of mother and infant, which are '*affectively supercharged* and which become central to organizing an array of precepts and memories, formative in their effect far out of proportion to their temporal duration' (Pine, 1981).

These moments of the experience of *non-differentiation* seem to be very important. Their presence can be felt in the child's early relationship with his mother and their mutual *mimicry and synchrony*. They are not only very enjoyable for both mother and child, but learning also seems to take place at a very great pace when there is plenty of synchrony. It probably forms a basis of comradeship, and friendliness of all sorts. It seems that transient or partial states of non-differentiation are both normal, in that they are frequent, and also probably essential for deep communication and health at any age.

The baby's emotional life

It will be apparent from this chapter so far that we see babies as being deeply emotional creatures. Young babies certainly soon manifest contentment, excitement, distress, rage and confusion. Perhaps after a few months it can be said that they can be joyful or elated and also depressed. There is no evidence in these early weeks for such complex feelings as disappointment, hope, envy, pity, concern or revenge. These emotions involve complex structures of intellectual discrimination and feeling, some of which may be put into words as: 'I have lost', 'I expect to get but haven't got', etc. It is also manifestly true that babies thrive on positive affect and become disoriented and disorganized if negative affects predominate. A major aspect of the mother's role is to help her young infant experience his *emotional arousal within manageable limits*. However, it is also of significance that in the process of providing this *emotional regulation*, mothers also gradually enable their offspring to make meaning of these emotional states. This can be thought of as arising through the parent's largely unconscious processing of the emotional experience of being with the baby.

Baby Leah (6 weeks old) was sitting in her chair, peering at the edge of the cupboard that was within her view. Her mother was sitting in a chair to the right, and slightly behind, not in the direct vision of her daughter. Leah began to frown, and over a period of a minute or so she became very restless and began to whimper. Her mother spoke to her from her seat in enquiring tones, wondering what was the matter. At first the sound of her mother's voice stimulated Leah to turn in her mother's direction, and for a few moments her face brightened. She looked at her for a short while and then turned away. Soon the frown reappeared; Leah squirmed in her chair, and her whimpering tones turned to cries. At this point her mother reached over and rocked the chair, again talking in soothing tones. Leah's cries hesitated but then became more definite, and then she began to cry lustily. Her mother was puzzled, and reached over and took Leah out of her chair, holding her close, chest to chest and Leah cried and cried. Mother spoke softly, asking Leah what was the matter, then conjecturing if she was cold, or suddenly hungry. Her mother rocked Leah and spoke of the different things that could be the matter, ticking off in her mind the likelihood of each. She wondered then if indeed Leah was suddenly lonely, only able to see her mother if she turned around, and she spoke of this. Gradually Leah calmed, and snuggled up to her mother's neck, and put her thumb in her mouth.

We can see here an ordinary everyday occurrence in the life of a baby and her mother; a baby starts to cry and the mother responds, not knowing what is the matter. The mother's attentiveness to the experience of her baby, and her own wish to understand the distress, indeed to take the cries as a communication, reflects the enquiry and *meaning making* qualities of these ordinary interactions. One of the consequences of this capacity in the mother is that the baby is helped to calm down, to *regulate* potentially overwhelming emotional states.

What makes an infant distressed?

What evokes distress in young infants? Babies are different in the ways they respond to stimuli, as some seem more sensitive than others from the very beginning to things like sudden loud noises or bodily discomfort. On the surface it seems that at the beginning most babies get upset predominantly because of bodily experiences: hunger, tiredness, pain, cold, etc. and over time we can see that both the cause and the meaning of a baby's distress will be very different. Crying is the *signal* that babies have to alert caregivers to their predicament and one of the tasks of those first weeks for parents is to learn what the particular sounds of the baby's cries mean, in order to respond in ways that console. Babies cannot use their cries to manipulate their caregivers – the capacity to do so is the product of development, and has no place in infancy. Babies are utterly dependent upon those looking after them to provide the soothing responses that will calm their distress. In fact the regulation of these highly aroused feeling states by caregivers is one of the primary tasks in infancy. This ultimately leads to the older child having a sense that there is a person to whom they can turn when they are upset, or if that person is not available and as they get older, being able to call upon their own *internal resources*, built up as a consequence of these consoling early experiences, to deal with their feelings.

Distress is relieved, of course, by stopping the disturbing stimulation and also by nursing, holding, caressing and cuddling. These all involve *gentle* movement and skin sense stimulation. Very young babies are most easily comforted when they are held chest to chest by the adult. This seems to give the greatest sense of comfort and security, from which soothing follows. These movements are *gently erotic*, rather than excitingly so, and have more than superficial similarities with a lover's embrace. By the second week of life, a soft comforting voice also often leads to distress being alleviated. Visually, the human face does not seem to be any more effective as a comforter until 1 month (Dunn, 1977).

In addition to the physical causes of distress, babies very quickly demonstrate that there are more psychological factors that upset them. Being left alone, for example, is something that many babies react to by crying. A young baby who cries in these circumstances will usually calm down pretty quickly if someone else comes into the room. He is not yet crying because of the absence of a particular person. It will be several months before the baby's cries will only be alleviated by the return of that special person. Also, as the baby gets older and more interested in things like reaching for a toy, he can become frustrated if teased and cry as a result. It is then the meaning of the object to the baby that is the key to understanding why he is upset.

Parents as sources of distress

Sometimes parents unwittingly can be the source of their babies' distress, such as being *over-stimulating* (e.g. erratic jigging which disturbs the sleep–waking rhythm), *confusing* (e.g. the mother becoming preoccupied with something which stills her face when the infant is expecting a lively interaction (Murray & Trevarthan, 1986; Tronick et al., 1979), and *rejecting* (e.g. parents' avoidance of their baby's gaze). Babies are amazingly in tune with the emotional states of their caregivers. They can intuit in the emotional atmosphere when it feels safe or not. This intuition goes on at a level outside of conscious awareness and is usually connected with most subtle cues that are detected in the minutiae of interaction between the baby and its caregivers. Sometimes, ordinary instinctive responses to a baby's distress do not work and the parents might be pushed to ask for outside help to understand what is going on with their baby and themselves. The following is an example of such:

Jilly was a baby who seemed to hate being separated from her mother, Jane. Every time Jane put her down, for example in her cradle or on a rug on the floor, Jilly would cry inconsolably. Jane got very upset. She was a first-time mother, a long way from her home and family of origin. She and her husband had moved to the city in search of work and better opportunities. Jane's father had died suddenly just before Jilly was due and she was born nearly a month late. At her 6-week check-up with her GP Jane burst into tears and described her worries about not being able to console her baby. After hearing some of the story her GP referred Jane and Jilly to the local parent and infant special project. There they were seen by a psychotherapist, who listened to Jane's story but this time got to hear another part of it – that Jane's mother had died when she was just 10 years old. She had not missed her, she thought, because her father had been such a good substitute. But now as a new mum herself she was feeling the need of her own mother to help her be a good mother to Jilly. In the first session Jilly was asleep in the sling on her mother's chest. They seemed stuck together like glue. In the next session Jilly was awake and when Jane put her on the mat on the floor she cried, her eyes screwed up. To soothe her, Jane tried rocking Jilly gently, speaking softly in her ear, walking around with her, gently moving, but nothing worked until she offered her breast and Jilly calmed down. Over just a few sessions the therapist explored with Jane both her feelings about the difficulties now with Jilly, but also something of her history. As Jane's trust in the therapist grew she was able to confide a terrible dread she had about Jilly, which was that she – Jane – would die and leave Jilly motherless, as she had been. Every time she saw Jilly smiling or beginning to play she felt sad and tearful as she thought of her dread. Following this discussion the change in Jilly was remarkable. As Jane grew able to confide in the therapist, and began to face the feelings about her own loss of her mother in her childhood, Jilly seemed less distressed and more able to tolerate the small separations that being put down entailed. They did not any more seem linked with the terrible dread – connected here with Jane's unresolved grief for her dead mother.

Here it was the opportunity to unravel the meaning to the mother of putting her baby down, a mini-separation which evoked all her unresolved grief, that ultimately allowed the usual means of consoling and comforting Jane's baby to be effective. If it is not an undiagnosed physical condition that is at the root of the distress, it is often the case that a more hidden emotional meaning to the parent is preventing them from being able to comfort their baby.

Unfortunately there are also situations in which parents, on whom infants are completely dependent, are also the *source of fear*. This can be either because they are malevolent towards the baby or because they are frightened of the baby. We will look in more detail at this in the later chapters, but suffice it to say here that this contradiction is extremely disturbing for the baby and gives rise to different manifestations of distress.

There are differing views about how parents, mothers in particular, can affect the enjoyment or distress of their children. There is by now so much evidence that in general ways parental influences on children are enormous that it is puzzling why anyone bothers to question it (Ainsworth et al., 1978; Bowlby, 1969; Fonagy et al., 1993; Fraiberg et al., 1987). Understandably, there is anxiety about 'mother bashing' – making mothers feel unduly guilty for the ordinary difficulties of life. However, there is value in such questioning for we can then argue different points of view; it is by this that we can continually refine our ideas about causes of enhancement and distress. For instance, it seems to be becoming clearer that it is often the general *atmosphere* emanating from a parent, given no doubt by subtle cues as in the example above, that distresses children more than any easily definable specific activities.

There has been even more controversy about the *lasting effects* on a child of infantile distress. Babies are certainly less fragile than we used to think, especially if periods of distress are made up for later (Ainsworth et al., 1978; Bowlby, 1969; Rutter, 1972). Children are often thought of as *resilient*. It is now clear that resilience is not something that babies are born with but develop as a consequence of *secure attachment* to their parents. Recent research also demonstrates the long-term consequences at many levels of severe and unmitigated distress in babies and young children. Perry and his colleagues have investigated the lasting impact at a neurological level, of repeated experiences of exposure to trauma and violence in families. They demonstrated how *'states' of distress* can be *hardwired* into the developing brain and so become *'traits'*, characteristic features of a person's disposition. Thus an infant who has been in a repeated and constant state of hyper-arousal may, as a consequence of the pruning of neural pathways (described earlier), become a chronically anxious older child (Perry et al., 1995). What has become more evident as a result of the explosion of knowledge of early development in the last three decades is that the child is indeed father to the man, as the poet Wordsworth wrote of in his poem 'My heart leaps up when I behold'. The earliest years are indelibly marked not only on the child's developing personality and character, but also on his brain structure.

Phantasy

We can see the baby as experiencing his world in profoundly emotional ways; surges of pleasure when the interaction with the caregiver mother is *contingent and modulated* at his pace, not yet expecting him to wait, as this capacity is the outcome of development based on experiences of satisfaction. Equally, surges of unpleasure (as Freud termed it) when satisfaction is too long in coming. Winnicott's view was that, through the accruing of these experiences, the baby's inherited potential as a human being is activated so that he begins to feel a sense of continuity, or a sense of 'going on being', as Winnicott put it. This is only possible when the infant has received care tailored to his needs, and 'primary maternal preoccupation' is the means by which the mother is able to adapt herself to her utterly dependent infant at the beginning. This is why general advice to mothers is largely unhelpful if it goes against their own sense of their baby. What mothers need from their partners or from health professionals or from friends is support to find and follow their own *intuitive knowledge* of their baby.

Now psychoanalysts say something more than just describing the acutely sensitive interaction between a baby and his mother. Because psychoanalysts are interested in the internal story of who and how a person *is*, they go beyond what is observable and speculate about what is in the mind of the baby who is feeding or looking, smiling or crying. Of course, they are not alone in this speculation, as anyone who has spent any time with a small baby will be familiar with the question: what is going on in this baby's mind? Only having our adult language to describe what we imagine hampers us. Babies do not have words and their experiences are felt at a sensorimotor level, with these waves of pleasure and unpleasure giving them particular qualities. Psychoanalysts postulate that the baby elaborates *phantasies* – derived from the sensorimotor, affective level – around their experiences (Isaacs, 1970). Our adult words might describe a baby feeding thus:

> She feels some urgency in her tummy and the mother's breast fills her mouth and the warm milk goes down her throat and into her gripey, hungry insides. She feels herself filling up and as she does she imagines her mother, not just the milk, filling her up and her whole sense of her body and her self feels full of this warm mummy and they are one, not two, as she is inside her and she has gobbled her up. At this point she may begin to feel sated and becomes groggy and sleepy, full of feed and mummy, and falls asleep as her mouth holds onto the nipple because that way she might hold onto this lovely feeling that she has mummy inside.

In this scenario we can also imagine the mother's unconscious, and perhaps also quite conscious, elaborating of another phantasy of being gobbled up by her baby, and wanting this as her mind meets her baby's in this encounter.

Another phantasy might include elaborations of the baby's experience of her hard gums as teeth begin to form and biting becomes a possibility. As this nipple is felt in the mouth the baby chews at it or really bites; the baby may imagine that her chewing and biting is tearing the breast to pieces, the gobbling-up becoming a much more aggressive affair. *Primitive love* is a strong business! Babies need to feel OK about their *aggressive impulses* as well as their loving ones, although of course the reaction they get will probably be quite different.

This is the stuff of *unconscious phantasy*, derived from the bodily urges meeting the experience of satisfaction (and non-satisfaction) from the outside world. We can equally speculate about other kinds of phantasies that might be more anxiety provoking, when the mother is unable to be so attuned to her baby and he has to bear frustrations before he is able to. Winnicott described these as *impingements* which, if they predominate in a young baby's life, provoke reactions which disrupt the nascent sense of '*going on being*', and might result in what he described as a *false self organization* where individuality and creativity remain hidden behind a compliant shell (Winnicott, 1960). The following is an observation of a 13-week-old baby girl, Lucy, whose mother Mrs A. was very reluctant to pick her up and hold her. In addition to a prohibition on holding, there were others relating to Lucy's exploration of her own body. Lucy was not allowed to touch her face with her hands. This had started at 3 weeks, and Mrs A. explained to the observer that it was because Lucy had long fingernails and her mother was afraid Lucy would scratch her face with them. Mrs A. was afraid to cut the nails in case she cut Lucy's skin as well. Thenceforth Lucy wore cotton gloves that prevented her from having any skin-to-skin contact with her hands. Additionally, any movement Lucy made towards her face was usually interrupted by her mother:

. . . Lucy found herself with her hands uncovered and sucked on them with great enthusiasm. She particularly seemed to find her left hand satisfying and sucked vigorously on the thumb when she could get it into her mouth . . . When her mother returned to the room, she immediately went to Lucy and said 'No! . . . No! . . . Don't do that, don't put your hands into your mouth'. So saying, she substituted the dummy and for a while Lucy sucked on it. Eventually it fell from her mouth and the left hand returned, the vigorous sucking being repeated. Again it was interrupted by the mother, this time offering baby rice, which drooled from Lucy's mouth as she appeared not to want it . . . Then Mrs A. took Lucy's hands and jollied her with a song which evoked giggles and smiles. The gloves were then replaced.

We can see here that Mrs A.'s worries about holding and touching were compromising her baby's sense that her own wishes and urges had any value; we might speculate that the rather manic conformity that Lucy had no option but to comply with could lead eventually to the false self-personality that Winnicott wrote about.

The feeding situation is prototypic of these early weeks: the imperative of the hunger, the ready response of the mother hopefully providing her infant with satisfaction, holding and handling with gentleness and close body contact. The mother draws on her own unremembered experiences that were registered at a psychic and bodily level, which enable her to connect with her baby in this way. She is able then to implement her baby's relationship with herself and thus the world in a benign and creative way. She is also able to provide for her baby the context within which his experience of these inner urges are really felt to come from inside himself, and not, as Winnicott put it, 'as a clap of thunder from elsewhere' (Winnicott, 1945).

The significance of the oral phase

We noted earlier that Freud (1905) and psychoanalysts call these days of infancy the early oral phase. This is because the mouth for breathing and feeding is obviously so important. Functions concerned with feeding must immediately get organized relative to his mother if an infant is to survive. Other parts of the body can, and do, wait until later months, but the mouth, gut and lungs cannot wait. We have, however, noticed that these early days are concerned not only with the mouth but also particularly with the use of the eyes and nose as well. We might better call these days the 'snout' phase. The mouth and the face are the focus and source of much, if not most, of the pleasure and unpleasure of the early months.

Early oral patterns certainly seem to persist throughout life and we can see that at one level they are linked with what we have said about *ph*antasy (that is, the unconscious imaginative elaboration of bodily processes in the context of the environmental provision. It is different from *f*antasy, which is used to denote a conscious thinking activity of the verbal mind). Consider for instance the social *expression of feeling* or *emotion* (it is a useful convention to reserve the term 'emotion' for the open *expression* or communication of feeling). Much of this is by the shaping of the mouth as well as in the use of other facial muscles, hands, and posture (Argyle, 1988). People often bear their teeth in rage, purse their lips in meanness, drop their jaws and open their mouths in wonderment or innocence and so on. Darwin, incidentally, noted all this years ago.

More than this, however, our everyday language is full of phrases about oral functioning. Here are a few: 'I've bitten off more than I can chew', 'He makes me sick', 'She's sweet', 'She's sugary', 'I can't swallow that', 'Trust not a lean and hungry man', 'This will make you choke', or 'I love you so much I could eat you'. These everyday phrases are not normally about eating or drinking. They are metaphors; they are in the evocative language of oral activity but about other things. They show the psychoanalyst and anyone else who dwells a moment on the subject, that *oral f/phantasies* infuse much of adult thinking, especially when we are being emotional (Segal, 1995).

The mirror and the sense of self

This chapter has described the building blocks of the new baby's sense of self. The kind of care that the young baby receives forms its core. The metaphor of the *mirror* is one that has been used to capture the essence of the interaction between the person who does the mothering and the baby. The mother, who provides her baby with an experience of being mirrored, i.e. the baby gazes into her eyes and sees himself, provides him with the kernel of a *coherent, non-alienated core* to his sense of self. Alternatively, the mother who is so preoccupied with herself, or who or what she wants her baby to be, will only show herself to him in the mirror of her eyes, and risks her baby taking in elements that are *alien, possibly hostile, to form part of his core self*. The long-term consequences for these alternatives are the difference between a *creative and coherent self-identity*, and an *alienated incoherent self structure* (Fonagy, 1999; Winnicott, 1960).

Observing young babies

Because babies can't talk and tell us directly, we have to rely on our imaginations to get inside their experience. We can also deduce a great deal from careful systematic observations, and in recent years this has been greatly assisted for developmental researchers, by videotaping and other forms of recording. Remember, it is important to observe babies for yourselves. Even if you can do no more, a few minutes comparing the facial expression of a baby of a few weeks with those at a few months will make you marvel at what happens in those early weeks of life. There are many opportunities, especially in London, to systematically observe a baby and his mother in their family environment in the context of a supervised 'mother–infant observation group' (see index). Failing that, as was mentioned earlier, there are very good films on the subject ('Sunday's child' for instance; see the film index on p. 304). In your professional practice you will probably come across mothers and babies quite frequently. Spend a bit of time looking at these babies; mothers usually love their babies being of interest and you will learn a lot.

Further reading

Baradon, T. with Broughton, C., Gibbs, I., James, J., Joyce, A., and Woodhead, J. (2005) *The Practice of Psychoanalytic Parent–Infant Psychotherapy. Claiming the Baby*. London: Routledge.

Boswell, S. (2004) *Understanding Your Baby*. London: Tavistock Clinic & Jessica Kingsley.

Klaus, M., & Klaus, P. (1998) *Your Amazing Newborn*. Reading, MA: Perseus Books.

Klaus, M., Kennel, J., & Klaus, P. (1995) *Bonding*. Reading, MA: Perseus Books.

Chapter 4

The second six months: the baby getting organized

Angela Joyce

So far, we have seen just how competent newborn infants are, and how poised and ready they are to relate to those who care for them. As they get established in these early relationships with those who, hopefully, will remain with them until they grow up, babies begin to show signs of what we will call '*getting organized*'. Those who spend time around young babies will see during these months that they change in very noticeable ways, at particular times. On the outside, the babies will move from eating only milk, breast or bottle, to solid food and, by the end of the first year, will probably be interested in a wide variety of ordinary foods and begin to show preferences for what they like or dislike; they will almost certainly be on the move, crawling if not already walking; they will probably have established a reliable sleep pattern where they sleep for some time during the day and have a long uninterrupted 10–12-hour sleep at night time; they possibly will also have uttered sounds remarkably similar to recognizable words and intended for communication about something. Increasingly, there will be a sense that the baby is gradually becoming a person. Internally, changes are also progressing apace, partly as a consequence of an inbuilt developmental programme with which we are all born and partly in response to the experiences babies have with those who care for them. In this chapter we are going to chart the changes that take place during the first year of life that we see as evidence of this 'organization' that is central to the internal emotional and social development of the baby.

Perhaps the first time this happens is around the middle of the second month of life, when babies begin to smile in response to a friendly face. Parents find their smiling babies immensely pleasing and often talk about feeling that their baby's intentional smile shows them something of their unique personality for the first time. However, over the next months babies become much more discriminating and, by the middle of the first year, their most beaming smiles are kept for the special people in their lives – usually mum – and dad – if he is around often enough, and of course older siblings who often find little babies of this age great fun and can contribute enormously to maintaining the positive feelings that are so good for the baby's development. This shift from the baby beaming at any person who engages with him to registering clearly the special-ness of just a few, reflects an internal development in the baby's experience of himself and of those people who care for him. It suggests that the baby's emotional investment in those who care for him has become heightened; one might say that the baby is falling in love. Psychoanalysts have called this the stage at which the mother, in particular, has become for the baby its '*libidinal object*' – a rather clumsy way of trying to say that mum is the object of the baby's passions. So what happens that the baby claims its mother in this way and, through her, the world? Let's start with an example of a baby responding to the realities of family life during the first 4 months.

When Mrs B. phoned she said she was at the end of her tether, as 4-month-old Jack was not sleeping. Her parents had just left to return to their home overseas after a visit to see the new generation of parents and their baby. She added that she had recently returned to work full-time and so would need an evening appointment. Both parents came with their little boy to the first session, when they initially presented the sleeping problem as stemming from the time when Jack had had his injections at 3 months. Before that he had been getting into a routine of being quite a reliable sleeper but this had been ruined by his upset over the injections. Mrs B., almost by the way, added that she had returned to full-time work at around the same time. She said that she had been at home for 11 weeks with Jack and he had been a real mummy's boy. She wondered if she had been too close to him. She was breast-feeding him and enjoying it, and now that was restricted, although when he woke at night he was fairly insistent on being fed by her. He also increasingly wanted to spend time up and alert at night, and two nights previously she had played with him from midnight to 3 a.m. At other times, she and her husband, at their wits' end with tiredness, and on the advice of an acquaintance, had allowed Jack to cry for an hour after he woke up in the middle of the night. He had cried all that time until they could bear it no longer, and he had fallen asleep 'instantly' when they had given him a cuddle.

A picture unfolded of a mother who had quite severe conflicts about closeness to her new baby, which seemed linked to her own history to her relationship with her mother. She was from the other side of the world and had come to this country with her new husband, as that seemed to be the only way to get away from her family. She had been unable to do this whilst living in her home country. Her husband did not seem to be so troubled by the same issues but agreed with her perception of her relationship with her mother as being claustrophobic. The therapist put to them that, with the birth of their first baby, she had become very anxious that the overly close relationship with her mother would be repeated with her son, and as a consequence she had created the opposite situation. She had gone back to work full-time, very early by her own description, leaving Jack with a childminder for 10 hours a day so that she was experiencing quite a distant link with him. His sleeping problems seemed very clearly connected to his wish for the close relationship with his mother of the first 11 weeks, to be continued.

Mr and Mrs B. were both pleased and troubled to think about their baby in this way. The idea that he was missing his mum and making up for it at night was very confirming to Mrs B. that she was a good mother to him, but she had very real anxieties about such closeness. Coupled with this were the economic factors which supported the solution they had arrived at: she earned more than her husband and they had a mortgage to pay. They had considered Mr B. staying at home to be the primary carer for their child, and on further exploration it seemed that he was not troubled in the same way his wife was about the intimacy and closeness involved in looking after a baby. She was struggling with her wish to be the baby's favourite, with all the exclusive closeness she also dreaded, and her wish to be a woman whose status as a mother need not disrupt in any way her previous solutions to these issues. Jack's sleeping improved dramatically after the first meeting!

We can see that there are possibly several reasons for Jack's difficulties in sleeping at night. For the moment, let us concentrate on the fact that Jack seems to have responded sturdily to a changing sense of mother's presence – a feature of *his external world*. He cries and is sleepless and we have a sense not only of his distress but his capacity to communicate his distress to his parents. We may infer that he is feeling anxious and unhappy – in *his internal world*. His cries obviously had emotional impact on his mother, whose responses seem likely to have been influenced by her own experience of being mothered as a baby and later as a child as she grew up.

The psychological birth of the self and the sense of external reality

In the last chapter we saw how the baby and mother have heightened moments together, of *symbiotic union* (Pine, 1981). We also described Winnicott's ideas about the young baby having an experience, supported by his mother, of feeling that he created the world – *the illusion of omnipotence*. Both these theorists were trying to grasp the emotional quality of the early mother–baby relationship when it is going well, full of feelings of *synchrony and closeness*, and which some developmental psychologists have now extensively investigated. They were also trying to set the scene for recognizing just how different babies are when they relate in the world in a much more integrated and directed, autonomous and 'separated-out' way. The baby who, at 4 months or so, is coordinating his hands and eyes so that the interesting-looking coloured shape can be grabbed and sucked, is indicating his *capacity for intentionality and agency* that has not been so evident before. The baby's physical capacity to reach and grasp also reflects his growing interest in things around him, in the context of the relationship with the mother. The intensely social time that Trevarthan and Aitken (2001) call *primary intersubjectivity* opens up to include playthings, which eventually also form the focus of *joint attention* and interest later in the first year.

Un-differentiation and separateness

There has been much controversy in recent years about whether the young baby is able, from the beginning, to experience himself as a separate and distinct individual. In fact, this had been a point of difference between the various psychoanalytic schools for much of the twentieth century, and is now added to by the findings of developmental psychology. The importance of the controversy lies in the significance attached to the baby's growing realization of the *otherness* of those around him and how this is related to the *development of mind* and the *integrity of the sense of self*. It seems the case that young babies have at a physical level, a sense of where they end and the outside world begins; that to suck one's own thumb is a very different feeling compared with sucking someone else's thumb. But what are the psychological or mind correlates of this? How and when do the accumulating experiences of the young baby's life, of being hungry then fed, of gazing into the mother's eyes then seeing her back retreating out of the door, of crying then being held, being smiled at, etc. etc. coalesce into this baby feeling that this is me and that is you, separate and yet connected? Theoretically, this area is called the development of the *representational world* (Sandler & Rosenblatt, 1962), and the next few sections deal with how this process has been understood by various authors.

Getting organized as a response to the external world

We have just seen an example of how the external world impacts on the early life of the baby. Mother, or her substitute, is the environment. But if mother remains in the state of *primary maternal preoccupation* for ever, her individual life will be compromised, as will that of her baby and the rest of the family. The special timelessness of those early weeks retreats and as the mother 'recovers' herself, so her maximum adaptation to her baby also changes. Mother begins to see that out of her adaptation, her baby has begun to experience the world and her, as *trustworthy, reliable and expectable*. Now the baby can begin to be relied upon to let mother know something of his wishes and needs. This usually corresponds with babies' motor development, so that at around 3–4 months, as they can reach out, they can indicate at a very primitive level something of their own desires, e.g. grasping a rattle that is just within reach. Mothers who are always ahead, always anticipating their babies' wishes and needs, do not help to create the space across which they can reach (Hopkins, 1996). Babies will now be able to wait a while, for example, as the imperative of hunger is assuaged for the moment by mother's voice reassuringly saying that dinner is coming, as she juggles perhaps to meet the inevitable conflicting needs of a busy household.

In this space opened up between mother and baby the most rudimentary thoughts form. When the baby feels hungry, for instance, we can imagine how the memory of a previous good feed will be drawn upon (Freud, 1921). Psychoanalysts, in trying to capture the essence of the young baby's experience, have talked about the baby relating to '*part objects*'. What they mean by this is that the mother is not yet felt to be a whole person but is related to as if she were parts of a person at different times. For example, the mummy who is the source of a good feed is one mummy, whilst the mummy who keeps the baby waiting just a bit too long is felt to be a very different one. It is a matter of time and development before babies can conjure up an image in their minds of the whole mother who contains all these different experiences, and it will still be many months before these babies point and show their mothers in these ways what interests them; but it begins here, around the middle of the first 6 months of life.

Psychoanalysts see early experiences of '*symbiosis*' as never being fully given up, but as providing the basis in experience for *fantasies of merger* that frequently occur in later childhood and adulthood (Pine, 1981). However, the process of '*disillusionment*', based on earlier adaptation to need, through which the mothers provide the setting for the babies to give her their '*spontaneous gestures*' (Winnicott, 1984b), is also the source of these babies coming to feel that they are living life creatively. Babies who can call their mothers and get her response, for instance, are beginning to experience themselves as effective people in the world. These are the earliest forms of creativity that Winnicott saw as essential to living a life from one's true self, in all its crude forms (Winnicott, 1971).

These processes can be easily recognized in everyday life. At around 5–6 months of age babies love to sit on their mother's lap and explore all the details of the mother's face and body. This is the time when necklaces and spectacles are grabbed and eyes are poked and ears pulled. The mother's ease in allowing this exploration reflects her capacity to receive her infant's curiosity and reaching towards her, across a gap that is coming to have meaning for them both. Another way in which this gap is evident is the almost universal game of 'peek-a-boo'.

Seven-month-old Peter was crawling around the floor, having just come in with his mother from a trip to the shops. His mother had taken off his jacket, which was lying on the cushion. Peter rolled on the cushion and the jacket ended up over his face. He whimpered underneath it and his mother took it from his face. Peter beamed at her as he rediscovered his recently disappeared mum, and she responded with a delighted 'Hello'. The game got going between the two of them.

The rhythm of being there, disappearing, followed by rediscovery with all the excitement and delight it invariably involves, captures beautifully the developmental task for mother and baby of managing creatively the space that is opening up between them. Not so long ago the baby will probably have begun to eat solid food and sometimes weaning from breast-feeding occurs, although many mothers continue to breast-feed for several months to come. This is a major transition and involves loss and mourning for what has gone before, in the opening up of the space between mother and child.

Daniel Stern (1985) observed that the 'mirroring' interactions of early infancy give way at about 9 months of age to the mother expressing her attunement in a different way, one in which the interaction functions more as a metaphor than an imitation. For the parents to be able to attune they must be able to read the infant's feeling state from the overt behaviour, and respond with a behaviour that is not an imitation, but corresponds in some way with the infant's own behaviour, and the infant has to be able to read this response as having to do with their original feeling experience and not just imitating the behaviour.

Stern gives as an example of this a 9-month-old becoming very excited about a toy and making an exuberant sound 'aaaah!' as she grabs it and looks at her mother. The mother responds by hunching up her shoulders and making her upper body shimmy like a go-go dancer, lasting as long as the daughter's 'aaaah!' with the same excitement and intensity.

Perhaps the term 'echoing' more accurately reflects what the parent does, reflecting in their unconsciously propelled actions, their registering of the baby's inner state. The parent also subtly opens up the space between, as a different modality is used to convey the resonance.

The father's role in this separating out process has been stressed by some authors (Lebovici, 1984). This 'triangulation' of the emotional space in and around the baby is of vital importance for the ongoing development of complexity in the child's mind. It enables the child to have the beginnings of experiencing group life, where, gradually, complicated sets of relationships occur, involving couples, singles, being on the inside or feeling left out, etc. etc. Ultimately, these will lead to what psychoanalysts have called the 'Oedipus complex' – but for most psychoanalysts that is for later on in early childhood.

Aggression

The inability to control must entail frustration, especially for the baby. And we know that this evokes distress and rage. To move from the position of feeling that they have created the world to beginning to realize this is not the case, involves the baby's recognizing that he does not control the world or the mother. Thus, development of a sense of external reality inevitably involves feelings of rage, which means destructive aggression as well as the experience of loss. Furthermore, if the sense of self is the counterpart of external reality, then the feeling of oneself as a separate individual is also born out of frustration, distress and rage. Without aggressiveness there is thus no self. This rather solemn conclusion is not widely discussed in the literature but it is explicitly stated by Freud (1915) and Winnicott (1984a, 1971). Winnicott stressed the vital importance of mothers in reality being able to tolerate and survive their baby's aggression: without this, the baby's senses of internal and external reality will be compromised (1971). Clearly, also, babies must develop differentiation of self from external reality by a tolerable rhythm of satisfaction and frustration. In a mixture of Spitz's and Mahler's phrases, the pattern of a mother's yes's and no's provides the background for this psychological birth. Without steady satisfactions and enjoyment from his parents, a baby cannot develop those hopeful ideas of future pleasure that make painful frustrations bearable. When distress becomes chronic, then it seems that a child's mind resorts to a variety of pathological defensive tricks of imagination where self and reality discriminations are distorted, if not disabled.

What we have discussed here are the first dim, vague but deep beginnings of an underlying sense of external reality. We are not yet talking about the clearly structured and precise thinking which we call rational thought, only its origins. The evidence suggests that realistic thinking only slowly develops throughout childhood and after; it is the product of imagination or fantasy being tested and refined by experiences. Children, if healthy, continuously create hypotheses about the world from their imagination. These are modified and also distorted by what they are told, and what they experience for themselves.

For a long time to come babies will need their mothers and the other caregivers to be attuned in a special way, based on intimacy and knowing. But this time of 'disillusionment' (Winnicott, 1982c) is vital for babies coming to know at a mental level who they are and who their mothers are; ultimately, that is, for the establishment of the sense of self and sense of the other, and external reality. Reality gradually disconfirms the illusory aspects of the 'belief' that mother and infant are one, a belief that was implemented and sustained by the mother's adaptation at the beginning. It is important that babies are able to experience this change in their sense of their mothers with her; for this beginning of separateness to be founded upon the real absence or retreat of the mother, perhaps through too early return to work, puts enormous strain upon the construction of the infant's developing internal world.

The organization of the developing internal world

Babies' everyday experiences begin to get more varied and complex as the first year of life unfolds. The early days of sleeping, feeding and being cleaned up become more elaborated as routines are established and their physical development proceeds. Nevertheless, the detail of these everyday happenings are the stuff of which the baby's 'internal world' is comprised. The way in which baby and mother settle in together becomes recognizably *their* way and in turn comprise the building blocks of the internal landscape of the baby's mind.

We can see that the baby has continuous moment-to-moment experiences every day; in the morning, for instance, waking and calling, crying and howling, being attended to by mummy or daddy, feeling relieved and calming down after being held and cuddled and reminded that they are here and have not disappeared forever; this may be followed by some time cuddling up in bed with both mummy and daddy, or perhaps some play time with one parent or an older sibling, then a feed just with mummy at her breast, or maybe breakfast at the table with the rest of the family. Each of these is made up of sequences of events that may be interactive with another, or may just involve the baby himself. What is essential to our understanding of these events is that they are all laden with feelings. These have both *quality*, what Daniel Stern calls *vitality*, surges of dynamic feelings that are felt in the body over time, globally positive or negative (Stern, 1985); and much later on, *discreet and elaborated* meaning such as admiration, envy, guilt. Over time, the baby accrues memories of himself and of others, which become '*representations*', and form the basis upon which he feels himself to be and how he feels others to be, in the world.

These sequences of interactions become expectable for the baby and begin to be represented in the emerging mind. Daniel Stern calls these *RIGS – representations of interactions that are generalized* (Stern, 1985) – and '*schemas of being with another*' (Stern, 1995). Joseph Sandler (Sandler & Rosenblatt, 1962) called them '*self and object representations*' or the '*representational world*', which becomes a structure in the child's mind that acts like a template for all later relationships. John Bowlby, who pioneered the theory of attachment, used the term '*internal working models of attachment*'. Another similar way of thinking about how these structures build up in the baby's mind is to see them as '*procedures*' – ways of being with another that become second nature, or indeed first nature to the baby. It is on the basis of these earliest experiences of being with the other that later relationships are approached. These procedures become part of the unconscious structuring of the mind and are evident in the person's customary ways of being – their personal style of relating.

Different theorists have described these processes in different ways, emphasizing different aspects. Within psychoanalysis, great emphasis has been placed upon the *meaning making capacities of the mind*, some schools seeing the operation of *unconscious phantasy* (see Chapter 3) as being primary in the creation of what is referred to as the '*internal object world*'. The term '*object*' has been used to stress the sense that in the unconscious, the external reality of the other person is distorted by the operation of *phantasies* and these are present and powerful from the very beginning of life. This is especially true of the Kleinian school of thought (Waddell, 1998). Others, such as those in the Independent Group of the British Psycho-Analytical Society (e.g. Winnicott, Bowlby), and those whose thinking is in the tradition created by Anna Freud such as J. and A.M. Sandler and P. Fonagy (the Contemporary Freudian Group of the BPAS) emphasize the significance of external reality, especially at the beginning of life, and see phantasy distortions as becoming important as development accrues. Theorists who straddle different traditions, such as Daniel Stern, who is a psychoanalyst and a developmental researcher, tend to see the infant as experiencing reality events that are not distorted by phantasy or defensive distortions until after symbolic thinking is available.

Adaptation

We can see from this description of the internal world of self and object representations, that the baby's mind is developing through its *adaptation* to personal relationships. It is through this relating and adaptation that the baby begins to use his developing mind. At the beginning, he is not yet doing what we might later call proper thinking, because he is not actively and systematically using these mental representations of the world in his mind. But the preliminary stages of adaptation are appearing.

Just a few words theoretically about these concepts. The term generally used to refer to an individual's mental processes that adapt to the world around him is *ego-functioning*. It applies to anyone of any age. Psychoanalysts introduced the term *ego* to refer to those aspects of the mind that are adaptive, in contrast to a person's drives and desires, which are termed *id* (Freud, 1923). The ego should also be distinguished from the *self*. The two ideas are related but the self refers to one as an *experiencing subject* whereas the ego refers to one as *adaptive*.

Infants, with their rudimentary ego functioning, are just beginning to know what to do in the world. They are starting to *register and memorize* relationships between things that are detectable within and around them. They seem to store them in organized systems, or in schemata (Piaget, 1953), using memory and beginning to make a 'same again' response. As we have seen, it is now thought that pre-verbal infants store their memories as 'episodes', that is, memories are not discrete perceptions but are a conglomerate of perception, action, and affect. In other words, what babies remember is a whole event or series of events that are generalized over time and are laden with emotional meaning (Stern, 1985). So a baby at the breast will have repeated experiences that are all largely similar, and these will be stored as a generalized memory of a 'breast feed'. If such a feed then is markedly different from earlier and now expected feeds, such as if the baby's nose gets blocked whilst feeding, this variant will be registered but not generalized unless it is repeated, and becomes the norm.

It used to be thought that very young babies had no functioning memory and that it took the best part of the first year of life for a baby to hold a memory of an absent object in mind. However, more recent researchers have been able to demonstrate that babies as young as 2 months of age can recall events. For example, a baby is lying in her cot with a mobile hanging above to which her foot is attached by a string. She quickly learns that by moving her foot she can make the mobile stop and start and shows pleasure in this. Weeks later when the baby is returned to the same cot but this time without her foot attached, she will try to move it, and will be perplexed at the failure to effect the move. If the mobile is different, the baby will not have the same response (Rovee-Collier, 1987). In this example, the baby needs the cot and the mobile to demonstrate that the previous event can be recalled. It seems that it will be many months before he can evoke a memory in the absence of such stimuli. Sometime in the second half of the first year the baby will begin to show that out of sight does not mean out of mind and will start searching for things that are hidden – he can evoke an image from his store of memories and it comes alive for him in his mind at that moment; this is termed *'object permanence'*.

The use of memory in the registering of sameness is, of course, one of the most widespread and fundamentally adaptive functions of the mind. We have here the rudiments of *classificatory activity*, which is used for *economy of thought and action*, from the simplest to the most complex and abstract. Infants and young children largely have to learn what things are the same as others and they often get it wrong. For instance, a baby grabbing at soap bubbles sees them in front of his eyes and thinks, 'Ah, the same grabbable things again', when they are not.

Note also that registration of sameness probably must precede '*the recognition of similarity*'. To register things as similar involves knowing that they are different but have an attribute in common, only after this does classification proper occur. The baby has nowhere nearly reached this complexity of thinking yet. In fact, Piaget noted that his 18-month-old child, out for a walk, saw a slug and then another one some minutes later. From her conversation it was clear that she thought they were the same slug. The idea of similarity had not occurred to her yet, at least with regard to slugs.

Defences

One of the most important aspects of ego functioning is to help the person deal with the demands that come from inside, e.g. in the form of wishes and wants such as hunger, and those that come from outside, usually experienced at first as whether these wishes are acceptable or not to significant people in one's life. This is another form of adaptation and it includes the person being able to take action to accommodate these two 'masters'. If a wish is felt to be unacceptable, a person may be able to take evasive action such as not demanding whatever is wanted. At the level of the mind, such action is termed by psychoanalysts *defence mechanisms* (A. Freud, 1936). A young baby has very few resources to deal with something that feels unacceptable, or even more so if that something feels dangerous, especially as at the earliest stages there is practically no ego function available for such adaptation. The baby, as we have said, is completely dependent on his caregivers for safety and adaptation. It is only over time, as the baby's ego develops, that he will be able to find ways to defend himself.

However, we can see that even a very young baby can muster some activity if he does not feel safe in a situation. For instance, no mother is able to sustain absolute adaptation to her baby, and even when this is no longer required, the exigencies of ordinary life mean that mothers quite often fail to be responsive to their infant's immediate needs. We have already seen that mis-attunements are part and parcel of everyday life for a baby and mother. Sometimes these mis-attunements might have a malign overtone, such as when a mother gets angry, or is preoccupied with something else in her mind. At its most serious, a mother might feel very angry with her baby, or even frightened of the baby for some reason. In circumstances like this, young babies may have to resort to tactics such as *gaze aversion*, avoiding the mother's look, so that they do not have to face the frightening sense of seeing the malign look in her eyes. Another such tactic is *freezing*, playing dead as it were, like an animal might respond in a dangerous situation (Fraiberg, 1987). These *defensive manoeuvres* are the early precursors to more organized defence mechanisms that become available as the infant's ego develops. For some babies this is the stuff of their everyday life and in a little while we will come to examine in more detail what John Bowlby and his theory of attachment has to say about babies in these kinds of circumstances. For the moment, however, we will pursue another aspect of this discussion of defences, and that is what is happening and what might happen in the baby's developing mind to deal with the sort of experiences that we are describing.

Good and bad experiences

Because babies cannot speak, we have to partly rely on our imaginations in conjunction with observation of their external world to understand their internal experience. To glimpse a baby's experience, we can see how he is likely to apprehend the detail of his day-to-day life in terms of feeling good or bad – (pleasurable or painful) – in global ways. As we have said, it will take time for these feelings to become more differentiated into discrete, categorical emotions. Putting these two sets of ideas together, we can suggest that babies' first attempts at classifying and ordering are to do with this discrimination of experience into good and bad, pleasure and pain; and that their representations of those who care for them will similarly be divided in this way. The mummy who responds to the baby's cooing with a smile and vocalization will be 'good', and the one whose face is immobile because her mind is elsewhere will be 'bad' in that moment. When the mother is experienced as enhancing the baby's pleasure she is welcomed with joy and when she is felt to arouse distress she is felt to be bad; babies tend to react in all or nothing ways, so experiences are either totally good or totally bad. This may not only be a matter of perception; psychoanalysts have also postulated that it is the primitive beginning of the capacity to discriminate, and serves defensive functions for the immature baby's mind. This defence mechanism is that of '*splitting*', a primitive way of preventing confusion (Klein, 1948). The infant's biological need to discriminate good and bad can evoke phantastic reactions, which have consequences in learning and adaptations for years to come.

These notions of good and bad refer only to the immediate experience of the child. They do not refer to what is good for him in the long run. Quite clearly, not only is it impossible for even the most devoted mother to be good in this sense all the time, but also, what is felt as bad by the baby in his immediate experience may well be really good for him in the long run.

Another psychoanalyst, Spitz (1965), stressed a similar distinction between good and bad in the mother–child relation, but in the opposite direction from Klein. Klein pointed out the importance of the baby splitting and hence feeling his mother was all good or all bad. Spitz, on the other hand, pointed out the importance of the mother feeling her baby to be good or bad. These states he suggests are signalled by 'yes' and 'no' gestures from a mother to her baby, reflecting her enjoyment and approval of her baby or the opposite. The 'yes' gestures convey to the baby that he is good for his mother, and hence a good person, worthy of being alive, and conversely 'no' gestures that he is a bad person, not worthy of being alive.

We can see here that the 'no' gestures probably lead, if only transiently, to the baby becoming distressed and the 'happy loving-ness' engendered by the 'yes' gestures is dead for the time being. We are not here talking about discipline, which becomes an issue in the second year of life. We are talking about a mother who is grudging with her child. Every exhausted mother will be grudging a bit of the time; what is being stressed here is that babies probably notice this quite as much as they do their mother's love.

Theory of mind

We are slowly getting to the point where we have to address some-thing beyond the experience the baby has of the various aspects of care administered by his parents. We have been stressing the feeling quality of the continuing multitudinous experiences of the baby and how contingent these qualities are with the provision from the caregiving environment. Feelings, of course, are an aspect of mental life and they are of central importance not only in these early times but throughout life. As the baby gets organized in the way we have been describing, we can observe the way the *reciprocity* of the early weeks and months gives way to what can be described as *dialogue*. Dialogue presupposes that the differentiation between the self and the other itself has become more organized, and is part and parcel of the baby's everyday sense of being in the world. Along with dialogue comes a plethora of indicators that the 'other' is rapidly being sensed as having qualities of aliveness that we recognize and refer to as 'mind'.

We have already described the 5–6-month-old who loves exploring mum's or dad's face. The baby and mum and dad have already discovered the delights of shaking rattles, bashing mobiles, grabbing a spoon, etc. as the baby's fine motor control has allowed him to manipulate and grasp things. This interest in a '*third*' object was built up on the foundations of the earlier mutuality of '*primary intersubjectivity*' (Trevarthan, 1979). Within a relatively short while, by 8–9 months, this same baby will become interested in '*the purposes of the other*', a new kind of interest in what others know about or are doing to things; truly cooperative activity with a toy becomes possible and the peek-a-boo game truly reciprocal; and mother's face will be viewed in a way redolent of inquiry – posing a question such as 'well, what do you think/feel about this?' The baby shows new clusters of accomplishments, such as requesting help (usually non-verbally), imitating conventional gestures like 'bye-bye' or hugging, responding to verbal requests by others and following the eye gaze or pointing of another. Perhaps one of the most potent accomplishments is in initiating *pointing* to communicate interest to another. It is around this time that many babies first show anxiety or caution when strangers are present and look to the familiar figure of mother (or father) to ascertain if this is a safe person. This is called '*stranger anxiety*'. Indeed, this caution is so common that its absence may well be an indicator of cause for concern – the failure of development of ordinary caution.

These radical changes in the baby's overt behaviour are predicated upon and signal profound internal shifts. They indicate that the infant is beginning to understand others as beings that also have minds, and that these other minds can be deliberately '*interfaced*' or communicated with through intentional signals. Bretherton (1992) has termed this '*secondary intersubjectivity*'. It is the beginning of what has been described as having a '*theory of mind*', i.e. having a sense in one's own mind, that one has a mind, and that other people also have minds that contain mental states such as feelings, attitudes, intentions, etc. All these capacities demonstrate an ability to identify with and assume the actions of another person, which requires an appreciation of the commonalities and distinctions between self and other. This does not mean that the baby can reflect upon his own mental states or those of others, but that he can operate with the knowledge of such states.

For instance, Robert Emde and colleagues (1978) found that towards the end of the first year, when a child is faced with an uncertain situation such as in the experiment of the visual cliff (the child is on one side of a pattern on the floor suggestive of a cliff and mother is on the other side), he will always look at mother's face to check if it is safe to cross, and if the mother's expression indicates it is safe the young child will cross, but if not, then the child will hold back. This is a highly complex interaction. It combines the seeking out of the mother's emotional expression and relating it to the current situation, which is seen to have meaning for both, reacting accordingly with feeling and with action. It demonstrates that, before infancy is over, very young children seek and are able to understand another person's interpretation of a situation. It will be several years before it can be demonstrated empirically that a child can hold a belief at the same time as knowing that someone else has a different belief about the same issue, but as is so often the case, this aspect of human functioning has its origins in these later months of the first year of life.

The form this development takes seems to have much to do with the kind of attachment that develops between the infant and his mother.

An example of this was when Becky, aged 8 months, and her mother visited her mother's aunt, whom they had not seen for a couple of months. When they entered the previously familiar house, Becky looked around with curiosity but her hold on her mother's arms tightened. The aunt said hello, and after a moment looking, Becky turned her face into her mother's chest. Her mother was surprised and exclaimed to Becky that she was usually not shy like this, and anyway the aunt was someone she knew. They went into the sitting room and mother tried to put Becky down on the floor, to no avail; Becky clung with an iron grip to her mother's arms. The aunt was sensitive to this show of anxiety in Becky and did not approach her but spoke in a friendly manner from across the room. Becky did not cry but she came out from her mother's chest and looked at the aunt and then at her mother's face and then back to the aunt. She was very serious in her study of the aunt's face and then she again looked at her mother who smiled encouragingly at her, at the same time as reminding her that she knew the aunt and that she was a friendly person. Becky once again turned to the aunt and at that point the aunt passed to her a very colourful toy. After a few moments' hesitation, and another look at her mother, Becky reached over and took the toy and put it into her mouth. It took a little more time before Becky could smile at the aunt and eventually be put down on the floor to play.

In this example we can see the complexity of Becky's experience. In relation to her past, she had been familiar with the mother's aunt, but in the present that familiarity is no longer strong enough to overcome the sense of anxiety engendered by the not-mother figure. Becky's relationship with her mother provides her with the *security* to retreat for a few moments into the *safety* of her body, and encouraged by the non-verbal emotional tone, as well as the encouraging sound of the mother's voice, she eventually responds with interest to the aunt's overtures and can play. For this to happen, much relies on Becky trusting her mother's view of the world. We can all think of examples of an over-friendly child who will 'go to anyone', but who in so doing may be alerting us to something amiss in the relationship with the familiar person.

Attachment

One of the most important contributions that psychoanalysis has made to our understanding of human development has been its emphasis on the personal context within which the baby's potential as a human being is brought to fruition. So far, we have been stressing aspects of the mutuality of this bond between the baby and its parents. Now we are going to look more specifically at the baby's *attachment* to its caregivers.

During the second half of the first year of life, as we have been saying, the baby does things that indicate more and more that the person or people who look after him are really very special. We have stressed the beaming smile kept just for those few, and sometimes only for mother; the preference the baby increasingly shows just for them. This attachment to the mother and father, but especially mother, was very closely studied by John Bowlby (1969, 1973, 1980) and by his colleagues, principal of whom were John and Joyce Robertson, and Mary Ainsworth. This has been lately elaborated into a specific branch of theory and greatly extended by such researchers as Mary Main and her collaborators in the USA, and Miriam and Howard Steele at the Anna Freud Centre in the UK, as well as others.

Bowlby's theory of attachment was originally developed to explain and understand patterns of behaviour found in infants and young children, as well as adolescents and adults. He drew upon ethological research into the behaviour of higher primates and linked it to the experiences of humans, whom he stressed had been living in similar environmental conditions to primates for most of their evolutionary history. Essentially, attachment theory examines the fundamental need in human nature to seek *protection, comfort and support* from parents or parent-substitutes early in life in order to ensure *survival*. The bonds formed at this stage – the second half of the first year, based on earlier experiences – persist, and our need for attachments figures remains central to our well-being throughout life. From a theoretical point of view, the emphasis is shifted from the realm of *subjective experience* and *unconscious phantasy* to *environmental and relationship* factors, specifically to the *sensitivity* of care given by the primary caregivers.

Bowlby and his collaborators were greatly influenced by observing the consequences for children of being separated from their parents, initially during the Second World War. Anna Freud had established the Hampstead War Nurseries to care for children whose parents were unable to care for them. In the early 1950s the Robertsons made a series of films about the effects upon young children of staying in hospital or in residential care. These were greatly influential in changing the policies allowing parents to stay with their children in hospital, as well as incorporating practices in residential and day nurseries that allowed the development of relationships between the children and child care staff.

Bowlby's research assistant, Mary Ainsworth, developed a research instrument known as the '*strange situation*' to assess whether a child of about 1 year old was securely attached to his parent. In this process, the infant is separated briefly (3 minutes each time, maximum) from his caregiver and his behaviour is carefully observed both in the *separation* but more especially on *reunion*. This research, which has been repeated numerous times across the world, reliably shows that approximately 60–65 per cent of children are *securely attached*, leaving 35–40 per cent who are deemed *insecurely attached*, and this category is further broken down into two different modes of insecurity, *resistant and avoidant*. Later, Mary Main identified a fourth category of attachment, called *disorganized*.

The *securely attached* child will be distressed but respond to the parent on reunion with the expectation that he will be comforted. The *anxious/resistant* child will be distressed on separation but is not comforted by the return of his parent. The *anxious/avoidant* child will appear not to be distressed at all, which is thought to reflect a lack of confidence in the caregiver's availability, leading to a strategy of coping with distress by downplaying it. These children, however, do have a high level of the stress hormone cortisol in their saliva if it is tested at this time. The *disorganized* infant seeks closeness but in strange ways, such as suddenly freezing when approaching the parent.

These characteristic patterns of behaviour associated with different categories of attachment seem to reflect different *internal representations of the relationships* that have been building up during the first year of life (Bowlby termed them *internal working models of relationships*) and, as previously mentioned, they are thought to be relatively enduring once they are in place. They have been particularly useful in tracking the *intergenerational transmission of experience*, and Mary Main developed the *adult attachment interview* to assess the adult correlates of these infantile patterns. Miriam Steele and her colleagues at the Anna Freud Centre have been able to demonstrate that the security of attachment of an infant to each of its parents at 1 year and 18 months can be predicted from the categorization of each parent in the third trimester of pregnancy (Steele et al., 1991)! This extraordinary finding suggests that parents unwittingly create a psychic climate of attachment within which their infants develop their own model of attachment. In itself, this might not seem extraordinary, on reflection, but it emphasizes that we can get a profound insight into how the infant internally experiences their external world and the different people in it.

The baby's internal and outer worlds intertwining

Anna Freud (1965) dated the latter part of the first year as when the baby has normally established a sense of 'emotional object constancy'. By this she meant that the baby could maintain a loving inner image of the 'object' irrespective of either satisfactions or dissatisfactions. It allows the soon-to-be toddler to have confidence that, when mother goes away, she continues to exist and that she will return. It is often in times of transition like this that the baby uses the transitional object, the special teddy or blanket to manage the gap, to imaginatively elaborate its personal meaning in the context of mother's absence (Winnicott, 1971). When a child has had too many caregivers or where there have been too many changes or losses, he will find it much more difficult to develop this inner sense of constancy (Edgcumbe, 2000).

The interfacing of minds and social referencing that Bretherton and Emde identified can also be thought about in a slightly different way, which reflects the growing organization of the infant's mind. The baby who checks out with mummy whether this floor is safe to cross, as well as demonstrating that he knows that she has a useful point of view to be taken into account is also indicating, perhaps for the first time, that this point of view matters (Winnicott, 1982a). In another circumstance, attending to the emotional cues on mother's face, the baby is also perhaps checking out how she is feeling; is she OK? what impact has the baby had upon her? What is important about mattering or checking out in these ways? We could say it is the beginning of the baby having a moral sense that is contingent with the emotional aspects of the early caregiving environment. Much later, the child will be operating within a much more internally structured system of what is considered to be right and wrong – what psychoanalysts call the superego, or conscience. For now, this sense of 'right' and 'wrong' resides in the important people who care for the baby but it is becoming of interest to him and the baby is beginning to feel that it is relevant.

The mobility of this older baby is also seen as having internal psychic or mental correlates and consequences. Margaret Mahler (Mahler et al., 1975), in particular, was interested in the process of separation–individuation, which comes into its own in the second year of life but which can be observed in this latter part of the first year. In her research she observed the exuberance and emotional elation that was so often a feature of these mobile children's affective state and she used the term 'love affair with the world' (a phrase coined originally by Greenacre) to describe it. The exploration of the world and the child's great narcissistic investment in himself and his own body and its functions are the central characteristics of this time. The child is seen as practising his growing ability to physically separate himself from his mother as the overt manifestation of an internal or intra-psychic process of separating from an un-differentiated state. The exuberance is seen as relating to escape from fusion with the mother, and is played out actively in peek-a-boo games, speeding away, etc. Mahler and her colleagues saw this as also expressing the fear of re-engulfment of the infant by the mother. (We can see here one manifestation of the psychoanalytic view of conflict in mental life.) Mother is still needed nearby as a home base for emotional 'refuelling', usually through physical re-contact.

Allan Schore (1994) proposed that what Mahler observed is corroborated at a neurobiological level. In the last few months of the first year of life the sympathetic nervous system, which is connected to states of high arousal, is in a state of rapid development. He stresses the importance of the mother's supporting this exuberance and notes that this is usually the case: he quotes Kagan as reporting that at 10 months, 90 per cent of maternal behaviour consists in affection, play and caregiving with only 5 per cent involved in prohibiting the child from ongoing activity.

The baby becoming a person

The findings described above from developmental psychology are of great interest to psychoanalysts because they connect with their ideas about what is going on in babies' minds during the latter part of the first year of life. These months are characterized by the sense that the baby is becoming more and more his own person, and relating to those around as people. This is the time when the baby's most beaming smiles are kept for his most intimate caregivers, and one has a sense that, in contrast to earlier times, the baby who is doing well enough developmentally now does have a sense of mother and others as being whole persons with minds and mental states that are of great interest and relevance. It is the time when *evocative memory* can be demonstrated – the baby being interested in where the toy has gone to, or where mummy goes to when she leaves the room. This older baby is probably mobile by now, almost certainly crawling, and is thus able to take himself across distances and away from or towards mother in that way. The space that we talked of earlier is becoming commonplace in the detail of everyday life, and we can consider the mental correlates of this manifest behaviour.

The space between mother and baby offers all kinds of opportunities, as we have seen, for the creation of meaning through shared and separate experiences. Winnicott called it 'potential space' (Winnicott, 1971). It reflects the growing differentiation of a sense of 'me' and 'not me', and also the possibility of playing with and in the areas of overlap between the two, increasingly incorporating a third or more elements. This is the time when many babies find a special thing like a teddy bear or a blanket. This often becomes mandatory to have at times of change such as when going to sleep, or when the child is left with a baby-sitter. This has been immortalized in the *Peanuts* cartoons by Charles Schulz, where the character Linus has his blanket which is clearly the source of his well-being, and is theorized about by Winnicott (1982b) in the notion of the *transitional object*.

The transitional object is one 'created' by the baby; certainly its meaning for the baby cannot be created by anyone else. It is often in times of transition that the baby uses the transitional object, the special teddy or blanket to manage the gap, to imaginatively elaborate its personal meaning in the context of mother's absence. The baby invests this thing with all the significance he or she wishes. This is a complex notion as Winnicott was trying to describe in what he called an *'intermediate area of experiencing to which inner reality and external life both contribute'*. It is an 'intermediate state between the baby's inability and growing ability to recognize and accept reality . . . the substance of illusion, that which is allowed to the infant and which in adult life is inherent in art and religion' (1951, p. 230). It belongs to the rich area of the infant's developing imagination and capacity for fantasy.

The very ordinariness and universal quality of the phenomenon of the transitional object belies its enormous significance. The capacities that have developed to make it possible arise from the emotional climate established for their baby by the parents. This, in turn, creates a pattern of attachment that enables the baby to feel safe. He can begin to distinguish strangers from those familiar to him and this distinction will support an emerging capacity to distinguish his own existent being from that of others. The phenomenon of the transitional object demonstrates the beginning of a capacity to move beyond simply being the victims of fate. From the launch pad of the ability to attribute meaning to an object, the baby can begin to claim the world.

Further reading

Boswell, S. (2004) *Understanding Your Baby*. London: Tavistock Clinic & Jessica Kingsley.

Stern, D. (1985) *The Interpersonal World of the Human Infant*. New York: Basic Books.

Waddell, M. (1998) *Inside Lives*. London: Duckworth.

Winnicott, D.W. (1971) *Playing and Reality*. London: Penguin.

Wright, K. (1991) *Vision and Separation: Between Mother and Baby*. London: Free Association Books.

Chapter 5

One to two years old: junior toddlers

Angela Joyce

The second year of life exemplifies the perennial phenomenon in human life: the tension between the impulse to explore and know the world with all its inherent benefits and dangers, and the need for protection and security in familiar surroundings with our loved ones around us. The junior toddler is on the threshold of moving out of his mother's orbit into the world to be discovered. The developmental changes, internally and externally, that this will entail are profound, and predicated on the good-enough provision of the first year. The tottering 1-year-old taking his first steps full of the exuberance and thrill of new discoveries will become the 2-year-old budding scientist, now with a nascent sense of his limitations and potential helplessness, and aware of his dependency upon his parents and other caregivers. By the end of the second year of life, the junior toddler's faltering steps will have become more confident – walking and running, jumping and climbing that take him away from mummy and daddy and bring him back, but still dependent upon the parents or their substitutes to watch out and protect him from danger. These toddlers will be able to speak to their parents across a distance in simple sentences, telling them what they are doing and asking questions, still with the full mastery of complex verbal communication to be achieved. The frustration of the tension between the wish for freedom and the need for security will often find its expression in the tantrums that are typical of this age – colloquially known as '*the terrible two's*', which usually start around the middle of the second year. This toddler will have a sense of being a boy or a girl, will invariably recognize this difference in others, and will be beginning to take control of his own bodily functions, claiming ownership of his body, possibly using the potty or toilet during the day instead of wearing a nappy. And his play will be markedly different, demonstrating his budding imagination in the beginning of story telling and narrative. This second year marks the time when the bundle of potential that was the baby of the first year is well on the way to being his own character, albeit with a long way to go.

Discovering the world

Acquiring the ability to walk gives the soon-to-be toddler a new view. Suddenly the world looks very different, and possibilities multiply. It epitomizes the creative tension between the *urge to explore* and the need for *a secure base* (Lieberman, 1993). Junior toddlers can now take themselves away from mother with increasing capability, only to find themselves much further away than was previously possible or likely. This is both thrilling and then potentially worrying. To be watched and encouraged in these explorations, to be followed and perhaps scooped up in an excited reunion is immensely reassuring; but what if mummy doesn't realize how far he has gone? What if she doesn't notice that he is a bit beyond his capacities and has now fallen and is feeling overwhelmed? The new and exciting world that a few moments ago was full of the promise of new discoveries is suddenly strange and frightening.

Being able to move around with skill takes the young toddler into all sorts of places hitherto out of reach. The child, who previously could crawl quite fast but essentially was floor bound, can now climb to reach that object so precious to the parent or older sibling. The world is full of things to find and explore, and mobility gives the child the independence to do this without waiting for mummy or daddy to carry and show him. It enables him to go into places that his parents would not have chosen to take him – not just the cupboard under the sink where dangerous chemicals can lurk, and which was known to be accessible since the baby was crawling, but to the medicine cabinet that was previously thought to be high enough because the child could not climb to it, or the sparkling dangling thing just on the edge of the table – now all are objects of great interest for the young adventurer.

This makes the parents' task very different from that in the first year of life. Allan Schore (1994) reports research indicating that mothers' ministrations to their offspring change from being 90 per cent 'care-giving' and only 5 per cent prohibiting behaviours up to the age of 12 months, to them expressing a *prohibition* to their

11- to 17-month-olds every 9 minutes. These prohibitions are not just to protect precious material objects, but more especially to keep the child safe. Moreover they begin to convey what is acceptable or not to the child and the whole area of discipline, and ultimately morality, i.e. what is deemed right and wrong, comes into the picture. They connect with the underlying question formulating in the child's mind – do mummy and daddy really love me if they curb my wishes? Anxiety about *the loss of the parents and of their love* is one of the fundamental building blocks of the child's growing awareness of the consequences of his actions and will ultimately contribute to the establishment internally of his own sense of right and wrong – his conscience. Of course, parents who threaten the withdrawal of their love to the recalcitrant toddler will not help the child deal with this question – it will only make him more anxious.

Separation, attachment and individuation

A very young child, and indeed still an older one, remains very dependent upon his parents or their substitutes to be at the other end of an invisible thread, reliably available, to be returned to for the 're-fuelling' (Mahler, Pine, & Bergmann, 1975) that reassures the child of his safety and protection in the face of feelings of helplessness and danger. At the same time, the psychological *separation* creating boundaries around the sense of self and other, paradoxically dependent upon the security of *attachment* between the child and the parents, becomes a central task of this developmental phase.

In the previous chapter we considered the importance of the security of attachment a child has with his parents as being reflective of an internal sense that these relationships provide a feeling of being able to rely on those external figures for a sense of safety. Increasingly, these external figures are '*represented*' in the child's mind, and become '*internalized*' so that we can observe the child having a sense of confidence in himself and the world around, being able ordinarily to trust in the predictability of circumstance. It is only on the basis of this trust in predictability that the inevitable unpredictability of the world can be countenanced. And so the discovery of the world through exploration, which is such a hallmark of the second year of life, is utterly dependent upon this sense of a secure base in the child's mind and its reality in the external world of his relationships. If it is not present then these developmental tasks of toddlerhood are made immensely more complicated.

In addition to this task is the related one of discovering the self. Mahler et al.'s (1975) term for this was '*individuation*' – the assumption by the child of his own individual character. As well as exploring the external world, our junior toddler is also extending his sense of being an active agent in that world, including having a new sense of his own body and what can be done with it. In this discovery, the *separateness* from mother, at both a *physical* and *psychological* level, will be central and the realization that her wishes are not the same as the toddler's will be fruitful ground for negotiation or battle. Some balance between the two will probably have to be found as the toddler flexes his muscles and makes this exciting and painful discovery.

Engaging with the world

Freud (1921) observed his little grandson, aged 20 months, playing with a cotton reel connected to a piece of string. He was repetitively throwing it away and retrieving it with the string, in the absence of his mother. As the reel rolled away he was heard to say 'fort' (interpreted as the German for 'gone') and 'da' ('there') as it returned. Freud understood this as the child symbolically *representing* his mother's absence and his mastery of the *passive* experience of being left by *actively* enacting it in his play.

We are now going to focus on these two features of development in the toddler period: first, the capacity to represent and, second, the use of these representations to engage with the world. Developmentally it can be thought of as an underlying tendency to move from a *concrete, literal experience* of something to being able to *represent* it in the mind in some way. This notion of representation also includes the linking together of fantasies and ideas with images which then 'give meaning, richness, quality and nuance to our inner world' (Tyson & Tyson, 1990). We will explore this in various different aspects of the child's life, especially the development of the capacity for play, language, and a moral sense as well as how character and personality form through the interplay between these experiences of the external world and what the child makes of them internally.

Play

Play is *sensory and manipulative*. For instance, sand is ladled from one cup to another and runs through the hands, water is splashed about, not only to see what happens to it, but also for its feel. 'Tools' are used to prod, push, pull and beat other things. The child will be feeding himself with a spoon, and using this to ladle food into other places as well as his mouth, partly through clumsiness but also to discover the relation of food to other things as well as to himself. As the second year advances, these sensory and manipulative qualities of early play are augmented by quite a different aspect that eventually becomes more obviously representational and symbolic – pretend play.

Initially, play takes place in the baby's very bodily relationship with the mother in such activities as touching, stroking, looking, etc. As we saw in the earlier chapters, many older babies then have a special toy or piece of cloth (a transitional object) that Winnicott understood to be reflective of the baby internally creating a sense of separation from the mother – the 'me' and the 'not me' areas of experience. In addition to this, Winnicott saw play and playing as the creative mode of relating to and exploring the world, internal and external. This is not confined to childhood but is the essence of a creative relationship with the world throughout life.

Anna Freud emphasized children's use of physical materials, whether they be toys or other things used for activities, as providing opportunities for pleasure, learning, control and mastery as well as the elaboration of fantasies and imagination (A. Freud, 1965). Additionally, as children develop, playing is the arena within which much peer interaction takes place and the whole complex area of friendship, cooperation and competition, etc. is elaborated.

Play provides a haven for exploration of internal and external reality, so long as the child's sense of reality or imagination is not challenged in too literal a way, which has the effect of puncturing the flow between inner and outer reality. Increasingly, as the second year advances, children gather whatever materials are available upon which their imaginations work to craft the expression of the sense they are making of the world and their place in it.

Jack, aged 19 months, was a restless child and on the whole preferred running and moving about to quiet focused play. However,

> he loved playing with a set of stacking beakers and from time to time
> would sit and concentrate on taking one after the other out of the
> sequence and then trying to replace them. He was especially pleased
> when his mother joined him in this play. He was intrigued by the
> different sizes that sometimes fitted together and sometimes did not,
> and showed remarkable frustration tolerance as he frequently failed
> to replace them in the right order. That did not seem to be the point
> of his interest, rather that sometimes they fitted and sometimes did
> not, and that the beakers had an inside and an outside.

We can speculate about what this very typical play might mean
for this young child. Undoubtedly it reflected his growing ability to
manipulate physical objects and his interest in what happened or
did not happen. But from a more psychoanalytic point of view we
can think about how this play represents Jack's exploration of the
properties of *inside-ness* and *outside-ness*, and fitting together or
not, reflective of his sense of his own body, what goes into it and
what comes out, whether things that come out of a space also can
go back into the space. This also harks back to his earlier babyhood, when contact with his mother's body perhaps also stimulated
phantasies about hers and what his body meant in relation to hers.
Interestingly this little boy was very reluctant to be weaned from
breast-feeding. More of Jack a little later.

Through play and exploration as in this example, we can see how
children find ways of knowing about and understanding their
experiences, at a symbolic, representational level. As their capacity
for creating a narrative develops they are able to explore, as trial
action, the contents of their minds, mastering the anxiety aroused
by interpersonal and intra-psychic conflicts, finding better and
more adaptive solutions to them. The adaptation to external reality
is usually hard won and play is an essential part of this process for
young children.

Beginning to form general ideas or pre-concepts

Towards the end of the second year the birth of *active make-belief*
will be apparent. When we look at this more carefully in the next
chapter we will see that make-believe seems to be rooted in *imitation*

(Phillips, 1975; Piaget, 1951). We have seen how fundamental this was in the early months. Now it is still vital in learning but with age takes on a more intentional quality. *Active choice* is becoming apparent. A toddler tries and tries again to do the same as his elders in finding the means to manipulate the things around him.

One of the results of repeated manipulation is to discover how many things can be experienced and treated as *the same* or, when more sophisticated, as similar. It is the beginning of forming generalized ideas; these too are constituents of make-believe as we shall see. By the end of the year most children clearly understand the meaning of such simple general ideas as in, out, up, down, heavy, light, big, small, few, many, water, wet, loud, soft and many others.

Such ideas cannot yet be called proper concepts; it will be a long time before, say, the concept of heaviness will have the constancy of application necessary for really logical use. There are many ways in which these early pre-concepts differ from what we know in adult logic, suffice it here to note that *primitive classification* often tends to be *wider* than is appropriate. For instance, any furry creature may be called a 'doggie' and on the next day a 'pussy'. Only later will the similar animals be more carefully clarified with appropriate attributes, into 'doggie, bow-wow' and 'pussy, miaow' (Leach, 1974).

Note again here that, as the *limits* of classes must be still vague for children, so puzzlements must infuse many things. For instance, when somebody is angry they roar, so is everything that roars angry? Are aeroplanes angry, are train engines too? This is the sort of world of unstable mysterious limits the toddler lives in. Because limits are vague and unstable there is probably a tendency to 'infinitize'. This seems to have its effect on how little children tend to *feel in extremes:* where infinity reigns one tends to be very, very frightened, or in ecstasies of delight. More of this in the next chapter.

Communication and language

Another central aspect of the child's underlying tendency to move from a *concrete, literal experience* of something, a symbol, to being able to *represent* it, is in the development of language. Buxbaum (1964) proposed that this symbol-forming tendency joins up with the genetically determined properties of speech at the point where the need to communicate becomes the central organizing principle in development. You will remember how the infant–mother mimicry of body movements in the first weeks of life, extended to communication by gesture and pre-word 'talking' in later months. In fact, human babies are born with the range of sounds capable of becoming any of the thousands of languages that have developed throughout human civilization. By the end of the first year, the range of sounds uttered by children are limited to those used in the language that they have heard during this time. The growth of understanding of the use of *words* and then the formation of these into *grammar* naturally follows. It has been the subject of very active research in recent years (Bower, 1977; Britton, 1985; Lewin, 1975; Pinker, 1994).

A symbol is something that stands for something else. For example, words are sounds that have been created by convention to stand for things, actions or relationships. On the whole they do *not* resemble the things or actions for which they stand. A few words do, however, have this resemblance, for instance 'cuckoo', 'curlew', 'bang', 'plop', 'hiss' and 'piss'; this is *onomatopoeia*. When we turn to non-verbal symbols, visual ones particularly, we see that resemblance is very common. In play material and dreams particularly, symbols do often have the same form as the thing signified. For instance, a stick as played with is a similar shape to the gun it represents.

Anyone acquainted with toddlers will know that learning to *understand* words as signs for things develops before learning to use them actively in *talking* recognizably. But this does not mean that young children are just passive recipients of language spoken by those around them. As readers will have gathered from the earlier chapters, babies are active participants in communication and learning from their earliest days The appearance of words and their use comes relatively late in children's development and 'disturbances in the pre-linguistic stages can lay the foundations for subsequent distortion and pathology in language development' (Edgcumbe, 1981).

Edgcumbe proposed a *developmental line for the acquisition of language* by children, very much in the tradition of Anna Freud (1965), taking the inherited potential with the environmental influence and seeing what use the child makes of it in various ways. Children develop at different rates but the sequence of development usually takes the following route:

- Stage 1: from birth the baby uses noises, including crying, and gestures that gradually become more organized into babbling, cooing, reaching in a more controlled way, and expressions, in what Trevarthan called 'proto-conversation' in response to the 'motherese' of the caregiver.

A young baby was placed in an orphanage shortly after her birth in a developing country. She was well taken care of in that she was fed adequately and kept clean. When the adoptive parents met her when she was 1 month old she was almost entirely silent, hardly even crying. It took a week or more of focused individual care for this baby to begin to cry, and it was only then that the new parents realized how silent she had been when they met her. It took quite a lot longer for her to begin the cooing and babbling typical of a young baby.

- Stage 2: there is differentiation in the baby's vocabulary of a range of sounds, linked with specific inner experiences and the value of the mother's sounds, in aiding the baby's tolerance of delay and frustration; there are indications that the first steps are occurring in remembering and organizing experience. This might be manifest in such things as the baby uttering specific sounds, when hungry or interested in something, that the mother then recognizes and reinforces by her replies.
- Stage 3: the child becomes aware that vocalizing has specific meanings and can be used to influence the behaviours of others and there is a greater sense of intentionality from the child. One little boy habitually used the sound 'adah!' when he wanted to draw his mother's attention to something. From stage 3 onwards, the infant develops the expectation of producing specific effects via appropriate sounds that are forming his language. The intention to communicate in this way requires sufficient development of the internal representational world for the child to have formed the expectation that the people who are important to him will respond in relatively predictable ways. There is also sufficient cognitive, perceptual and memory development to support these mental representations; and sufficient motor and vocal development to express the communication externally in gesture and in word.

> In his first two years, Jacob's mother thought that because he did not understand words, there was no point talking to him. When he was presented at the local child and family mental health service, aged two and a quarter, with a query of autistic spectrum disorder, he used no sounds to communicate. The child psychotherapist who saw him with his parents, spoke directly to him and the parents were astonished that he stopped his wild running around and looked directly, in an interested way, at the therapist. Because he did not make sounds to them they thought that he had no interest in language. He was a severely under-stimulated child whose language development was grossly impaired because of this.

- Stage 4: words are used to express wishes as well as the release of impulses and feelings. This involves increasing linkage between words and inner experience, words helping to differentiate between feelings and experiences as well as amongst objects. Words are used to convey commands and prohibitions from adults, contributing to the formation of the moral sense.
- Stage 5: children's vocabularies increase rapidly; words are used to communicate a wide range of experiences, questions, and ideas, beginning sometimes to use words as a substitute for action, and using familiar phrases from parents; reinforcing the normal identifications that take place.

With playful trial and error, children approximate closer and closer to voicing recognizable words. When parents think they recognize a word they are usually delighted with their child for his brilliance. The child for his part is then usually delighted with himself too, often repeating the word to get more of his parents' pleasure. Parents are perhaps not absurd to be so delighted; finding words is an impressive feat of perseverance and discrimination. After this the child usually races ahead trying out and finding many new words. Early speech usually involves comical mistakes or approximations, which are nonetheless delightful, for instance: bissica for biscuit, blabbi for blanket, wowies for trousers, toon for spoon, pisgetti for spaghetti, even coddispeeper for compost heap. These approximations indicate the *creative* invention that goes into learning to talk. Invention comes first; testing their conformity to rules comes second. Perhaps adults find such delight in children's early language because it is so freshly creative with a freedom that they cannot hope to match, engrossed as they must be in the routines and rules of adult life.

By the age of 2 years, children will usually be linking words into simple grammatical sentences and will have a vocabulary of approximately 200 words. It used to be thought that this comes about by a process of *reinforcement*, that is, the simple repetition of phrases becomes implanted in the mind by the pleasure of sounding the same as grown-ups (Skinner, 1953). However, Chomsky, a linguist and cultural theorist (see Britton, 1985), says this model is naïve. A child does not just copy adults, rather he actively, of his own initiative, uses language-acquisition devices, which are probably of innate origin. He *discovers* grammatical rules for himself. For instance, at first a child (usually a bit older than two) will imitate adults and use 'went' as the past tense of 'go'. But then, after discovering the general rule of past tenses, will use 'goed' instead. Only later will he revert to 'went'. Children seem to be largely independent of their parents' habits. For instance, adults will consistently say, 'I don't think it will rain today' – not, of course, meaning that they are not thinking. Although children hear only this idiomatic form from their parents, they will use the more simple, logical structure which is, 'I think it will not rain today'. Only later will they take over the adult usage.

Chomsky has suggested that, no matter where a language comes from, there is a universal similarity of deep structures of grammar and there must, therefore, be an innate readiness to acquire these forms. How this might be remains uncertain and there has been much argument about the question. Probably there are common bases to the structuring of thought generally, which rest on the innate propensities for mimicry as suggested in the last chapter.

This thought structuring is then reflected in grammar. With speech and grammar, the 'flattish' world of infantile impressions is broadened and deepened immeasurably. By using words children begin to be able to communicate more precisely what their inner wishes and feelings are. To say 'drink' when thirsty is much more economical and peaceful than the crying and shouting resorted to before speech. Words help children to be aware of inner states and differences between wishes and reality. By 3 years of age they will speak of them coherently. For instance, 'I feel sad (or cross, etc.), Jenny wouldn't play with me', or, 'We had a super picnic in the park'. Also, with language children are brought into a clearer apprehension of other people's wishes and feelings. They will recognize parent's wishes – 'Don't do that, it is very annoying', or, 'Mum feels tired now', or, 'Well done, that is a lovely sand pie'. Later still, the vast, moving and intricate web of other people's inner feelings will be opened up through everyday speech, novels, biographies, poetry and drama. It might be said then that a primary function of language is to gossip, that is, the talking to others about relationships, feelings, happenings, outcomes; the stuff of everyday communication (Dunbar, 1996).

The realm of physical facts is widened immeasurably. By attaching known words to a new object, that object immediately gains meaning. For instance, walking down a strange road a mother points to one building and says, 'That is where they bake bread, it is called a bakery', and points to another, 'That is where the milk van has its garage'. With this, unknown buildings are brought into contact with familiar things and, in a flash, gain meaning for the child, and augment his growing ability to engage with the wider world.

It is not only in the communication of feelings and wishes and facts that language has such value. Language helps in the development of reality orientation and in problem solving, and what psychoanalysts call *the secondary process* – being able to think logically, with a sense of cause and effect. It retains a connection with *primary process* – a form of thinking epitomized in dreaming, and characterized by visual imagery, condensing of meaning, symbolization and the displacement of meaning from one thing to another – through such things as poetic form and imagination. Many writers have stressed the interweaving of primary- and secondary-process thinking as ways in which the unconscious and conscious parts of the mind connect with each other (Rycroft, 1979; Tyson & Tyson, 1990). This connectedness is often apparent in the play of young children, especially as they become more able to weave a verbal narrative to accompany the drama of the play.

Language can, in certain circumstances, be condensed into signs and symbols to such a degree that they seem to be unrelated to ordinary words. This occurs in mathematics, where symbols condense what might take pages to write in ordinary language. It is perhaps a good exercise to try and imagine what our world was like before we learnt the meaning of words. With a little imagination we can get the impression of an inner and outer world where sound is

only noise, where there are no sure signs to indicate hidden connections, and which is thus full of mysteries and terrors.

Volatile feelings

The exuberance that is such a characteristic of young toddlers is
not the only emotion that they feel; indeed toddlers are often
known for their *volatility* and increasing *complexity* of their emotions. They can be apparently supremely self-confident one minute
and then, faced with something new and strange, become scared
and clinging. Having been content to play alone they might suddenly demand company, or seemingly out of the blue be tearful
when going to sleep at night, or when the parent is going out and
leaving them with a baby-sitter, familiar or new. When thwarted in
his desired plan, the toddler might increasingly become angry, and
tantrums become commonplace for a while.

We have seen how the exhilaration so characteristic of the young
toddler is underpinned at a brain level by the surge in development
of the *sympathetic component* of the autonomic nervous system,
responsible at a physiological level for heightened emotion. A little
later, towards the middle of the second year, the *parasympathetic*
component also has a surge of growth and this aspect of the
autonomic nervous system underpins more *low-keyed feelings*, and
coincides with a noticeable lowering of affect in toddlers as they
begin to realize that the closeness of babyhood has been superseded
by this more distant link. This is the time when the explorations
of the earlier months of the second year now are augmented by
a seeming return to the mother – Mahler et al. (1975) called it a
'*rapprochement*' – culminating in a time of crisis: the conflict
between the desire to remain so close to mother that it feels like
they are merged, both *secure and omnipotent*, and the urge to be an
autonomous individual, who fears *re-engulfment* by the mother. The
realization that increased autonomy requires a sacrifice of the
toddler's belief in his *omnipotence* can lead to a dramatic loss of
the *ideal self* that was so enjoyed during the earlier period when he
was just beginning to move away, which Mahler et al. called the
'*practising*' period.

These apparently capricious changes are indicative of the complex development going on inside. On the one hand, it is likely that
the child is working out his sense of *safety and security, attachment
and separation*. To seek *proximity* in danger is what the attachment

system is all about: the junior toddler is finding out when he feels safe and what he needs in order to do so. Seeking the real presence of the parent, the *attachment figure*, when worried and anxious is the precursor to the child having a sense inside of *safety and security*, which later can be drawn upon in the absence of that person. The wish for closeness to one's loved ones in times of anxiety will remain a lifelong tendency. On the other hand, the tension between the wish for *autonomy and freedom* and at the same time for *attachment and security* is an awful lot to bear; to be told 'no!' when at that moment the only desire is to do the opposite can feel like the end of the world to the young person, and the temper tantrum is its expression.

The young toddler is struggling with the powerful emotions of love and hate, passionately felt and potentially overwhelming. This can feel to be such an all or nothing affair that the idea that this mummy who just thwarted me and I thus hate, is also the one that I passionately desire, can feel just too much. It is at this point that *conflict and ambivalence* are the main characteristics of toddler behaviour. At this stage the toddler realizes that his wishes and desires are not identical to mother's, and he is increasingly frustrated by interventions that challenge his newly created and fragile boundaries. The role of the mother, more particularly her emotional availability, and the quality of caregiving are fundamental to the successful resolution of this crisis: 'It is the mother's love of the toddler and the acceptance of his ambivalence that enable the toddler [to develop a sound sense of self-esteem in these circumstances]' (Mahler, 1975). Although conflict at this stage seems inevitable, the mother's tolerance of both the toddler's *regressive tendencies* and *autonomous urges* can help the child to separate successfully – in fact the mother's 'gentle push' towards the outside world is essential.

How the junior toddler deals with all this

Even with all the sensitive handling in the world, internally the young child also has to develop capacities to deal with feelings that are intolerable. They are very much linked with what is available from the parents in terms of sensitive support, but not entirely. In the earlier chapters we mentioned *defence mechanisms*, and the defence that is called upon to help with intolerable ambivalence is *splitting*. It concerns good and bad feelings and their all-or-nothing quality. It is easy to observe how a young child gets deeply absorbed in a thing and then suddenly switches off it to become deeply absorbed in something else. So engrossed is he that it is as if the previous thing is of no importance at all. This switching is very frequently used to recover from distress. One moment the child is in a rage kicking and screaming at his mother then, if he is attended to and cuddled, he switches, the rage is gone and he is all smiles. 'Bad' mother has become 'good' mother again; indeed bad self has gone and good self returns. The bad experience seems to be forgotten, or perhaps denied in the moment of the good feelings being restored.

Splitting helps a young child to recover from the helpless confusion that ambivalence can engender at its greatest intensity. Structuring his awareness by splitting allows him to retain some sense of self-coherence, even if it is inadequate in the longer run. The young child will need to be helped by his parents to integrate these passionate feelings of love and hate that make up the feelings of ambivalence. The underlying proneness to dichotomize is omnipresent throughout life, and indeed is at the heart of being able to order, categorise, discriminate and judge, all vital ingredients for reality testing. At an extreme level, splitting leads to fragmentation and breakdown, but on the way to integration it is essential in helping the young child to bear the intolerable.

The importance of the mother, father and other caregivers supporting the 'love affair with the world', and being sensitively attuned to the contradictions of the toddler's fears and desires, cannot be underestimated. It is complicated also when coupled with the need to keep the young person safe, as well as making sure that those precious objects so tempting to the toddler are not damaged. It is a very common sight to see a young toddler bringing all kinds of 'gifts' to mother, to them endlessly interesting items that are closely inspected, all equally delightful in their newness. It is equally common for mothers to be rather anxious about this, especially when the young toddler has got hold of something they 'shouldn't' have.

The crestfallen look on such a toddler's face when confronted by mother's less than pleased response can be thought about as the first indicator, in this interpersonal setting, of the emotion of *shame*. The expectations of their exhilaration being met by a sustaining response are punctured, leaving the child with the painful task of suddenly feeling let down and *self-conscious*. Other situations also contain the possibility of the emotion of shame being stirred in the youngster.

Jack (of whom we heard earlier) was a lively 20-month-old, just beginning to register awareness of his bodily processes of defecating and urinating. He and his mum were visiting his great-grandmother one day and, being summer, he was out in the garden naked. Suddenly he began to poo and he trod on it, becoming very distressed as it stuck to his foot. His mother responded calmly and helped him but his great-grandmother was upset and in her response laughed – possibly out of anxiety. Jack became distraught and screamed, and as his mother endeavoured to calm him and clean him he was overwhelmed. It seemed that the laughter had really touched a chord in him, perhaps of something resembling shame, and for quite a while after this event he became distressed every time he sensed himself doing a poo.

We saw previously how Jack was fascinated by the stacking beakers, suggestive of his interest in his body and what went into it and came out of it. When the incident just described happened, his interest in the beakers became more intense for a while, as he gradually worked out something of this principle of something being inside his body and coming out of it. Later we will consider the link between these bodily processes and the child's f/phantasies about them in more detail.

Sometimes these ordinary exchanges between toddler and mother can be infused with something much more malign from the parent or other caregiver – something like contempt or scorn might well creep in for all kinds of reasons to do with that particular person. If this happens, and especially too frequently, it can put undue strain on the young toddler and cause hurt. Perhaps it is odd that we should use the word hurt where no physical damage is caused, but the feeling of shame is close to feeling scorned, and we do feel almost physically hurt. Perhaps something of the following happens in these events. We are hurt most by those we love most. In love there is perhaps always a fantasy at least of finding a near-physical unity with the loved one. When that loved person is, or feels to be, scornful or contemptuous, the sense of a loving bond, with all its tender physical feelings, is savagely cut; we feel dismissed or disowned and our self-esteem is broken. It is as painful, often more so, than a physical wound. You will notice that here is an instance of the strange workings of emotional logic. The self and the body are experienced as identical, both are hurt.

The experience of shame can be dodged by using the same mechanisms of defence associated with the splitting already mentioned. These are *projection and denial* (Segal, 1973). After these are used, the end result can be that a person feeling shame can convert it to contempt. Here are a couple of examples of projection and denial.

> I feel rather ashamed of being very incompetent at foreign languages. However, I am very competent in my knowledge of the London Underground. When a lost foreigner hesitatingly asks me the way, I find myself sometimes welling up with a superior, scornful feeling of, 'You fool, don't you know your way around', and 'You can't even speak English properly'. I think I hide this well enough and perhaps am often over-solicitous, for I particularly dislike scorn.

> Georgie Porgie pudding and pie, kissed the girls and made them cry, when the boys came out to play Georgie Porgie ran away.

In both these instances a person feels inferior about himself. Myself at languages; Georgie Porgie was, and must have felt, a coward. But this shame can be denied in perceiving weakness in others for it relieves one of feeling weak or incompetent oneself. I might feel superior in seeing foreigners flounder with their English; Georgie Porgie presumably got a similar pleasure in making the girls cry. When an attribute *originally experienced about oneself is emphasized about someone else, projection* is said to occur. Violent projective processes probably underlie all bullying, shrewishness, scorn and contempt. As will be obvious, these malign activities abound throughout the world, not only individually but also particularly rampantly when shared in groups, by cultures, nations and races. Projection and denial are here like twins acting hand in hand.

A process in the opposite direction from projection is also common; this is termed *introjection*. Here an attribute is first experienced as belonging outside oneself, but is 'swallowed' so that it becomes a possession of one's own self. It is a common occurrence when a person feels distressed by a loved one. Blaming a loved one is often frightening, so a person will readily leap to the idea that it was really his own fault. Blame is introjected into the self. In a less painful way, it is also probably used by older children a great deal, for example when they themselves feel posh if their parents do or have something grand. Introjection is a very common activity with both beneficial and malign aspects. It can be less malign than projection because it does not unfairly attack another person, but it can lead to the self being attacked or spoiled in some way. It goes on daily when learning skills from a teacher or parent. It is a fantasy associated with imitation and hence with identification. But it should be distinguished from full identification. This involves not only imitating another person and introjectively feeling like him, but also repeating and testing out to steady mastery of the actual skills involved – becoming like that other person.

Lastly, in the context of shame, scorn and contempt, the feeling of *envy* should be mentioned. This occurs when an individual is unable to *introject* and then identify with something he wants badly, but still perceives it as the possession *of* another. It happens when imitation, introjection and identification fail. It can, of course, be corrosive because of the desire to steal or destroy the envied thing, but is also a spur to learning. It is hard to say how often it is acutely present in little children. In older ones it is very prevalent indeed, and, as the younger children are actually surrounded by people with much more than they have, it is probably very active in them too.

Primitive guilt

Very close to shame is the experience of guilt. Both involve actual or fantasized awareness of being observed by others. They differ, however, in that shame is a reaction to failure to meet up to an *aspiration* of one's own. Guilt, on the other hand, may involve this but is essentially the experience in fantasy or *fact* (conscious *or* unconscious) of one's *effect of causing damage* or *distress* to another. The essential point is that it is concerned with the individual's experience of his effect on others. Psychoanalysts have stressed for many years that *fantasies of effects* on others are often much more powerful in experience than are actual effects. Such fantasies are not precise knowledge and thus tend to infinity of feeling.

Many psychoanalysts have pointed out (Klein, 1932; Winnicott, 1965a), that manifestations of guilt can be detected in the behaviour of children under 2 years old. One can see gestures of fending off expected retaliation, running away and also attempts to kiss mother better or to offer her titbits of food to placate her after a misdeed.

The credit for first investigating the natural personal development of guilt, rather than assume it as a given of human nature, must go to Freud (1915, 1917). Since then, academic psychologists have largely shied off the subject with a few but growing number of exceptions. Piaget (1935), for instance, investigated the development of moral concepts in young children. Also, in particular, Kohlberg (1969) developed and refined Piaget's experimental methods, indicating subtleties in the later development of moral conscience that Freud and other psychoanalysts had not articulated (see also Dorr, Zax, & Danner, 1978).

Psychoanalysts themselves have not been very interested in statistical, experimental studies of guilt and conscience. Rather, they have been concerned with their presence, genesis and habitual structuring in individual minds. Melanie Klein (1932), for instance, was the first to point out the omnipresence of intense, guilt-ridden, primitive phantasies in the imaginings of very young children that were paralleled by adult patients. She tended to envisage primitive guilt almost solely as a process internal to a child. However, our presentation envisages guilt as a product of social processes, coming particularly from parents, interacting with mental ones internal to the child himself.

The toddler's primitive guilt is, as Piaget pointed out years ago, pre-moral, that is, he has not developed a stable, coherent mental structure of conscience that he identifies or possesses as his own.

It seems that in the first instance, as would be expected, commands, pleas and threats about a child's actions are experienced as coming *predominantly* from *outside* the self. This is natural, for it is from outside a child that they do in fact often come. We observed the precursors of commands in the first year of life in a mother's 'yes' and 'no' non-verbal gestures. It is in these and in the infant's reactions to the gestures, that we must look for the origins of guilt. We have noted how a mother's 'no' gestures and rebuffs evoke depressed distress in an infant. This depressed distress seems to have fantasies akin to a sense of *death* in them, so we would expect ideas of death to be closely associated with profound guilt and remorse. This is certainly heard in the remorseful utterances of suicidally melancholic people. It is also seen more widely in culturally shared fantasies like, 'The judgement of sin is death', and 'Hell is for the wicked after death'. In young children, and indeed in older people who remain stuck in this mode, there is an underlying concern with *losing the loved parent*, on whose person one's very existence feels to rely.

As time goes by, young children develop *expectations of punishment*, often fantastic in quality, based upon their experiences of mother's rebuffs. This can be observed in little children behaving in some way indicative of an expectation of punishment when none has in fact been meted out. Here it is plain that, although punishments are felt as coming from outside the self, the child is beginning to develop representative *schemata* or mental structures about punishment or revenge that have a lasting quality.

This observation is confirmed when we note a slightly older child talking to himself, saying such things as, 'Don't do that John, it's dirty', using his mother's voice. From our point of view, the child is clearly internalizing his mother. But, from the child's point of view, expected punishment still seems to him to come from the outside, not from within his own conscience, and here is linked to *loss of the love* of the parent.

In general, up to this age children predominantly (but not exclusively) experience their 'self' consciously as a *passive recipient* of influences and effects from the outside rather than as one affecting others. This is natural enough because they are really small and powerless, very much at the mercy of huge, almost infinite, mysterious adults. Their anxiety is largely concerned with what others will do to them rather than what they do to others. In psychoanalytic language it is said that these anxieties tend to be *persecutory*. That is, these children feel their 'self' as small, weak, and innocent in the face of powerful, unpleasant outside forces or persecutors. It is also said that, because they tend to experience themselves as predominantly *passive* in the face of powerful, possibly cataclysmic, forces, they are primarily in a *paranoid–*

schizoid position with regard to this image of themselves and the outside world. This is perhaps not a very happy term because it suggests serious pathology, which is not intended. It is used to indicate a normal developmental stage and to draw attention to the nature of the anxiety involved in it.

This assertion that children settle first into a passive position might seem puzzling, for it has already also been suggested that they probably have fantasies of their omnipotent effects on others, and this seems to contradict the assertion. Indeed, it is probable that junior toddlers are very caught up internally with the confusion about their sense of smallness and fragility, and their sense of omnipotence and strength. Frequently they can be observed oscillating from one to the other. The reality is much nearer the latter than the former and it is from this that the sense of being done to rather than doing to derives.

But, as has been noted already, toddlers grow up, walk and very evidently gain confidence in their own powers and cannot help noticing their *active effect* in pleasing and distressing others. With this they seem to begin to experience *concern* about the, often fantasized, damage they have done (Winnicott, 1965b). For instance, they kiss or hug mummy better, or make other reparative gestures. These are only rudimentary at this stage, but the work of internalization is beginning to take effect so that a new form of representation is developing. Around 2 years old or so, it is possible to hear little children say, 'Mummy, John will be a good boy today.' Then later, perhaps at about 3 years old, more internalized, 'I'll try to be good today.' Because this process is primarily concerned with the *effect of self on others*, and consequently with self-accusations and remorse, it is referred to as *a depressive position*. Note that this implies a similarity to but is not identical with pathological depression. It is a normal valuable mental activity. Klein's distinction between paranoid and depressive functioning is a fundamental one. We can see it everywhere, every day.

It is of note that, although the philosopher G. H. Meade (1932) was no psychoanalyst, nor particularly interested in the development of guilt, both he and Klein had a similar point of view about the sequence from passive 'me' to active 'I' in the development of a child's awareness of himself and his world. It seems that, rudimentary though it may be, the achievement of stable feelings of concern is of the most fundamental importance. Genuine sympathetic kindliness and then the formation of a moral conscience seem to originate in them. More than this, the very sense of self in a setting of a real external world seems, in part, to be dependent upon them. This is because depressive feelings are concerned with the self's effects on the outside world. And without an awareness of the effect of self on others, one is being only half realistic. Thus *concern about effects on others is an essential component in being realistic*, both morally and intellectually.

However, this concern can be enormously exaggerated, especially in children. We have already noted this in our earlier discussion of fantasies of omnipotence. So this concern and guilt can be very painful and frightening. All sorts of tricks or defences might be used to avoid full conscious awareness of them, thus guilt is perennially defended against, but without its experience we cannot be fully realistic. This seems to be a problem not only for children, but for older people too. As any person comes to a new situation he is faced with the question of his effects on others. Painful fantasies of inordinate shame and guilt might make him avoid awareness of this. But if he does not face these experiences and *test out*, at least subconsciously, his effects on others then he cannot be realistic in the new situation. This depressive experience has to be 'reworked' at every phase of life. Without this happening, a person is weakened and probably prone to breakdown. It is also to be noted that with the coming of these depressive experiences more wishes and intentions are felt as coming from *within* the self. The feeling of things *inside*, of an *inner world* is getting stronger and potentially richer.

Defences against primitive guilt

It has just been re-stressed that little children often seem, albeit quietly, to experience guilt in fantastically exaggerated, all-or-nothing ways. For instance, a 2-year-old boy, seeing a broken chair, said, 'Michael (himself) didn't do it'.

The play of disturbed children often shows obsessive preoccupation with fantastic guilt. Many less disturbed people can look back into their childhoods and remember dim, omnipresent, helpless feelings of responsibility and unworthiness, especially if their parents were unhappy in themselves.

With guilt being such a painful, all-or-nothing experience it is no wonder that it is vigorously defended against in the mind (A. Freud, 1936; Smith & Danielson, 1982). One of the most frequent mechanisms or tricks (and the most malignant socially and personally) is the use of a combination of *splitting*, then *projection* with *denial*. In the instance of the broken chair just mentioned we can see denial operative. First of all Michael must have thought 'Did Michael do it?' then denial, 'Michael didn't do it.' In this case, the denial matched reality and his mother confirmed it, but this does not always happen. Another instance shows projection operative:

> A 4-year-old boy was severely reprimanded by his mother for some misdeed and she shouted the words, 'You horrible little boy.' He spent the rest of the morning interrupting his little brother in his play, hitting him and screaming, 'You horrible little boy, look at all the mud on you, look at your vest, look at your filthy hands.'

Here, apparently after experiencing guilt himself, he spent the rest of the morning actively projecting it into his brother while he presumably felt clean and pure by comparison. Here, badness, originally felt as belonging to the self, has been split from it, denied as in the self and projected into his brother, so that the boy can feel his self to be pure and good.

The splitting, projection and denial, the syndrome of, 'it's not me, it's him', 'it's not our fault, it's theirs', is particularly pervasive in little children but continues on throughout the adult world. In psychotic form it becomes paranoia. It is present in 'goodies' and 'baddies' games, and thus in all goody-and-baddy hero–villain films, which appeal to millions. It can also be seen in wicked witch–fairy godmother, beauty–beast, God–devil fairy stories. It is, more seriously, prevalent in the group behaviour of chronically acrimonious party politics, in racism, sexism, class wars, belligerent nationalism and religious intolerance. It is very prevalent in private, but often equally painful, ways in marital conflicts. At an individual and marital level it has been much studied and is well documented (see Chapter 11). It seems a great pity that, although we are beginning to understand so much of what happens in people's minds, the leaders and participants in horror-ridden social conflicts often utterly ignore what they are doing. Perhaps violent *splitting and projection* are essential ingredients of 'evil' activity anywhere. Our growing knowledge of these processes seems still to be virtually powerless to call a halt to people when they desire easy thoughtlessness. This comes naturally when splitting and projection hold sway.

Dreams, nightmares and phobias

The sorts of experience just mentioned are complex, contradictory and confusing. Each child's mind must have to work hard to make *some* coherence of them, however inadequate. It seems likely from research (Palombo, 1978; Wolman, 1979) that *dreaming at night* is one of the ways by which day-time experiences are digested into *coherently structured memory systems* to be stored for future use. We know from examination of brain rhythms that dreaming, from before birth, in all mammals is a regular and frequent feature of sleep. How much lower animals assimilate experiences into long-term memory is an open question. But humans certainly need to, and we would thus expect disturbed sleep to be associated with problems of assimilating experiences into memory. This is a fascinating and mysterious question. Little babies can have very disturbed, panicky sleep, which is probably associated with dreaming but they do not manifestly have *nightmares* which leave them awake in terror. These, however, do begin to appear at about 18 months. They seem to arise only after a certain level of intellectual and emotional development has been reached, but perhaps earlier the terrified states that can be observed in young children who have not yet reached the level of representation. For instance, as we have seen, language is developing apace at this time. Here, as we know, one set of mental events (sounds) is being used to *stand for*, or signify, other mental events. Dramatization, as manifest in make-belief play, is another form of symbolization. Perhaps fully *dramatic* nightmares, which use symbolization, only occur after the child has actively begun to signify in a general way.

It is interesting to note that specific *phobias*, 'unjustifiable' fears of things, people and places seem to take root in children at about this time. These are in some ways rather like nightmares when awake, they involve the *condensation* of intense feelings into a *class* of things, a certain sort of person or animal, say, or particular situations like dark places, very open spaces, or crowded areas. Here again, one sort of thing, a sort of animal, say, seems to *stand for* some other set of emotional ideas in the child. Thus the coming of signification and symbolization seems to bring not only language but also dramatic nightmares and phobias.

It seems that not only does each child have his own idiosyncratic forms of activity, but also each family presents its own mixture of enjoyable impressions and useful information interwoven with confusing or stultifying, contradictory fantasies. Furthermore, not only do families differ in their competences and crazy fantasies, so also do cultures. As each child is exposed to and has to adapt to a different environment from other children, he must structure his mental life differently from the child next door or in the next continent. He is being socialized in ways particular for him.

As the second year of life proceeds, we can how see the child develops these capacities for taking in experiences of the outside world, representing them in his own idiosyncratic way at a mental level, and then uses these to explore the world, both external and internal. In the next chapter we will see how the complexity of the internal and the social world increases as these mental representations are further elaborated as the child's experiences multiply.

Further reading

Gustavus Jones, J. (2004) *Understanding Your One Year Old*. London: Tavistock Clinic & Jessica Kingsley.

Lieberman, A. (1993) *The Emotional Life of Toddlers*. New York: The Free Press.

Mahler, M., Pine, F., & Bergmann, A. (1975) *The Psychological Birth of the Human Infant*. London: Hutchinson.

Chapter 6

Two to three years old: senior toddlers

Angela Joyce

Passion and zest in movement, feelings and ideas

Junior toddlerhood was epitomized by the discovery of a rudimentary trust in movement of the whole body and the consequent internal conflict between the urge to explore and the wish to remain close to the loved parents. Vitality, full-blooded feeling and fantasy are the hallmarks of the toddler period. In discussing this time of life it would be wrong to separate out each year too strictly from the others. Many things that apply to a 2-year-old can also be said of a 4-year-old, and vice versa. Developments are taking place at a rapid speed; one child will develop in one direction but not in another until later, whereas with another child it will be the other way around. Indeed, some of the issues considered in this chapter, e.g. toilet training and taking control of the body, might equally have been considered as part of the last chapter.

What must be remembered is that all aspects of development are intermingling at all times and that although some functions seem particularly important at each phase, it is probably best to think of the developmental process as being multi-modular. How sequences of development occur in any individual child's life is 'highly influenced by the context of the child's experience, including the emergence of other sequences – and whether one domain becomes integrated with another, and under what circumstances is an open question' (Coates, 1997, p. 46).

This chapter will be concerned with a range of different aspects of this developmental stage: what psychoanalysts have called the anal period – that time when children become preoccupied with what is going on inside their bodies and what comes out of them, and the establishment of bodily ownership and control; the formation of gender identity and the elaboration of make-believe or symbolic play.

Ownership of the body

With the firm knowledge that autonomous movement is possible, the 2-year-old will be seeking out new and more refined movements to achieve. From toddling, he goes on to walking steadily but, not content at that, will want to run everywhere, practise climbing, jumping, and skipping. The most immediate impression one gets of a group of senior toddlers is one of continuous flowing movement, eager, excited running, bouncing up and down from dawn till dusk. This sense of physical autonomy is perhaps reflected in a child's conception of himself. As a junior toddler he referred to himself by his first name, which had been given to him by others. Now, less passively, he uses the word 'I'. This reflects a growing sense that the young child is living in his body, that he has a more elaborated and secure sense of where he begins and the outside world ends; that he has a mind that resides in a body. The child who can rely upon his feet to find their way around without tripping over all the time was described by Winnicott as having eyes in his feet, i.e. a sense of his mind living in his body that knows where it is in the world (Winnicott, 1982).

The sense of living in one's own body might seem to adults as something to take for granted but in fact it is a feeling that is won only through developmental time. In fact it could be said that the child's body is only 'on lease' (van Heeswyk, 1997) from the parents until adolescence, when the adult sexual body arrives and has to be accommodated into the sense of the self. In toddlerhood, this wresting of the ownership of the body from the adults is often at the centre of battles for control, whether it be around general issues of behaviour or more specifically over toilet training. Parents have immense power over children's bodies, not just by virtue of the difference in their size but also because of the responsibility that parents have for the care of those bodies. Feeding, cleaning, nappy changing, carrying, cuddling; all involve the parents in intimate access to the child's body. For the toddler asserting his autonomy, control of the body will be central, and will not only involve using his body in ways *he* wants to that might be different from the parents' wishes, but also taking control of his bodily functions that previously had happened automatically.

Developing control of the body

We know that at birth the nervous system is neither structurally developed nor functionally organized to cope with the complex organization that has to come into play to achieve sphincter control. Let us look at the sequence of thought that must take place in children for control to be acquired.

They must first be aware that they *have* wetted or soiled themselves. They must then become aware of the sensations *just before* they wet or soil. They must next understand that other people want them to *communicate* this inner state of affairs to them. They must also inhibit the relaxation of their sphincters long enough for them to be brought to a pot. Lastly, they must learn to relax their sphincters when over the pot. It is quite a complex sequence to learn.

Clearly, not all children necessarily learn the sequence in the order presented here. Many children, for instance, quickly grasp the last part – opening the sphincters over the pot – long before they master the first part of the sequence. Early in the second year children might simply not remember what has happened even a few seconds after wetting or soiling. Engrossed in some new interest they will go on as if nothing has happened. In the second half of the second year they are likely to be able to indicate that they *have* wet or soiled themselves. In the last chapter, we saw how Jack responded when he became aware of these sensations and their consequences in his great-grandmother's garden. A month or so later children are just about able to say they are *about* to do so. After this they can begin to *voluntarily* clench the anal or urethral sphincter muscles. Around the second birthday they can begin to control themselves to hold on and *move* to a pot. Toilet training may be well under way but for many children it will happen later or will have happened sooner. Incidentally, control of soiling usually comes before being dry.

One suspects that there are as many methods of achieving the sequence as there are mothers in the world. Perhaps we could distinguish two main schools of thought. First, the 'start it early and repeat it often' school who advocate potting from the earliest months to get the child used to the situation. Some mothers of this persuasion emphasize routine, and will put their children on the pot for half an hour or more after meals to establish a routine and a habit. The other philosophy could be called the 'wait till he wants to' school. This emphasizes that a child will learn quickly and easily when the situation of potting means something to him so that he *himself wants*, for his own as well as other people's sakes, to control his bladder and bowels.

Those who wait will not necessarily have to deal with dirty nappies for longer than the 'start them early' school, as those who begin earlier do not necessarily get their children reliably clean and dry before the late starters. It seems that they are relying on a baby's proneness to void himself at certain times, immediately after a feed for instance. There is no harm in catching the motion then. But parents are under an illusion if they think a child is really learning to control himself. Relapses are common until children have really discovered they want to be clean and dry. The final stages for this won't really begin to be assured before at least nearing the second birthday during the day and probably much later at night Those who wait are likely to find that learning control has an element of fun and pleasure for the child as well as the parent, and in addition promote a greater sense of autonomy and ownership of the body in their offspring.

Some considerations about anal and urethral impulses and fantasy

Potty training is not usually an openly difficult affair, whatever method is used. What adults usually have forgotten (or repressed) is the range of emotion they experienced as young children as they went through this stage. As children develop control of their sphincters for urinating and defecating they then become able to regulate whether and when they are to perform such functions, and these are thus open to other influences, not just the pragmatic fact of needing to excrete. These other influences may be more obvious in the relationship with the person who is trying to toilet train the child. During this period children will experiment with holding in or letting go of their urine or faeces, feeling the bodily sensations and undoubtedly elaborating fantasies around these experiences. These fantasies may well be related to the issue of who controls their body – Mummy or me? – and then be imbued with a range of feelings and impulses around control and mastery, domination and submission.

This phase is known in classical psychoanalysis as the *anal–sadistic phase* as this is often the first time that cruel and tormenting behaviour is observed in young children. It is usually a displacement from these aspects of the relationship with the adult who 'demands' that the child now abandons the previous practice of urinating and defecating when the feeling happens, to controlling the body and only evacuating its contents into a suitable receptacle. Parents can promote the transformation of these impulses into something more benign through not reacting in an aggressive and controlling way, but encouraging compromise. For example, children of this age often show the first signs of possessiveness, and conflicts between children, which might involve biting, hitting, kicking, etc. can become frequent. Settling such conflicts usually needs adult intervention of the kind that encourages concern rather than indulgence of these aggressive impulses.

Other influences apart from pragmatic ones will equally be associated with internal process of the balance of pleasure and unpleasure in the body. The sensations of holding in and letting go are very satisfying to the young child, and often such children can be observed becoming quiet and self-absorbed as they focus inward on the feelings in their body. At a fantasy level these can be associated with benign good impulses and their opposite – destructive and cruel. It will be some time before the more ordinary or familiar attitude of adults to their faeces and urine – of disgust and the pleasures of cleanliness and order – become apparent in the child. These are dependent upon identifications with the caregivers that promote the opposite impulses to the wishes to soil and mess that are so apparent in the young child's play. For example, young children at this stage are often fascinated with playing with water coming out of taps, or playing in sand and making squishy messy sand and mud pies. The beginnings of the opposite tendencies can be observed when they might exhibit fastidious mannerisms, hating having dirt on their hands, refusing to use finger paints, etc. However, any parent of teenagers will testify to the continuation of the pleasures of messiness throughout development – they are given up often with great reluctance!

Toby became quite anxious about progressing from using the potty to the toilet. He would be hesitant and sometimes distressed when his mother suggested that he was a big boy now and could use the toilet like his older siblings and his parents. One day he agreed to use the lavatory to do his poo and when he was finished he did not want his mother to use the flush. He became upset and said that his poo was his friend and he was worried about his friend getting lost down the loo if it was flushed.

Toby's feelings and fantasies are very common in young children and connected to the sense that what is inside their bodies is part of themselves and therefore to be kept and protected. Often these fantasies involve the growing interest children have in an increasingly important question for them – 'Where did I come from; where do babies come from'. Commonly the spontaneous answers that children of this age give to these questions are based around the influence these anal concerns have on their conception of bodily processes. They may well have observed that mummies get round in the belly and then they have a baby, or they might be told in answer to these questions that first of all the baby grows in the mummy's tummy and then is born. Often, senior toddlers arrive at the conclusion that babies are like their poos, they are in their bodies first and then they come out – they are 'born'. In fact, if poos are like babies it means that they can have babies too – boys and girls – there is as yet no differentiation in these terms; that is for later. So Toby thought of his poo as a friend but he might equally have thought of it as a baby. In some children these fantasies can become exaggerated and interfere with the ordinary developmental process of agreeing to use the toilet for these bodily functions (Hayman, 1974).

General considerations

Anal and urethral fantasy is an omnipresent mental activity not only in young children's minds and the psychotherapists' consulting rooms but in everyday life as well. For instance, pleasure in dirty jokes is pretty well universal in spontaneous children who naturally get very excited about lavatorial humour. Later, having learnt to talk about sex, these are transformed into sexual joking, but the underlying lavatorial-ness seems to remain.

Less fun than joking is the continuation of anal fantasy into the habitual *character structure* of many adults. For instance, there is strong evidence that *obsessional* features like meticulous cleanliness, meanness about possessions, self-righteousness and preoccupation with obedience to rules do all tend to form constellations together as characteristics of some individuals (Kline, 1972). There seems little in common to bring these together except an underlying, often unconscious, concern about control of contents, which at a body level is excretory control.

If toilet training itself is not usually a desperate struggle, why then should phantasies about it continue so troublesomely to cloud many people's adult lives? The answer to this seems to lie somewhere in the following direction. First of all, because the anal and urethral zones of the body are highly sensitive, they easily arouse erotic sensations and these particularly stimulate exaggerated fantasies. In addition, these zones mediate the expulsion of contents from inside the body. We know, too, that the body and its contents, in phantasy, are some of the self's most necessary and private possessions. And in toilet training some of these apparently precious possessions have to be controlled and then surrendered – often, it is felt, to another person. This being so, toilet training would epitomize, and generate exaggerated phantasy about the *surrender* of aspects of the self and its capabilities to others. This problem of the surrender of self to others is not a trivial business for anyone, and for some is catastrophic.

It seems that *conflicts, originating in many other areas, easily become unconsciously focused onto excretory functions* because these, being so excitable, are, above others, readily represented in phantasy (Abraham, 1927; Freud, 1905; Segal, 1985). One of the characteristics of mental activity at a highly emotional, often unconscious, level is seen to be working here. Functions that have a *similarity* are experienced as the *same* or *identical*. We have spelled this out before. Faeces, body contents and the self are all similar in that they are 'possessions'. However, at an emotional unconscious phantastic level they are felt not just as similar but identical. The self is precious and faeces and other body contents, being identical to the self, are precious too. What is more, if faeces are surrendered to others, so too, at this level of imagining, is the whole self. When this carries on into adult life the idea of the self can be treated as if it were faeces. This will seem a very weird, slightly mad reasoning to those used to everyday logic. But if one is closely involved with intimate emotional problems it will be seen happening every day for many people.

Another facet of the frightening importance of faeces is their being fantastically equated with *dead* things. After death, animals rot and smell very like faeces. A child quickly picks this up. As we have just noted in the last paragraph, things that logically are alike are phantastically experienced as absolutely the same. So faeces and dead things can be the same, and, since everyone has faeces inside them, then they have dead things inside. Thence, using the peculiar logic of the imagination, our selves can be full of deadness; even our selves can be dead! Perhaps this sort of phantasized imagination is at the root of the traditional Hell. This is never up in the sky nor on the surface of the body of the earth even, but in its bowels, in the underworld, usually entered through a hole in the ground, where devils eternally torment transgressors.

Freud was the first person to explore systematically the vagaries of logicality at these primitive emotional levels of thought (Freud, 1900, 1915) followed recently by Matte-Blanco (1975). Our example of anality and the self is just one more instance of the strange classificatory logic used unconsciously by the emotions.

Parents

Returning now to childhood. It is not simply the child's fantasy systems that are involved but his parents' as well. He grows up, throughout childhood, fighting with and submitting to his parents' fantasies. Toilet training is only one event in a long, often benign, sometimes chronic, history of struggle. Here is an illustration, evidence but not proof, of this contention.

A boy was brought up by parents belonging to a religious sect, which was strict, rule-ridden and unquestioning. His mother was kind but a convinced believer and also meticulous, very busy and matter of fact, did not play games and was rather joyless, certainly not erotic. She toilet-trained her boy successfully by routine from an early age. He remembers being fond of his family and passionately wishing to conform. But an underlying element of dreariness in life was epitomized for him by hours in chapel, which were appallingly painful because he had to keep still all the time. However, the rebel was still alive in him. He secretly discovered how to explore erotically with pet dogs, and also how to play more open, ordinary games in fun with other children. When he went to school the relaxation of other families disturbed him and he became overtly rebellious. He seemed to express this by peeing on the carpet outside his mother's prized and very clean kitchen at night.

As he came to adolescence, the revolt became more open by refusing to accept his parents' ideas and challenging their beliefs and habits. Neither side could budge and at home he lapsed into a generalized sulking mood. Rebellious and intelligently free thinking in his general philosophy as he was, his parents' ways had nevertheless entered into him. He found himself in obsessive dilemmas about petty things that wasted hours of time, prissily meticulous about other people's faults and hair-splitting in arguments. He tended to find himself mean and over-careful about money. As an outlet he took to obsessive orgies of gambling, priding himself, however, on the meticulous, carefully worked out systems that he used before staking his money at the tables.

This illustrates not only a child's long-term struggle with parental habits but also suggests the association, which has been generally recognized for a long time by psychoanalysts, between early childhood control, rebellious aggressiveness, and *obsessional* thinking and activity (Abraham, 1927; Fromm, 1973).

Many other desires seem also to focus around discipline, which, you will note, is always *against* some immediate impulses, with the aim of forming controlled habits. Passivity, for instance, the wish to punish and be punished, desires for torturing and being tortured and *perversity* generally, all seem to centre around excitements about control and the desire to lose control. It is a vast subject for which we have no more space here.

Girls and boys

Along with all the other things to explore, a child will have been investigating his own body from earlier days of life. Contours will have been examined and erotic sensations aroused in all parts of the body. The main agents for this autoerotism will be the hands. With toilet training the encumbrance of nappies will be laid aside and the child will be much freer to explore the contours and sensations of the genitals. Here will begin the rudiments of genital masturbation. The shape of the sensations will be different for boys and girls, just as the shape of a penis is different from clitoris and vagina. It is usually about 2 years old or a bit earlier that a child shows signs of awareness of sex differences, but some recent research has shown that it takes quite a long time for children to link the recognition of genital difference to the idea of being a boy or a girl.

A study conducted by de Marneffe (1997) has shown that boys and girls begin to communicate recognition of their own genitals between 20 and 30 months, with most children over 24 months able to do so. Following this, both boys and girls show a preference for dolls whose genitals are like their own. Contrary to classical psychoanalytical theory, developmental research of this nature has shown that children's representations of their own genitals precede any more conflictual recognition of genital difference, which would involve a sense of inferiority in the girl. Indeed, it infers that such sense of inferiority is most likely to arise from other factors such as family relationships than any inherent sense of the nature of the genitals. Children in this study seem to have a clear and valued sense of their own bodies and can distinguish them from the bodies of the other sex. But children's ability to link the accurate gender label with the genitals is often confused in younger children and takes time to be securely established. It seems that the coordination of the recognition of genital difference with gender difference often follows a circuitous route and a child who has a rudimentary understanding of genital difference does not necessarily link this with gender for quite a long time.

Following the recognition that 'I have a vagina' or 'I have a penis', children of each sex begin to show a preference to play with same-sex peers. Susan Coates (1997) links this with the child's enhancement of their sense of self. Indeed, other research has demonstrated that 2–3-year-old boys and girls positively ascribe attributes to activities that are stereotypically associated with their own gender, and conversely negatively describe such activities for the opposite sex (Kuhn, Nash, & Brucken, 1978). So here we have the first open glimmerings of feelings of affinity with those of the same sex and difference from those of the opposite sex. In addition, in a child's play one will notice girls often beginning to model themselves actively on their mothers, and boys on their fathers. The great class distinction between male and female has begun! Before long, and certainly before going to school, 'both boys and girls will seek out activities consonant with their sense of their own gender and a majority but not all will come to prefer, albeit not on an exclusive basis, same-gendered peers' (Coates, 1997, p. 39). In Coates' view this leads to different experiences of peer socialization for boys and girls, which is a very important arena within which the gendered sense of self is constructed.

This seems to suggest that young children grow up with a sense of certainty about their gender, but this is not borne out in many subtle ways. For quite a long time children play around with their sense of gender. This will be evident in their play, such as dressing up as different characters, pretending to be one of a different gender, such as a girl being a prince or a king and a boy a mother. We have already seen how children's fantasies about procreation and their wishes associated with their sense of what goes on inside their bodies, often leads to boys, for instance, claiming that they are having a baby, just like mummy. Very often, young children believe that by changing clothes they can become the other sex. They may lack both gender constancy (the knowledge that being a boy or a girl does not depend upon outward appearance or activity) and gender stability (being a boy or girl does not change during development) for a long time. One 4-year-old boy told the author with great conviction that his little sister, aged 1 year, would grow a 'willy' as she got older.

Psychoanalysts have theorized that these subtle indications that all is not certain suggest that, unconsciously, children are very conflicted about this conscious knowledge of sexual, gender and bodily differences. Freud's view was that the recognition of sexual difference evoked much anxiety in both boys and girls; anxiety about the precious possession of the penis being lost, castrated. Boys would fear castration and girls had to accept the fact of it. Girls would experience envy of their male counterparts for their possession of the penis and would blame their mothers for their own castrated state. This view has been immensely contentious both within and outside psychoanalysis over the past 80 to 100 years. Recent developmental research has joined the challenge to this classical Freudian view. However, many psychoanalytically informed clinicians and observers of young children often say that these young people have read Freud before they have, such is the preoccupation with their bodies that many of them demonstrate!

Children also become interested in the different body contours and colours of other people of all ages, and in the differences between female and male. This also reflects the breadth of identifications that young children make in their family environment – both parents and other significant figures are used as objects for identification at many different levels, and gender is one of them. Girls will notice and ask questions about similarities with their mothers and differences from their fathers; boys vice versa. It is interesting to note that parents seem often rather coy about giving their children names for their genitals, especially girls. In de Marneffe's study she found that girls were often given the word vagina for their genitals, which is inaccurate anatomically. Girls were never just given a name for their own genitals but also for boys', but some girls had been given no name for their own. Boys were usually only given names for boys' genitals. When parents were asked about this they sometimes stated or inferred that they were reluctant to draw their sons' attention to female genitals if they had not spontaneously expressed curiosity.

At this point it is useful to summarize findings on some of the differences between the sexes. There is a great deal of research material on the subject collected in recent years (Archer & Lloyd, 1982). Very briefly, we can say the following. Until about the seventh week of pregnancy, human fetuses are identical in form, except, of course, for the chromosome pattern; this form is essentially female. At the seventh week the male hormone testosterone begins to be manufactured and its action generates the development of male characteristics. Female development is not the same process, it simply occurs in the absence of male hormone; it is the default position in the absence of testosterone. The development of male characteristics entails the following sex differences after birth. Boys tend to be stronger-muscled, have a higher vital capacity and metabolic rate than girls. They thus tend to be more physically aggressive (in the sense simply of using their muscles thrustfully). Girls, on the other hand, have more body fat; this, together with a lower metabolic rate, tends to make them less muscularly aggressive. Perhaps partly because of their imbalance of X and Y chromosomes, males statistically tend to extremes more than females. More male fetuses abort. There are more male stillbirths and more males born defective. In intellectual achievements there tends to be an over-weighting of males at both the dull and brilliant ends of the scale (although this is undoubtedly coloured by cultural factors). In childhood, girls tend to develop intellectually earlier than boys, and currently the previous tendency for this to even-out in their teens has abated and girls continue to achieve higher academic results to degree level. This reflects the power of cultural factors in determining these outcomes. Girls tend particularly to be higher in verbal abilities, whereas boys excel more at spatial-motor abilities (this again may be culturally coloured).

Apart from these and the primary sexual characteristics of the reproductive organs, there seems to be little evidence of real differences between males and females. Ideas of superiorities and inferiorities have been formed over many centuries, fantasized, often shared between people to become prejudices, which are sometimes of a brutality that is now only too well known. However, it is also cruel to deny the differences between boys and girls. They are physically different and metabolize differently. This must mean that they generate phantasies differently because these originate in body sensations as we have noted. As phantasies are different, so too are interests and ideas more generally. Those who argue that girls' and boys' differing play preferences, for instance, are just a function of cultural indoctrination are simplistic; they ignore the body functions that give rise to play. They thus do serious, often very hurtful, injustice to children's vital spontaneity. What is wrong with sex differences anyhow? How boring life would be without them.

Vitality, movement and fantasy

We will now turn to more general aspects of the senior toddler's development in this third year of life. In both movement and ideas, children will throw themselves into one activity and then switch, often without warning, to something quite different. This flow of imagination, shifting from one activity to another, is exhausting to an adult as well as a delight. It is tiring not only because of the physical movement involved, but also because adults, to keep up with the children, must allow their own imagination to range freely at the same speed as that of the children. They must give up their well-tried modes of thought and action and allow free play to their own 'childish' fantasies. To be childlike, and at the same time remain a realistic, responsible adult, is not easy; it requires being mentally coherent at several levels at once. However, to many parents the pre-school years of their children are unforgettable. There is enough drama of joy, anguish, comedy and violence from one family to fill a hundred theatres.

The 2-year-old's capacity to speak gives us the opportunity to understand his point of view with a precision that was not possible in the earlier years. We are less dependent upon inference to understand. However, we must also remember that many aspects of children's development and functioning is unconscious and therefore we still need to rely on thoughtful inference to get at what is the hidden meaning and subjective experience of what is out-wardly observed. We see that, whereas 2-year-olds are usually zestfully interested in the world, it is a puzzling place that often frightens them. They still rush back to mother when it all gets too much. Mother, or a well-trusted substitute, needs to be kept well in sight except perhaps at home; even then she will be frequently checked up on (Bowlby, 1969).

As children go about the place they often seem to be talking all the time. Their speech may be about what they feel: 'I want a biscuit', 'Don't want to go to bed', 'You are horrid'. Most often it communicates an observation: 'We did go to the swings today', 'We did see an elephant', 'There's the moon', and so on. Although stated as observations, these require an answer and children will become very upset or puzzled or angry if there is no reply. They are not only making an observation but also asking for confirmation that their idea is correct. They are trying, as we have mentioned before, to build up coherent and meaningful representations of the host of impressions that impinge upon them. A lot of their obser-vations can sound silly, but are perfectly sensible from their rudi-mentary point of view. For instance, many children search behind a television set or look under a telephone to 'find the people'. Or when told, 'We are going to post a letter to Granny', may burst into tears at the pillar-box because, 'Granny locked in there'. Again, on seeing a chimney smoking, they puzzle and say, 'Bonfire on the roof'. Such observations indicate the feats of learning, which every child must accomplish (Fraiberg, 1959; Isaacs, 1930).

Learning from others

Children are usually quite content to have their observation simply confirmed by the adult companion. But they also rely on the adult to explain and fill out their direct perceptions. Obviously it would be a very careless person who just said 'yes' to the observation about bonfires on the roof. Children's parents and siblings are continuously required to correct, fill in and expand the child's knowledge of the world. Thus a child when drinking says, 'Milk', and his mother may reply, 'Yes', and no more – in which case his concept of milk is confirmed but not expanded. On the other hand, she may say, 'Yes – do you remember the cows we saw yesterday? Well, milk comes from cows.' Children usually readily pick this up, and may speculate with quite vivid approximations or fantasies as to how milk comes from a cow. They might say: 'Cut cow open and milk comes out', or, 'Milk in cow's tummy'. This would be refined, perhaps, when the mother and child again see a cow, and she points to the udder and says it is where the cow makes the milk, and that it is sucked out through the teats by a machine and then put in bottles or cartons.

We have just noted how very seriously a child of this age needs coherent and amplifying replies from the parents. A lazy mother leaves a child ill informed, puzzled and with only his own ideas to go on; intellectual development is then very likely to suffer. An overworked or depressed mother, burdened by external or internal preoccupations can unfortunately also leave a child unsatisfied, puzzled and even frightened of the world. Still more confusing can be the replies and amplifications of a parent prone to paranoid ideas; suspicion and mystification can then intrude upon explanations given. The social chemistry of information exchanges varies from one family to another. Remember also that these illustrations are mostly British, and that children from other cultures will often be exposed to quite different information and misinformation. They are then likely to form different competencies.

Mother, father, the family, the outside world and a child's ambivalence

The physical movement of children at this age indicates their eagerness to get to know the world outside the family. We have noted their fear if separated from those they knows well for more than short periods (Bowlby, 1969, 1973). But this does not mean they are uninterested in and cannot learn from other people. Many people will testify that other members of the family – grandparents, aunts, uncles, siblings – and nursery workers can become most valued objects of affection. Many children these days have started in some kind of playgroup or even a nursery, where they have to manage for many hours in the day being looked after by people not part of their immediate family. How they manage this transition will depend very much on the experiences that have gone before, but also the sensitivity with which their feelings are recognized in making such a radical change in their daily lives. Too often one hears of situations where the child's ordinary anxiety is ridden roughshod over: 'Never mind her crying – she will be fine when you [the parent] have left.'

Often, the best way children can be helped to make the transition into a nursery is for the parent to stay for a while and gradually enable their child to become acquainted with the new surroundings and people. This requires nurseries to be more flexible and understanding. They need to know that the children in their charge are best helped by being supported in recognizing their feelings about their new situation so that reassurance is based upon real knowledge of how the children are experiencing it, rather than something which is false and based on ignorance of the child's feelings.

At this point it is important to stress the question of a child's ambivalence. We have seen how children of this age are passionate; they can switch instantaneously from ecstatic idolizing love to vehement dislike of one and the same person. They shift from all good to all bad experiences. This is splitting; we have already noted that it is useful in saving the immature child from confusion but it seems that, if equable enjoyment and tolerance of other people is to develop, then a child must develop a structuring of ideas in his mind whereby he can experience good and bad feelings about one person at the same time.

It is one of the major tasks of growth throughout childhood to coalesce together into coherent ideas the conflicting ambivalences of loves and hates. Without it wisdom, intellectual and interpersonal, cannot be attained. For instance, an adult who gushes in adoration one moment and then is full of loathing or contempt the next is a tiring pest to others and often has poor intellectual judgement as well; he is immature. Such immaturity can happen anywhere, it is tied to no one culture. It seems that close family members, mothers in particular, play a vital part in helping or hindering this tolerance of ambivalence. If a mother is present to receive and respond to all forms of her child's mood, good and bad, then he can slowly create an image of a person, his mother, who is good, bad and in between. She is then experienced not so much as either wonderful or terrible but as lovably interesting. Forming this representation of a person as a whole, with continuity between the multiplicity of feelings of good and bad, sadness and joy, rebuff and gladness, takes a long time of exploration and experience. In times of extreme distress it may shatter: for some children it is never remotely achieved.

Psychoanalysts stress that young children's splitting and ambivalence means that they relate only to part-objects at any one time, a loved one or hated one for instance, not both. The process towards integrating good and bad feelings together is a vital aspect of what is called whole object formation. It will usually take years, if ever, for this to be stably achieved.

The importance of this development argues strongly for children having at least one person (most frequently their own mother) to both love and hate, with continuity, at this age. If loving and hating is chronically split so that they only hate one person and love another, for example, then the children's tolerance is not so likely to develop. This argument, however, does not imply that children ought to have only one person to love and hate. On the contrary, if there is only one person they have no one else to turn to for comfort in moments of intense hatred. This is often intolerably distressing and they will resort to some distorting defensive trick to find comfort.

The easy presence of another person, a father perhaps, allows a child to run to him crying, for instance, 'She's horrible, horrible, I'm going to smash her into little bits'. The other person can hold and comfort the child in a way the hated mother could not at that moment.

Quite clearly the role played by the other person in helping to resolve a child's ambivalence depends on the position taken. If a father, for example, replies by gesture or word, 'Yes, she's horrid. I'm much nicer than she is', then the splitting is exacerbated. On the other hand, if he replies, 'You are to say no such thing about your dear mother', then the child is left all alone with his hatred. But if he says something to the effect of, 'Yes, she's horrid sometimes, but lovely too', then a child is probably helped to resolve his splitting.

This instance is in terms of a father as the 'other person'. It could equally apply to anyone else to some extent, an elder sibling or grandparent, for instance. However, a father can be particularly well placed for this function because he, above others, is likely to know, love and be annoyed by his wife as deeply as the child, yet also can be dispassionate. He can share feelings with his child with both conviction and fairness (Backett, 1982; Lamb, 1981; Parke, 1981).

This argument is laid out in the language of a British nuclear family. In more universal terms, the necessities for maturing out of primitive ambivalence into more 'whole' experiences of people simply seem to be: at least two, mutually intimate and tolerant grown-ups. These can be found in family patterns other than the stereotyped nuclear one. However, even with people who have grown up in large, extended family networks in other countries, the nuclear triangle or mother–father–child within the wider network very frequently remains of vital and long-lasting importance to the growing person.

Now let us turn to more intellectual aspects of play and exploration.

Symbolization and pre-concepts

In the last chapter we noted the beginning of signification and symbolization not only in language but also in drama and play. In *signification* generally one thing or event stands for another. Many forms of signification arise through cultural convention as well as verbalisation. We also noted a quite different form of *symbolization*, which seems to arise more spontaneously from within a person; here the symbol resembles the form of the thing symbolized. Such symbolizing, most evident in dreams, seems to arise from the depths. Its source seems to be the unconscious.

Piaget has stressed that signification is rooted in imitation (Piaget, 1951). You will remember how mother–infant synchrony was an early instance of imitation. It is certainly present in a baby from the earliest weeks in automatic form. Later in the first year and on into the second we noted this imitation becoming more actively intentional. For example, Piaget noted that a girl, on seeing a child jumping up and down and thus moving his playpen, soon started jumping up and down herself clearly with the same intention of moving the playpen.

An imitation that is clearly a symbolic wish fulfilment is instanced by a child trying to re-open a box and at the same time opening his mouth very wide. At about 18 months the first symbolic imitations emerge, for instance, rubbing hands together to represent washing, or jigging running to be like a horse galloping.

Dramatic symbolization or make-believe proper has begun. Let us stress again that here imitation is occurring; a body action is actively made to signify another event. Remember also that verbalization rests largely on a vast background of imitations; but, as we noted in the last chapter, words rarely have the same form as the event or thing signified.

Another point, in the case of verbal language a child comes to conform to general usage as he gains in skill. This conformity has a lesser place in dramatic symbolism; here personal invention remains more idiosyncratic. Even so, people or children dramatically playing together can usually mutually understand the meaning of the symbols.

With symbolism comes the full beginning of interest in the similarity (as opposed to sameness or identity) of things (Piaget, 1950, 1951). We have seen in earlier chapters how synchrony and imitation seem to give rise to primitive feelings of sympathy, of being the same as another person. We have also noted the baby registering sameness in the first steps of classifying. With symbolization, from the second year onward comes a gigantically freeing step for the intellect. This is that something the same is recognized as common to instances that are themselves different. What is more this attribute in common can be actively and intentionally signified, either verbally or in dramatic symbols.

General ideas have arrived but they are not yet by any means logically consistent. For instance, as we have noted earlier, a child may easily distinguish a set of boys from girls and know that boys have willies and girls have fannies, etc. But put the boys in girl's dresses and he will say they are girls. Or again: take a ball of plasticine, roll it into a long sausage and a child will say there is more of it 'because it's longer', or there is less of it 'because it's thinner'. These two examples show quite different sorts of pre-conceptualization; one is qualitative, the other quantitative. But they both indicate that, even though our children have achieved the beginnings of general ideas and the use of signification about them, they have little idea of logical consistency. This inconsistency involves incomplete comprehension of the constant attributes that run through things that are similar. A child will be seven or eight before he gets into the way of checking his inconsistencies systematically even in concrete situations. But a start has been made (Overton & Gallagher, 1977).

Dramatic symbolization or make-believe play

Brief reflection about any sort of play will suggest that it rests on an active but relaxed manipulation of materials (in adults these materials may be purely mental). During play, distress must be at a minimum. The pleasures of play can be erotic but are more frequently those of meaning-making. From the earliest days of life, the infant plays in sensori-motor ways; so do other animals.

The dramatic or make-believe play we have just introduced is not confined to humans. It has been noted, for instance, that monkeys make characteristic 'let's play' gestures before gambolling together. In the absence of these, serious fighting can ensue. Bruner (1976) argues that some measure of discrimination of a separate-self is necessary for true make-believe, even in animals. In other words, in order to play, a person must be able to experience, 'I'm me and it's it and now I'll pretend that it's something else'. Or if two individuals play together they must both be able to agree, 'I'm me and you're you, now let's pretend we are doing something else'. Bruner and many others before him (Millar, 1968) have stressed the importance of play as essential in acquiring serious skills.

Although oddly ignored by multitudes of parents and educators in the past, the importance of play is well recognized today. However, it seems that there is a resurgence of disbelief in early years education that play is also 'work' – that is, the child's equivalent. Play is serious work for a child!

We have already stressed how, towards the end of the second year, the toddler will begin to state explicitly that such-and-such is something else, and then play with it as if it were the real thing. For instance, he will pick up a stick and gleefully say 'saw', and start a sawing movement with it. In the third year (when he is two, that is) he will probably multiply his instances of make-believe. Here are just a few. A stick can be a saw, screwdriver, fishing-rod, sword, gun, crane, hosepipe, TV aerial, telescope, kerb to a road, aeroplane wing, or knife. A grocer's box can be a cot, bath, seat, car, train, aeroplane, boat, pigsty, oven, table, cage or house.

Make-believe takes place in two directions. First, the stick or box is made to stand for something imagined. The visually recognizable similarity between a toy and the thing for which it stands makes this possible. It is here, of course, that the child is using his rudimentary capacity to generalize. What is more, each symbol (stick or box for instance) here stands for, or signifies several sets or classes of things that have similarity between each other. But also a child pretends that he is somebody other than himself. Thus when he uses a stick to saw he is perhaps 'being Dad', or at least himself as a person who can use a saw. Again, in using the box as an oven, he is being 'Mum cooking'.

In make-believe there is an 'as if' suspension of reality. This is naturally only partial. Children usually know very well that they are playing. We have already mentioned how both children and adults may on occasions doubt whether their fantasy is real or not. When this occurs, play ceases and distress takes its place. There is something oddly paradoxical about play; it is an essential means of acquiring skills: in mastering reality, but in doing so a person stops bothering about reality to enjoy fantasy. The reality gains are a spin-off of the weaving of fantasies.

Make-believe play is at least partly moved by phantasy, and this in turn is aroused by ever-present body feelings. One particular feeling about the body that underlies so much of a small child's life is his helplessness or incompetence. We noted this in the last chapter as a vague, not necessarily unpleasant, feeling of general or *existential anxiety*. With this children play at being bigger or stronger. Nearly always they play at being adults: big, strong, clever or grand, Their play is of lions, horses, cooks, nurses, dancers, mummies, soldiers, cowboys, doctors, tractors, aeroplanes, acrobats and cars. Sometimes they play at being little things like mice, but then they are usually clever enough to escape, or good enough to be preciously quiet. There is *wish-fulfilment* in play.

We see ph/fantasy, probably arising from different parts of the body, in play. From the skeletal muscles there is play of diggers, cars and tractors and dancers. From the mouth there is lions, tigers and doll feeding. From the bowels and bladder there is messing and splashing, cleaning and tidying. From the penis, there is probably boys' enjoyment of thrusting, sticks, guns or spears. Fantasy from the penis is seen as more evident when a boy puts a broom between his legs saying, 'Look at my willy'. And from a girl's clitoris and vagina probably come fantasies moving her often to enjoy such things as dancing and also playing with the insides of things such as doll's houses as well as dolls themselves, flowers and frilly clothes. Her working over her response to the recognition of sexual difference might involve her playing with a hose pipe between her legs and greatly enjoying the experience of wetting everywhere.

But it is not simply body functions that are played over; it is the child himself in relation to things. When a child plays at being a digger or at being a mother with a doll, he can forget his smallness in relation to the world and for a time is its master or mistress.

This also happens in relation to people. What has been passively experienced can be played actively. For instance, having been nursed and fed by his mother, a child can play at actively nursing a doll. Having this in mind we can infer that active games of killing have been preceded by passive experiences of things going dead for the child. Play is, as it were a triumphant assertion of aliveness over deadness. Herein, perhaps, lies an argument against preventing little children playing battle games on the ground that they are too aggressive. In doing so adults may deprive them of the opportunity to play over and possibly find ways out of experiences of being made 'dead' or depressed. Battle games tend to be enthused about most by boys because of their interest in muscularity. Girls' play of triumph over deadness is more likely to be about having babies.

Perhaps the morality of allowing some forms of play and not others should centre not on the content of the play but on the material of the playthings. We have, for instance, no reason to believe that dolls or little soldiers object to being knocked about. But when the plaything is another child it is another matter. When a child who has been physically punished goes and spanks a doll it is one thing. But when, as described in the last chapter, a child goes off and sets about hitting another child without any 'let's play' agreement beforehand, it is quite another matter.

Let us now turn briefly to a general consideration. Play obviously does not cease with childhood; in the adult world creative play takes place with the minimum of physical objects, for instance a chess set, a writing pad, a drawing block or a musical instrument. Playing is embedded in all satisfying work, particularly in the design stages of a task that require the work of the imagination. But the childhood need for physical objects in play often goes on into adult life without recognition. A child, being small, needs only a patch of mud to play in. Adults can readily enlarge this bit of mud to vast tracts of the earth in the urge to play their games – albeit unconsciously and no doubt with rational or rationalized motives.

Adults and children's play

The arguments given above stress how children need time and space to play. The need to give physical room in which to play is now well recognized. More subtle are the limits set on play by adult attitudes. A child is prevented from playing over an activity not just by materials being unavailable but also by forbidding and rebuffing gestures spoken and unspoken. An 'Ugh', or, 'Don't do that' prevents relaxed play as much as any wall. It seems only fair to a child that his adults should, except in emergencies, reflect 'Why?' before they forbid a game. Otherwise a child is surrounded by incomprehensible fantasy-driven rules, which are not realistic rules but whims.

But children need adults in play, and not only as rule setters. Under about 3 years old, children can usually only play solitarily or at most in parallel. But even at this age they often seek to play with an adult. Parents on the floor, and songs and stories at bedtime are usually remembered as times of bliss long afterwards. Adults who play with children are remembered with deep gratitude. In addition, when these children grow up they have inside them the often unconscious but also conscious memory of these experiences, which they then are able to reproduce in their parenting of the next generation. A most painful sight is one where a parent who has not experienced their own parents playing with them when they were children, being at a complete loss as to how to play with their own children.

When adults play with their children, the children can feel that an otherwise huge adult is a human with experiences like themselves. The wholeness of the parent is enhanced. It is a time of sharing democracy. In particular, many of the frightening fantasies and puzzles, which assail them in solitude, can be transformed into fun when experienced with an adult who has similar fantasies but who is humorously unafraid of them. In this, lie the principles of play therapy and most other psychotherapies for adults as well as children (Winnicott, 1971). It seems more economical, as well as deeply satisfying, if parents can pre-empt such measures by having some fun themselves.

Further reading

Hobson, P. (2002) *The Cradle of Thought*. London: Macmillan.
Miller, L. (2004) *Understanding Your Two Year Old*. London: Tavistock Clinic & Jessica Kingsley.
Trowell, J., & Etchegoyen, A. (2002) *The Importance of Fathers*. London: The New Library of Psychoanalysis and Brunner-Routledge.

Chapter 7

Three to five years old

Eric Rayner

Playing with ideas

Be warned, this is probably the most difficult chapter in the book!

As a toddler, even as a baby, a child will have been interested in other children without quite knowing how to get on with them. His general view of the world will have been *egocentric*. Around 2 years old, children begin to seek out the company of other children, but the games will still essentially be private. Piaget called this 'parallel play' or 'collective monologue'. At this stage there is often quite a lot of squabbling over toys, interspersed with quiet periods while children go separately about their own business (Winnicott, 1964, 1986).

At about 3 years old, the first group games emerge. Here children share ideas and begin to help each other. It is starting to be *social* in the real sense, with *sympathy* and *comradeship*. It is a manifestation of the beginning of solid *friendliness* between equals. This leap forward depends upon a child's growing capacity to feel a coherent person in a world of other people. This in turn is dependent not only upon an intellectual grasp of the similarities and differences of self and other, but also on an emotional capacity for sympathy and *empathy* – this term is used to indicate an emotional sympathy for another person that discriminates further by using intellectual thoughtfulness. Then, out of ordinary everyday friendly sympathy and empathy, comes fondness, love, identifying with others; and from this comes the ability to disagree but still be friends (Emanuel, 2005).

In the intellectual sphere, *bafflement* about the world must still be to the fore in a child's mind. But now, having grown mental structures, which take in more and more experience, he begins to be able to formulate clear, *conscious* puzzles in the mind. At the same time, word *vocabulary* will be multiplying fast, so he will be *asking questions* – often going on from morning until night (Sroufe, 1996).

Skills broaden and become articulated. A child will be able to ride a tricycle or bicycle with stabilizers, and can probably keep a playground swing going by themselves. He begins to make recognizable drawings, scrawl 'pretend' writing and even form some recognizable letters. He can usually get absorbed by simple constructional toys.

Play becomes less centred on learning simply how to manipulate things, for children can now enjoy things for their *ideational* content. For instance, they try drawing for what they can *reproduce* as well as for the pleasure of the feel of the pencil on paper and the control that is being achieved.

Conceptual and emotional development

Now, with a greater ability to talk, a child can begin to make plain to others the essence of his puzzlements about the world. The questions asked by a 3-year-old show how far they have got, and yet how uncertain is their conceptualization (Piaget, 1953, 1955; Sugarman, 1986). Here are a few examples of 3-year-olds' questions – taking representations and concepts of *space* first:

> How big is a ship? Is it as big as the moon?
>
> Can you hold a star in your hand? It isn't as big as an electric light is it?
>
> Could I touch the sky if I stood on the roof?
>
> Are clouds as big as a house?

A child has a similar puzzlement over *time*. For instance, 'We did see Father Christmas yesterday' (said in late spring). It seems that 'yesterday' is often used for any time in the past, just as 'tomorrow' is used for the future in general. If you are a parent you have to be on guard not to promise a treat too far in advance. If you say 'next week' the child may expect it the next day and be bitterly disappointed. It is the same with unpleasant things, like being left with a strange childminder or going to the dentist. With so much that is indefinite, it is not surprising how full of '*infinities*' a child's ideas can be.

Number is similarly undifferentiated to begin with. The 3-year-old can usually recite some numbers in order but cannot count objects one by one. He may count up to ten in speech but nevertheless be unable to count out this number of objects placed in front of him. He will often forget which ones have already been counted and end up making a wild guess. There are great variations in this ability. Some children can count quite young, whereas others are unable to get up to more than three by the age of five. The use of the idea of *constancies* between things in the external world, needed in counting, is often still shaky. Incidentally, the average ages, or statistical norms, at which these various intellectual skills come to fruition have been studied by psychologists for nearly a century when developing *intelligence testing*.

Some time in the fourth year a child usually gets hold of the idea that *written* words stand for speech, and thence for things, actions or ideas. A few children can actually read and write by this age, but most are content with scrawling 'pretend' writing. However, they have usually begun to grasp that writing is *symbolic* – that it stands for something; and thence that words on paper carry meaning. A 3- to 4-year-old usually recognizes at least a few letters and may even be writing them in an unsteady way – although many children will not be doing this until they are four or more. At the same time, he may be getting a sight vocabulary of a few whole words. Likewise, although children of this age might not actually be able to read yet, they can often accurately retell stories from book illustrations, which naturally helps them grasp a story's sequence.

A child is also becoming more articulate in representing his *own inner feelings*, as well as recognizing those of others. Here are a few examples which show how intellectual and emotional developments are interwoven:

'I don't like you, Mummy, when you are angry.'

'"This Little Pig Went to Market", that is a sad rhyme.'

'David is cross because his mum smacked him.'

These are all about inner feelings, but you will notice how their conceptualization and communication must involve highly articulated *intellectual* processes. Think how complex the ideas within these emotions are, compared to the amorphous feelings of a baby a couple of years earlier.

Now a child is also becoming coherent in *multiple sympathies*. This is dependent, on the one hand, upon his ability to recognize that he is a coherent individual who has a physical place in time and space and has inner feelings as well. On the other hand, he is recognizing that other people also have their places in time and space, together with their feelings. Children will have 'gone out', put themselves into other people's shoes, identified with them and begun to see things from their point of view. *Dramatic play* or *make-believe* must be part of this achievement – it is truly marvellous when you think of it. Many intellectual or cognitive processes together must have played their part in the articulation of the feelings behind such dramatization (Erikson, 1963; Piaget, 1953, 1955).

Optimally, cognitive and emotional developments go hand in hand. However, the two can become grossly cut-off from each other, or *split*. For example, some clever people can be highly articulate in thinking about the physical world and in having abstract ideas about it; but they may remain emotionally and sympathetically awkward or cold about other people. Likewise, a person who is backward intellectually can sometimes be emotionally and sympathetically sensitive and astute, but not always. An uneducated person can, of course, be emotionally mature. But he must have some intellectual competence to manage the subtleties involved in emotional relationships.

Children playing together

Going back to earlier years for a moment, we can see that quite young babies, of less than a year old, show great interest in others of their own age. They may even be carried away in imitation of them – for instance, they often burst into tears when another baby starts crying. When they are out in their push-chairs, they will turn to look at each other while more or less ignoring other people. They are, however, also noticeably vulnerable to other people's moods, not only their parents' but also strangers' feelings, and particularly other children's.

Toddlers are more coherently interested in others of their own age. They often greet each other and want to be together. There seems to be both pleasure and relief in being with others who are the same size, whose faces are on a level with theirs, whose hands are as small as theirs, and who are puzzling about the same problems. But each child's game is still usually a monologue, and egocentric. When paths cross there can often be a fight because two children want the same toy. Then, probably towards the age of four, children begin to want to play at the same game together. We begin to hear, 'Let's play at houses', 'You be ill and I'll be the doctor', 'I'll be a shop-lady, you be a mummy' (Erikson, 1963).

Just as solitary play is of central importance to intellectual development, so mutual play is a keystone in social development. It seems to be vital in the growth of humane morality, but it is also subject to gross perversions: war, for instance, has, with much truth, been called 'the great game'.

What mental functions are involved in ordinary, friendly, mutual play? The most obvious is *language*. The *non-verbal* language used by animals to communicate an intention to play together was mentioned earlier in this book. The human child can, of course, do much more than this by using speech, not only to indicate an intention to play but also in the dramatic content of the game itself. Incidentally, those who have worked with deaf or blind children will recognize the very special difficulties that they have, although they can often be very ingenious in finding special ways to communicate.

As well as involving spoken language, play centrally requires a child to *sympathize* with others. He must be aware of the others as *like* and yet different from himself, with feelings and needs that must be recognized. There has to be a *sacrifice of egocentricity*. For this to happen, a child must develop some ability to inhibit his own impulses and whims for the sake of a wider pleasure in communality. One can hear this happening in children's conversations: 'Oh all right, you get the water this time, I'll get it next.' Note that the necessary inhibition here needs a complex coordination of ideas by the child. Without intellectual achievements, a child can only remain impulsive. And of course giving up egocentrism is deeply rewarded by the joys of communal feelings and friendship. Growing up is worth it.

Play, conscience and rules of conduct

The ability to make the step of sacrificing some egocentricity usually becomes explicit from about 3 years old. It seems to depend upon the formation of a coherently structured, if still rudimentary, *social conscience*, or *superego*, as it has been called by psycho-analysts (Freud, 1905, 1915). We discussed the origin of this in the last chapter. In order to play mutually, a child must be able to enjoy *sympathy* with and *concern* for others. Central to this is the coming of an inner 'depressive' or self-accusatory *guilt*. In a similar way, egocentricity must be inhibited for the sake of the sociability of a game with others. A child must check the violent expressions of indignation, rage and hatred that often arise naturally when whims are frustrated. Put briefly, it can be said that social play, like all sociability, depends on the happy working of conscience (Piaget, 1935).

Thinking within a developmental framework leads easily to the realization that a child's particular growth of conscience is dependent upon a long chain of earlier experiences with his parents and others. There will have been commands, demands and requests on a background of parental delight, warmth, love, devotion, conscientiousness, frustration – and neglect. These have all been described in earlier chapters.

However, a parent's task does not end with a child moving off into mutual play with other children. For example: when children have established rudimentary consciences within themselves, they can generate simple *rules of conduct* amongst themselves, but these can work only for short spans of time and can easily be swept away by the surge of a child's impulsive whim. An adult needs to be around to mediate sharing and to re-establish fair play. Equally, children of three can be sensitive to the *fairness of sharing* but they have not usually developed the steady breadth of vision needed to re-establish fairness when it has been shattered.

Watching the growth of mutual play, one can sense the development of the beginnings of the fundamentally important ideas of *fairness and justice*, as well as of social enjoyment amongst peers. *Mutuality* is a great step forward from the primitive dependence upon the autocracy – both of the little child's own imperious demands, and also those of the early colossi – parents. Mutuality provides a breeding ground for true democracy.

It is of note that, throughout much of history in both East and West, the step to mutual play seems often to have been left to children themselves. Children have tended to find their own games while the adults got on with their own work or pleasure. The development of *fair play* has thus probably largely arisen naturally among the young children themselves or their older siblings. Even so, the example given by parents, older siblings, nannies, child-minders and other supervisors will also have been crucial. Incidentally, it is probably only in recent decades that parents have really made self-conscious efforts to get down on the floor with their children to play mutual games – probably to everyone's pleasure as well as benefit.

Serious research and theoretical thinking about these vital phases of play and development are of fairly recent origin. The pioneer playgroup work of Froebel, Montessori, Susan Isaacs and Piaget (Sroufe, 1996) is less than a hundred years old.

Distress, dreams, disturbance and dramatic play

So far, we have only discussed the virtues of mutual play; but it can sometimes become dangerously destructive. With this in mind, remember that one fundamental motive for the use of playing was distress and anxiety. Let us look at this.

We have already thought about *dreams*. It was probably Freud's greatest discovery to find that remembered dreams are coded or *symbolized dramatizations* of distressing or otherwise *significant experiences* that have not yet been fully assimilated in memory. Dreams are now known, from psycho-physiological evidence, to be regular and frequent in every night's sleep. There are clearly defined sequences of physiological response associated with them. These include, oddly enough, *genital arousal* – of the penis in males and of the clitoris in females. It is now well researched how day-time experiences are worked over in these regular dreaming periods in sleep, probably to reformulate them for ease of *memorization*. If this has been successful, we probably wake refreshed. If dreaming is unsuccessful in this way, we may remain disturbed and wake up fretfully. Sometimes the inner distress produces a nightmare, which leaves nothing but puzzlement, anxiety and disturbance as its aftermath. Incidentally, a characteristic of dreams, probably to facilitate memorization, is to *condense* highly charged emotional ideas into *symbolic images* – and this can make them useful tools for the psychoanalytic therapist. Dream laboratory research has been widely extended in recent decades.

Following Freud, it was later noted, particularly by Anna Freud and Melanie Klein, that children's symbolic play bore some striking similarities to dreaming (Edgcumbe, 2000; Segal, 1973:

Sroufe, 1996). Children's play often seemed to be, like dreams, a symbolic repetition of anxious and *dramatically felt* situations. Further relaxed interest from parents or carers, and freedom to play, seem to have a settling effect. Children need to play certain games for themselves – and when tense, they are even compelled to. A really good, exciting and dramatic game usually leaves a child calmer and satisfied – like a good night's sleep. A disrupted game can leave a child in distress. There is a great deal that is not yet understood about the mechanisms involved but it seems that both *dreams and play can be a means of assimilating puzzling or distressing experiences.* What is more, if a stress-provoked game remains uncompleted, yet further distress is created, and the game often needs to be repeated in an urgently compulsive way.

We can roughly distinguish two particular problems that might prevent the satisfactory completion of a dramatic game. The first lies before the game: the stress may have been so intense that the 'central control system' or 'ego-functioning' breaks down. In this case, a child's, or adult's, mental activity is likely to have shattered into such chaotic, or bizarre, *bits* that coalescence into a game is impossible. This is not uncommon – it can often be seen when a child is too terrified to play.

On the other hand, a child may not be as shattered as this but be prevented from playing by the limitations of external circumstances. This will usually involve the parents somewhere, for they are usually the organizers of their child's environment. They might explicitly forbid certain games; or they might order the children to 'go out and play' to get them out of the way, or carry them off to do something else. They might simply provide an over-strict home climate where playing is devalued, thus emotionally robbing their children of this resource.

At all events, when playing is prevented, for whatever reason, it seems that frustration in itself creates further distress, and this then brings a *hatred* of the frustrator by the child. The need to play may then become compulsive with an underlying mood of fear and vengeful rage. Feelings of being *tormented or persecuted* will have swamped friendliness and *sympathetic concern*. When this happens a child will not feel for other people or things. He will simply want to use anything at whim. Other children can become *playthings rather than playmates*. This is, unfortunately, not uncommon. There was an instance in Chapter 5 when a boy cruelly smacked his little brother after being beaten by his mother. This game was *sadistic,* and *without concern* for the little brother. It is very important to distinguish this kind of *ruthless play* from genuinely *mutual play*, for, although they may have similar origins, in the child's need to assimilate an experience, the two sorts of play can have very different consequences. Ruthless play will have an unempathic, cold, suspicious, cruel, hating – even delinquent or *psychopathic* quality. The underlying mood will be full of frustrations, which seem to be mocking and torturing the self. One usually then wants to torment others in order to feel active and to 'even the score'. Almost anything is better than feeling a humiliated, weak, passive recipient. As with any play, ruthless games do not end with childhood. The fantasies in such play are easily seen in adult life, even though they may be covered by polite or diplomatic smoke-screens. For instance, *ruthless play* seems to have been rampant in all those millions of adults who have been active in *empire building*, whether for economic or political reasons, and whether the empires are Assyrian, Greek, Roman, Germanic, Nordic, Islamic, French, Spanish, British, Russian, German, Japanese, or American.

On a small scale, ruthless play can usually be detected in any crooked, criminal, delinquent or *psychopathic* activity. Here, one or more people ruthlessly use others with no consideration for their needs. In intimate ways it can occur within families – as in the tyranny and torture in some unhappy marriages – and also in parents who treat their children like dolls. The multiplicity of forms this sort of play can take was first dramatically emphasized in Eric Berne's classic book *Games People Play* (1964). This was joking in tone, even flippant sometimes, but his message was a deeply serious and important one. Even friendly comradeship can become dangerous when there is ruthless combination against another. Two or more people together are stronger than when alone. Ruthlessness can then be doubly cruel – and more.

Many ruthless personal games can go on *without clear conscious awareness* of their aim and theme by the perpetrator, and without awareness of their effects on others. Yet an observer may see the cruelty being repeated with such consistency as to rule out accidental occurrence. The theme will then probably be *unconscious* in the perpetrator, so psychological *defences* must be operating. An array of defences – such as splitting, projecting and denial manoeuvres – can often be recognized in ordinary life (as when politicians – and ordinary people – adeptly lay blame on others for a man-made catastrophe, while portraying themselves as blameless).

However, whatever the blotting-out manoeuvres, the ruthless game can often be seen as omnipresent. Forced forgetting of this sort is termed *repression* in psychoanalytic language. It can be used throughout life.

Psychoanalysts have emphasized that *unconscious* play is active in *psychoneurotic* symptoms. If these are limited to simply *forgetting* fraught emotions, then *repression* is said to have taken place and the resulting symptoms are said to be *psychoneurotic* in nature. Here, the individual sufferer is prone to be *inappropriately anxious* but not seriously assailed by confusing ideas produced by the self with external reality. When someone suffers psychoneurotically from *obsessional* symptoms, ideas of inner and outer remain relatively distinct. However, the sufferer is compulsively caught in worries about highly charged *ruthless imaginings*, or 'games' locked within the mind.

Another psychoneurotic symptom takes the form of highly emotional ideas being *dramatically enacted* at other people, but without much self-awareness: this is then said to be *hysterical* in nature. Or the dramatic themes can emerge less flamboyantly and, while still probably using the gross forgetting of repression, they do not involve other people so insistently. The symptoms are then likely to take the form of *hysterical conversions* and *phobias*, often mixed with obsessions. These deserve a great deal of attention in their own right, for they are very common indeed, but we only have space to point them out briefly here.

The Oedipus complex

Turning now to less tortured and more ordinary activities, we will start this crucial section by briefly going over again the main emotional developments of the first three years. We have seen that a child begins to play by simple sensorimotor manipulation of any objects around, thus using them as playthings. Out of this manipulation, joined together with vocal imitation, develops *symbolization*, and from this comes the use of words. Out of this comes *make-believe*; this at first appears to be a monologue, linked at times into dual play with an adult.

In the ordinary nuclear family, the first main adult is usually mother. Even though nowadays many fathers have gained in emotional intimacy with younger children, she is still 'the sweetest, most loved and hated one'. Then, during their second year, many children become interested in, and obviously feel affinity with, other little children like themselves. They start by playing along-side, or in parallel with, other little ones. It is probably only towards 3 years old or more that a child will have developed ideas and feelings about others enough to engage in truly social or *mutual play*.

At about the same time, you will recall that we began to see a growing articulation of a child's relationship with their parents (Freud, 1905, 1915; Hamilton, 1982). In earliest infancy there seems to be no distinction in the child's mind between what is self and what is not. Only slowly in the first year does the sense of being a different entity from others begin to crystallize. Even then, mother often appears to be conceived of as an extension of the self. Likewise, conversely, in a deeper and more long-lasting way, a child still feels the self to be either a possession of mother's, or that she is a possession of theirs. Even so, all being well, differentiation is taking place. A child slowly comes to accept that mother has an independent mind of her own. This probably comes especially from a mother's strong 'yes' gestures and words of love, and her 'no's' of disapproval. With the no's comes the pain of loneliness, as well as the freedom of solitude. However, it is still usually mother who centrally ministers to a child's world. Even when interest turns to things beyond the home, it is still mostly mother who interprets and explains (or confuses) it for him. A child in an ordinary family feels that life itself depends on her – no wonder most of us are passionate about our mothers.

A father usually seems to be experienced in a similar yet different way. In the first place, he has a different physical feel from mother. It is also usually he who goes out into the world and comes back bringing ideas and things that are different from mother's. He is usually bigger, probably more 'hard-angled' and muscularly stronger than her, and this is sensed quite early – in the second or third year. Maybe there is a bit of a triumph for the child on discovering mother's frequent dependence on her husband. It is something like: 'Ha, ha, you have ruled me, now I've found some-one who can boss you'. It is quite common to hear a child threatening his mother with, 'I'll tell my daddy of you and he'll smack you'. But then this can, of course, be easily contradicted in a child's mind if they hear father being ordered about by mother so that he appears to be her compliant slave.

The previous chapters will probably have given some idea of what giants, if not gods, parents can be to a child. They are big, complex and mysterious because the child is small, unlearned, immature, and full of fears – but, insofar as they are kind and intimate, they are also felt to be equals. However, being at their parents' mercy, a child will naturally want to be self-assertive – by charming, manipulating and tyrannizing them. It seems important to recognize that this particular parent–child constellation must be *a given of the human child's condition*, no matter what the conventions of rearing.

We have been arguing that the pattern of a two-parent nuclear family has many natural advantages for the rearing of young children. We are not saying it is the only setting in which children can grow up feeling secure, and later on we will be investigating its weaknesses. But even on the small scale of a contented nuclear family, parents are mysterious giants to their toddlers. Add to this the frequent contradictoriness of most parents, and the family, while still the most intimate of human groups, must at best be puzzling for a child,.

It might seem that this is an over-dramatized picture. A small, chuckling child shows no obvious evidence of being baffled by their parents as complex giants. But we cannot expect a child to say everything that rumbles through the mind. In addition, what can be more enjoyable for a small person than to live in the safety of friendly, loving giants? Let us not forget that adults can still carry admiration like this on, finding comfort in the idea of a benign, protective God, or in adulating a leader, or the royal family. At the same time, comfort can be found in the reverse of this – and it is not just children who love to emulate the gods, kings or queens by fantasies of manipulating, dominating or tyrannizing others.

Erotic stimulation and the Oedipus complex

Turning now to *bodily* experiences – we have already seen how the tension of muscles, changes in blood supply, the secretion of hormones, ventilation of lungs and so on are central to all feelings. It has also been noted that *erotic* pleasures are important in feelings. The very word 'feeling' has a double meaning, standing either for an emotion, or for the physical sensations of touching, which are intrinsic to *eroticism*.

It is worth noting that erotic sensations arise when there is a *sequential stimulation* of tactile, or touch, neurons close to the surface of the skin. This happens when *stroking* occurs; it is central to *sexual love play*, and to *masturbation*. When the stimulation of touch neurons is *not sequential* but is steady and simultaneous, then a feeling of *holding* occurs. Parents, when cuddling and comforting their young, will probably be doing a bit of both, but true comforting will predominantly need to be by *non-sequential* holding. If there is too much stroking, a child will get over-aroused and excited, and if repeated insistently by an adult it could become the beginning of sexual *abuse*.

Having prepared the background, we can now move towards the somewhat controversial conception of the *Oedipus complex*, introduced first by Freud (1905, 1915; also Erikson, 1963; Edgcumbe, 2000). This is centrally associated, in both boys and girls, with genital erotic excitement, pleasure and anxiety. This complex of feelings of desire, envy, triumph, rage, fear and guilt is likely, in one form or another, to be part of every child's life. The simple outline that follows will differ only slightly from Freud's original view, which will briefly be discussed later, and will resemble in its essentials that given by most present-day psychoanalysts. One or two aspects introduced here, such as the role played by dreaming in the resolution of the Complex, have not been much stressed until recently, but there is nothing very unusual about the formulation here. Needless to say, many non-psychoanalytic psychologists and psychiatrists still disagree with the whole Oedipus complex idea. You must decide for yourself what you think.

We know that a child's sequential touch stimulation of their own body – masturbation, particularly of those highly sensitive erotic zones the genitals, anus, nipples and mouth – arouses vivid and enjoyable fantasy. We have also seen how a boy or girl of about 2 years old begins to be aware of, and curious about, which sex or *gender* they belong to, and of their similarity to the parent of the same sex.

The genitals, being erotically excitable, become particularly interesting. You will probably remember something of your own secret, exciting and 'exquisite' explorations at about this age. Genital play by boys or girls – *masturbation*, both alone and mutually – is pleasurably exciting, comforting and evocative of fantasy. But it is an embarrassment to – and often fiercely forbidden by, or flustered about – worried parents. Most important of all, genital arousal, so easy to get started, is *never* fully climactically satisfiable in childhood: full *orgasm* must wait till adolescence. Frustration, with all its anxieties, is never far away.

There is another function centred on the genital region, which makes it even more precious. It is common knowledge, among gymnasts and athletes, that the 'centre of gravity', or centre of *articulation* of the body when making *complex movements*, lies somewhere just above the *pubic* area and below the navel. Thus, in our body image, the pubic–genital–sexual zone is close to the *organizing axis*, not only of our dancing, gymnastic and acrobatic competence and grace, but also of our everyday handling of ordinary physical objects. The joy and freedom of dance, gymnastics, athletics, sports, or physical vigour generally, is obviously important to most youthful people – of all ages. This is especially so for little children, who are uncertain about themselves, and are discovering how lovely is the freedom of body movement. They will hopefully go on to find out that this physical articulation plays a part in developing a happy and flexible imagination – and sexual feeling is not far away from this.

Another function associated with the genitals has already been mentioned. This is that *genital arousal* normally and consistently occurs at certain stages of the *dream cycle* in sleep. We have also noted the importance of dreaming in assimilating memories and in resolving the distress and anxiety coming with apparently *contradictory ideas*.

Adding together all these genital zone functions – urination, erotic pleasure, fantasy, the gymnastic axis of the body, making love, reproduction, and the integrative function of dreaming – it is no wonder that the genitals are felt by the little child to be marvellous, precious organs and organizers. But, apart from urination, they have as yet no immediately apparent social use. What is more, the genitals are often surrounded by intense parental taboos. For instance, sexual pleasure can, in many religious families, very easily lead to fears that masturbation could be a 'mortal sin'. The threat 'Don't fiddle with yourself like that or I'll see it gets cut off' is rarely explicitly made today, but expressions of dread of sin, disapproval and embarrassment are still all too common. For instance, even in today's time of freedom, many parents never quite work out how and what to say about their children's masturbation. It is not easy to strike a useful balance between being too permissive about sex, or being 'uptight' about it. It is a topic full of fun and giggling for children together, but also a serious matter, and an adult needs to see both the fun and the serious side at the same time. To most adults, the genitals can sometimes seem to hold a secret of sanity and madness. Many would say something like, 'Best antidepressant there is – a jolly good fuck!' At other times, they seems to be at the root of our troubles.

How does genital arousal and its precious fun affect a child's feelings about his parents? This will be easier to answer if we first distinguish the child's *inner sexual fantasies* about parents from what parents and children *actually do* with each other. The former, the *private* sexual fantasies, is referred to as the *Oedipus complex*; the latter – the real, external, *social* triangle of child and parents – is usually termed the *Oedipal situation* or *Oedipal triad*. The two are clearly related but not the same.

We have already noted how all parents differ somewhat in the ways they relate to their children. Thus the Oedipal situation is at least slightly different for all individuals. Then, because social experiences affect inner fantasy, every child's inner fantasies will be both similar and different from others. Each individual has his own *privately patterned* Oedipus complex of feelings and ideas. However, some common outlines, based on the bodily structure of the two sexes, can be made out.

As has been traditional, we will start with a boy of three or four, then turn to a girl of that age. We have said already that, in *general, non-sexual* ways, he usually both passionately loves and often hates his mother because of all the particular experiences he has had with her. At 3 or 4 years old he is usually clearly feeling himself as physically different from her (and she will be giving indications that she feels sexually about him – and different from him).

Now, any ordinary, vigorous little boy wants to love and hate with all the organs of his body. This includes teeth to bite with, tongue to lick with, lips to kiss with, feet to kick, hands to hold and to punch with, anus to shit with: and then his penis, which sticks out and is so nicely exciting – what to do with that? Mother probably usually seems very interested in those parts but is a bit shy of them, so it's somewhat wonderfully mysterious. He wants to stir her and himself with his penis. As it is a sticking-out thing, he will probably want to touch her with it, to stroke her, and have it cuddled. He even dimly yearns to get inside her with it, as, incidentally, the whole of him was not long before. What is more, in hating her, he will want to use it to attack her. These are urges or fantasies not often openly heard, except by children when very excited, or out of control, or by children in therapy. Such expression of sexual imagination is of course much less taboo and more readily heard in ordinary families today than it was a few years ago, so what is being described here will not sound very strange. But embarrassment, disgust, mystery and taboos are still ordinarily, and often usefully, present.

Turning now to a boy's sexual ideas about his father. He, like mother, is loved and hated for all the child's past experiences. These urges, too, have to be expressed with all his body, penis included. However, he tends to see his father as being like him: both are male, but his father looks like a giant. He is bigger in every way, including the size of the precious penis. So we have rivalry by son against his father, and vice versa. This is the celebrated Oedipal (or phallic) *rivalry*, named by Freud after the Greek tragic character King Oedipus, who was fated to kill his father and unknowingly to marry his mother.

Lastly, a boy at most times cannot help seeing his parents being intimate with each other, in both love and anger. In particular, they usually sleep together while he is shut out and alone, or left with mundane beings like siblings. This emphasizes that a boy's mother is not his sole possession. Sexually at least, his mother is more intimate with his father than with him.

Being highly charged with imagination, the boy can experience this situation of being shut out as a re-arousal of bitter, but non-sexual feelings from the past – of being *neglected, unwanted and scorned*, giving rise to moods of depression, despair and hatred. A boy's pride is often wounded. 'How can she do it to me, when I am her most loved one?' Here is one more blow, and a necessary one, to the comfort of infantile egocentrism. Because of this, psychoanalysts stress the importance of the experience of being shut out when parents are together sexually. It is often referred to as *the primal scene* (Freud, 1905, 1915).

This cannot really be a catastrophe in itself. But, when stirred up with mysterious feelings, it can be deeply imagined as a cataclysm in the emotional recesses of the mind. However, it also has its compensations – a child can easily feel safe if his parents are clearly fond of each other. More than this, the experience of *not being unique* is crucial to the development of a sense of oneself as being *just ordinary* in a real world. This is vital for sanity, but it can, for a child to begin with, be felt as a painful wound to his own grandeur.

All boys must feel this some of the time. For instance, when young we usually cannot easily imagine our parents making love together and being totally absorbed together in it. It seems such a peculiar business for respectable grown-ups to get into! Children are often very touchy and upset about this, so it is not a laughing matter. Later in life, most people are glad of their parents happily making love together, but at this early stage it is embarrassing and difficult to imagine. What is more, parents who ignore their children's feelings and indulge themselves without thought in front of them are usually felt as ruthlessly selfish and are not forgiven. A child can easily get over-excited about these things and, unable to relieve himself, feels small and humiliated. Such occasions are often reported as a source of resentment for years afterwards. To stop this getting out of control, every stable culture, however open or naked its ways with the body, appears to have strict rules of decorum for sexual intercourse itself.

Now let us turn to a typical little girl, with her own body structure and sexual arousal patterns. She, like a boy, will have loved and hated her parents non-sexually for her early experiences with them. She is also sexy, like a boy is, but in a girl's way. She will want to love and hate both her parents with her whole body, which includes her mouth, anus, clitoris and vagina. These genitals do not stick out like a boy's, but are both outside and inside her. She will also clearly see her father as physically different from her, even if she is unlikely to have more than a few glances at his penis. And she, too, wants to love and hate him with all her body, including her genitals. This means that, as far as sexual love is concerned, she, *in fantasy*, wants him both *outside and inside her genitals*, to love and hate him, either to caress or crush him in rage. But, of course, like the boy, this is never actually possible, except perhaps in incestuous and sexually abusive families – so, optimally, the urge must continue frustrated until she finds a sexual partner in her adult years (Edgcumbe, 2000; Hamilton, 1982; Miller, 1992).

With regard to a girl's mother, there is, of course, as with the boy, the non-sexual love and hate arising from past experiences. However, in her body and sexually, she feels like, but smaller than, this gigantic, magic person, her mother. What is more, when she sees her mother and father intimately together, her feelings of smallness are compounded by realizing that she has lost her father to her mother – and her mother to her father. So, the little girl feels an underlying rivalry and envy, especially of her mother.

Like the little boy, she is often quick to notice that her envied mother is smaller, physically less strong, and even nowadays may be financially dependent on her father. This can especially accentuate one of two predominant fantasies. She can easily use it to deride her mother – as if to say, 'You think you're big but Daddy is bigger than you and he specially loves me'. On the other hand, she can side with her mother and cool her envy with the idea, 'My poor mother and I are like each other really, kinder, cleverer, wiser and more beautiful, but enslaved by this gross, giant father'. This easily generalizes to dislike of all men.

Freud called this the situation of *penis envy*. Believing a girl's patterns of sexual feelings were the same as a boy's until about the age of three or so, he considered the stage when she realizes she lacks a penis as central to her sexual development, and that she breaks into envy of males because she herself has been deprived of what they have.

However, the formulation we are making here is slightly different from this. Most psychoanalytic thinkers now agree that Freud's theory – that the girl's very early pattern of sexual feelings was identical to that of boys – was not quite right. There is now plenty of physiological evidence that a girl's sexual development, psychological and physiological, is different from a boy's from the beginning. However, this does not mean that Freud's concept of penis envy – or, more generally, that of envy of masculinity – is totally invalid. There is much clinical evidence to confirm that such envy of masculinity can be a consuming passion for some girls and women – but it is probably not so central in normal development as Freud thought. For instance, most girls these days know that their vaginas and ovaries are vital for child-bearing – and are thus more important than penises, which, after all, are only needed for a very short time! There is no doubt that in Freud's day, before women's suffrage and liberation, men naturally ruled the roost socially and at home. The point of view of this present book is that it would have been natural, in these circumstances, for women to envy men for their power, and for this envy then to get focused onto bodily parts. Seeing this, Freud attributed its origins to purely instinctive factors, and not social ones.

Lastly, it must be emphasized that the little girl is as sensitive as a boy to her parents' intimacy and love-making together, when she is left alone. So the primal scene can, with some modifications for the gender difference, largely be transposed from our description of the boy's Oedipus complex, a few paragraphs back, to apply to a girl as well.

Some conclusions concerning the Oedipus complex

Thinking generally about the Oedipus complex, there is probably no reason to assume that parental sexuality itself causes neurotic disturbances. These seem to arise when the parents have, through insensitivity, aroused a little girl or boy to excitement, and then left them embarrassed, small, lonely, envious and humiliated in ways that cannot be coped with. This seems to happen often when the parents have been brashly exhibitionistic or have intruded upon the child's genital privacy. The child will then be, at least over-excited, and at worst chronically disturbed by sexual abuse. There is perhaps a multitude of different ways of arousing the stress of over-excitation in a child, who will naturally not yet have adequate methods of resolving it.

However, the Oedipal situation focuses many old problems into one simple, yet highly charged, 'zone' of fantasy creation. The excitable *genital core* of the Oedipus complex, which also has its dreaming and playing functions, makes it central to sane resolution of conflicts. It thus becomes an axis for either future development or long-standing disturbance. The genitals are a 'gathering ground' of a child's early passionate life. In this light, the present-day habit of laughing at the Oedipus concept as old-fashioned is regrettable. Thus, whereas considering the Oedipus complex as the only experience of importance to a child is frankly blinkered, ignoring its significance is perverse and pig-headed nonsense. It is perhaps like any drama on the stage. To go to a play only for the dramatic climax of the last act makes it meaningless, because the earlier build-up of tension has been missed. But to miss the climax and resolution at the end makes the play equally pointless.

Our description of the Oedipus complex highlights the impossibility of resolving its conflicts and contradictions if it is only seen from the child's sexual-impulsive point of view. For instance, any ordinary little girl wants to love her father with all her body including her genitals. But, if a girl does in reality experience her father incestuously, then the privacy of her genitals is invaded. Their sensitive use in essential dreaming, playing, and resolution of distress, is thrown grossly into disarray. This is *sexual abuse* – a most serious catastrophe for a girl. However, if incest does not occur, which fortunately is nearly always the case, a girl's genital yearning will naturally and normally remain unsatisfied and irritable. It seems a no-win dilemma, except that, when one feels content to live with it, *dignity* and *self-respect* do eventually grow happily, just as with a boy and the urges of his penis.

How can a resolution, or at least a partial one, of these apparently impossible conflicts come about? We have already emphasized the importance for *sanity* of a child's genital *privacy*, because of its close association with *dreaming*, which is vital to steady memorization and thence to maturation. The age-old incest taboo thus protects a child's vital sanity in emotional and intellectual development. We can then go on to detect that children, if developing healthily, *want* to surmount erotic attachments to their parents because they have an intuitive feeling that, if unchecked, they would bring on a sort of erotic–compulsive imprisonment. This desire for self-control is reminiscent of the way we saw toddlers wanting to control themselves to be clean and dry. Now, in order to get a general view of how one comes to accomplish the second great feat of self-discipline – surmounting the erotic attachments to one's parents that we have just been describing – let us start by looking at social and intellectual development.

The inhibition of eroticism

You will remember the description of a pre-school child's all-or-nothing spontaneity, and propensity for eager, engrossed happiness. We also noted their tendency to switch quickly from one interest to another. This was termed normal *splitting*, or proneness to *dichotomize*; it enables a child to be deeply absorbed and to learn about minutiae very quickly. It also means that, when seriously upset, this dichotomization can make one feel totally panic-stricken and distressed – but then, at the next moment, the trouble has suddenly been forgotten. This all or nothingness of response also creates confusion, both intellectually and emotionally, for as one grows older, and learns more, new and wider puzzles are created as the smaller ones are solved. Splitting in thought and feeling can give a quick, immediate relief, but it tends to fracture the capacity to make *dispassionate overviews* of complex situations. These are at the heart of mature thoughtfulness and mental integrity.

We have already thought about the healthy child's urge to solve puzzles, and seen that Jean Piaget (1953, 1955) was a pioneer thinker here. A child, even more than an adult, is always attempting to make sense of phenomena by thinking out wider and wider meaningful mental structures. To make understandable what was incomprehensible before, new data, which have similarities with the old, need to be brought in continuously, otherwise anxious puzzlement lingers on fruitlessly. However, we noted in the first chapter that every new idea involves a serious task of a new integration – it is a small, *private revolution*. We owe a great debt to Piaget for emphasizing that this *urge to integrate* meaningfully is fundamental, although it can very easily be disturbed and disturbing.

We are now presented with a paradox. The infant's proneness to split allows him to learn certain things quickly; but it also tends to prevent integration of wider meanings. However, if, after mastery of the elements, a child *waits*, or stands back for a moment, he can find that the mind is able to ponder over a wide variety of other phenomena and memories. These, too, can then be integrated. The child has discovered that *inhibition* of impulse can be *rewarded by the pleasure and power of greater understanding*. Thus, in a normal child's growth from infancy onwards, there is a continuous *dialectic* between *impulsive zest* and a spur to *self-inhibited appraisal*. Each aspect can easily be helped or disturbed by parental pressures and taboos.

This dialectic obviously occurs in toilet training, but Piaget showed that it happens in many other developmental activities as well. It seems to be especially important in one particular situation. As children grow up during the fourth and fifth year, they usually find pleasure in spending more and more time *away from their mother* in the company of other children. It has also been noted that, when children are young, these periods of enjoyment away from mother are short, but that when they grow older they seem to become centrally interested in the advantages of self-contained independence. Thus, they may be anxious about their mother's absence but, when this is held in check, they triumphantly find the freedom to enjoy their own new experiences.

Here, one finds that, through inhibition, it is possible to resolve conflicts that have arisen out of impulsiveness and all-or-nothing splitting. With *growth in thoughtfulness*, the disturbingly opposing sides of ambivalent feelings tend to be able to be related to each other, and can become relaxed in their integration. Among other things, the *representations of parents* in the child's mind become more available to be understood as *working together*. This combination of images can become usable when thinking about things in many situations. Inhibition can be frustrating and infuriating, but it is also essential for reflective thinking, and this then offers new mental freedoms through fluidity of imagination. In particular, inhibition plays a vital part in a child's fateful steps out from home into the wider, strange world, and especially to school. This is especially important, so let us look at it further.

Latency, self-containment of Oedipal feelings, and school readiness

If you compare a group of children of, say, 3 or 4 years old with children of 6, you will probably notice that the younger children are full of eager, impulsive bounce but are easily given to tears and need to be hugged and kissed better. The older children still show signs of bounce as well as tears; but a subtle, more erect *dignity* has appeared in their posture. Their heads are held higher, and they survey the world from a more *detached*, but still interested, point of view. They are beginning to *overview* things – to see them from, not just one, but several different points of view. This dignity, which involves *inhibition*, not only shows the child's wish to integrate wider experiences but is also a sign of being able to be alone away from the comfort of their mother and her body. The finding of this dignity is a sign of *school readiness*. The child is beginning to be able to stand the puzzlement and anxiety of being in the strange school environment for as much as 6 hours or even more at a time. (Erikson, 1963; Freud, 1905, 1915; Holditch, 1992; Sroufe, 1996).

Going to school not only means being separated from home, it can also be a positively exciting journey into *new patterns of culture*. There is, of course, the culture of the patterned habits of the classroom itself, presided over by the teacher. More than this, a child also meets, and is called upon to relate to, many other children who have come from the different cultures of their own families. Many of these will be from familiar backgrounds, whereas others may come from different social climates and countries. Detached dignity seems to be a very important achievement for any child who has to face this *culture shock* more or less alone. One can see that, as a child goes through the early school years, the detachment is often lively and gains in strength. The period when this has got steadier and more usable, from about 5 years old until puberty, is usually referred to as *latency*.

Looking at this dignity of latency rather more closely, we have already noted that a child stands more erect, both physically and mentally, surveying the world around with the characteristic detachment. The posture is very similar to the one a child will have seen his parents taking up when they were being protective, dispassionate and thoughtful. It is thus perhaps a fruit of good, active parenthood.

Psychoanalysts and therapists think that children, in being dignified like their parents (assuming they have been), have not only found the stance for themselves but have also unconsciously *identified* with them. It is probably the fruit of long periods of imitating them. Grown-ups will now be felt to be rather less like mysterious giants and more like ordinary fallible and interesting whole human beings. A child is getting 'grown-up-ness' in sight.

Recapitulating, this adoption of a parental posture, using identification, allows the child to be less swayed by switching from, or splitting (Segal, 1973) between, one impulse and another. It also allows him to need less immediate comfort when distressed. It helps to resolve, at least for the time being, a proneness to the clinging intensity of loves and hates which bind young children to their parents. Inhibition and then identification with a parent's dignity also helps them to identify with many other people, both children and other adults. There is thus a start to achieving the ability to see things from *many points of view*, and then thoughtfully reaching an overview. This is the very essence of *argumentation, debate* and *discussion*, as well as *reflection in solitude*. Without these mental and social functions, serious *wisdom* is impossible.

In summary, we have noted the following. The young child's accumulated welter of loves and hates about their parents now tend to focus into genital and aggressive fantasies about them. These have an especially embarrassing, baffling and pressing quality. However, at about the time of going to school, with the achievement of some detached dignity and with some ability to overview situations – all helped by identification with parents – a child can make a start on resolving these sexual and aggressive conflicts.

For instance, a girl in the throes of Oedipal feelings is swept by envy of her mother and yet loves and needs her too. While immature splitting prevails, this must seem an impossible conflict to solve, except for a short time. But with the coming of detachment, a little girl can find that it is deeply enjoyable to feel the bitter–sweet emotion of envy and love interwoven. It is similar with a boy.

The fateful formation of character in the resolutions of the Oedipus complex

The different ways of partial resolution of infantile and Oedipal ties to parents are multitudinous. Each child has his own idiosyncratic pattern of loves and hates for parents. This will be partly because of genetic make-up and partly will result from personal experiences. An aspect of these developments will be a particular *patterning of identifications*; this will be used to achieve some dignity from the conflicts with parents. This patterning will be quite personal, idiosyncratic and *characteristic* of an individual child. Each child 'chooses', probably unconsciously, different aspects of their parents to identify with and reject.

There is evidence to show that each person's future is affected by events from early infancy onwards, and by genetic inheritance. The course of life will also certainly be altered by later happenings. But there seems to be something particularly poignant and fateful about the characteristic stances a child takes relative to his parents as he sets off on his solitary way into school. One child will find his way easiest by proudly being his father's son, aiming to follow him. Another will 'settle' for a life that is 'morally better' than his mother or father, or more potent. Another may naturally become kindly and nurturing, like a good mother, and then take this on into later life and adulthood – and so on.

These combinations of identification are near infinite, and later experiences will change them, sometimes nearly out of recognition. But the threads of this early character formation seem to go on through life, providing both strengths and weaknesses in the time to come. Let us look at a few simple examples:

A self-assertive man married a more humble woman who tended to do as she was told. They had two daughters. For reasons no-one was conscious of, the father felt an affinity with one daughter, perhaps because she looked like him, and she naturally responded to his closeness to her. The other daughter missed this closeness. The mother, on the other hand, felt equally close to both girls. Now the first girl 'resolved' her Oedipal feelings by tending to dismiss her mother as dim, while being eagerly devoted to and modelling herself on her father. The second girl, less favoured by her father, sided with her mother, accentuated her virtues, and seemed to reject her father as a male chauvinistic martinet.

This is an over-simplified picture but it shows how fateful the partial resolution of infantile attachments by identification can be. The form of the resolution must depend, not only on the patterning of early experiences, and on the continuing stances of parents, but also upon the pressures put on a child from outside the home. For instance, a boy prone to identify with his sensitive, artistic mother is likely to find it hard to display this identification with her if he goes to a sportive, pugilistic, all-boys school.

Here are two more brief histories, which show differing patterns of partial resolution:

The eldest of three brothers was the son of a kind but rigidly conforming mother and of a father who was a footballer. The boy himself was rather sickly as an infant, and his inexperienced mother was prone to react with horror because of her ideals of good health. Later, when his brothers were born, their mother became more confident and easy-going than she had been with him. The boy felt he was the sickly horror in the family and was frantic about it. Yet his sickliness had its compensations: his mother fussed over him all the more. He found his compromise. From the age of five or six, he quite consistently chose the path of being the 'oddity' in the family. Everything that shocked his mother – and she was easily shocked – he found a pleasure in doing; for he got more doting attention when being shocking, even though he was quite sadistic about it. His father on the other hand treated him with irritable dismissal and ill concealed contempt. Later, in his mid-school years, he loved to investigate everything that was 'alternative' or 'different'. By ten or twelve he was absorbing himself in oriental mysticism. In his teens he naturally espoused any activity, philosophy or causes that were different from Western standards. He was erudite upon Buddhism, Taoism, Zen, Shinto, acupuncture and macrobiotics. Athletically, he could not be a beefy footballer like his father and brothers, but he found athleticism with a vengeance in great skill at karate. He was very adept at strikes that could kill.

Apart from an athleticism somewhat similar to his father's, this example hardly shows positive identifications with parents. Rather it appears to be a life-style centred on rejection of them both, and of all they stood for.

Here is another example:

In her first years, a little girl adored and was thrilled by her father. At work he was a carpenter while at home he was artistic and imaginative. However, he was rather irresponsible and tended to let the house go to ruin. The little girl's mother began to grumble about her husband, and a chronic rift of bitterness grew up between them. By the age of six or so, the little girl had at last become convinced, from her mother's continuous arguments, that men in general were no good, and her father in particular was a useless mess. Later, in adolescence, she entrenched her sense of contempt for him. In the early years of her adulthood she consorted only with women who likewise held men in contempt. Later, when forced to work with men, she tried very hard to hold to her old beliefs. It was only with great pain that she allowed her good feelings about them, which she had had as a very small girl, to find a place in her conception of them.

These were people from two countries in mainland Europe. But the 'working out' of childhood family ties ranges very widely and is a fateful question, especially in cultures in flux. Here is a quote from China:

Mao Tse-Tung, speaking of his mother and family, said: 'She pitied the poor and often gave them rice when they came to ask for it during famines. But she could not do so when my father was present . . . We had many quarrels in our home over this question. There were two "parties" in the family. One was my father, the Ruling Power. The Opposition was made up of myself, my mother, my brother and sometimes even the labourer.' (from Snow, 1968)

This, of course, is not the case history of a crippling neurosis fit only for an analyst's couch, for Mao is humorously and convincingly recounting the origins of his life's political passion, explicitly relating it back to his family as well as to the social and economic conditions of his time. From our point of view, it stresses that personal Oedipal feelings may be fateful for an individual – and even for a whole nation. They cannot be considered as just neurotic or sick.

Further reading

Emanuel, L. (2005) *Understanding Your Three Year Old.* London: Tavistock Clinic & Jessica Kingsley.
Hamilton, V. (1982) *Narcissus and Oedipus.* London: Karnac. Serious theoretical thinking, clearly written.

Chapter 8

Early school days

Eric Rayner

The family and the outside world

The law in Britain requires that children must go to school by the age of five. This means that for 6 hours a day some people outside the family – school teachers – take statutory responsibility for them. This means that a child is formally under the orders, and thus partially in the *possession of*, a stranger. They probably have been to a play-group or nursery school, but a child's view of the world will still have been much filtered by their parents. A child will have attuned to their habits and morality, so that their standards would sometimes have seemed the only ones possible. Now the child belongs also to the school and its teachers, who may have quite different habits from their parents. The other children will also have unfamiliar habits and beliefs, and their parents are likely to be from other countries, continents, and cultures. Lastly, a child will be in a classroom to learn intellectual skills and, for the first time, will have to submit to doing this in a *formal setting* (Barrett & Trevatt, 1991; Green, 1968; Sroufe, 1996).

Parting from parents

It is very common for children just going to school for the first time to make a slip of the tongue and call their teacher 'Mummy'. Here are a few memories that distill some of the shocks of this new situation.

'We were Welsh-speaking, but had to sing hymns in English. I know what they mean now, but I can still remember the incomprehensible jumble of words from those school assemblies.' (These days, of course, the opposite might well happen, with English-speaking children at school in Wales having to sing in Welsh.)

'I remember going to the medical room with a cut knee to have what I thought was 'flints' (lint) put on it.'

'I jumped on a see-saw to show off to the Mother Superior of our convent school, who was standing near. The other end shot up and knocked her over. I was frantic – I thought I had killed a saint.'

Here is a teacher's description of an abnormal separation:

'Jack started nursery at the usual age of 3½, but his mother took him away when the nursery teacher expressed concerns over his speech and language development. He was returned to the nursery class when a new teacher took over. His mother was visibly distressed at parting from him, inducing tears in the child. When she saw another child crying at the nursery gates she made comments in front of Jack, such as: "He's crying because he doesn't want to come to school". She also allowed Jack several days absence due to her own illness, rather than make arrangements for someone else to bring him. She said "He's very funny about who he'll go with". In Jack's first 22 school days he was absent for 13 of them.

'When Jack is left at nursery, he stops crying almost immediately and proves to be pleasant, friendly and very interested in the nursery class setting. The teacher once rang mum to reassure her that Jack had stopped crying and was happily playing. The following day, Jack was kept at home. This was a repeat of the pattern right at the beginning. It had also happened with the older child, a girl now 6 years old, who continues to display abnormal attachment behaviour into her second year. The teachers feel that mother is projecting her own severe anxieties onto her children.'

The following memory from a retired Nigerian teacher highlights some differences from these European instances:

'There were few cars in our town and everyone wandered around and played in the streets. Most people knew each other. We Yoruba are rather proud of being friendly, so you might spend the whole day out, even if you were very tiny. Going to school was not seen as a great change and was eagerly looked forward to because it was very important to be educated. There weren't any birth certificates so you had an entrance exam. All those wanting to go to school were lined up and told to put their right hand over the tops of their heads. If you could touch the lobe of your left ear you were old enough – you could go to school, and you jumped up and down with joy.'

Some families who have settled in Britain from overseas have little or no experience of socializing and mixing with other children outside the immediate family circle. That is, they do not go to toddler groups, toy libraries or mother and baby groups. So it may be that a child is having to adjust to school after being in a family where, say, mother has very little English, but father is fluent and well educated. The child may feel confident and exploratory when able to stay close to mum, but if mum tries to leave she will become very distressed. It may take all the efforts of the nursery teacher, the bi-lingual support assistant and the parents to work out a programme where the child can be left for increasing lengths of time over a month. With this kind of help in bridging the gap between home and school, the child may be happy to start forming relationships with other children.

The shocks of going to school are, of course, well recognized and most teachers take a great deal of trouble with the early months.

Yet, however ready a child may be, and however kind the school, there is often a susceptibility to being torn apart in efforts to conform to and placate the multiplicity of people and expectations which are encountered. Let us briefly examine the three main groups involved in this: the family, the teacher, and other children.

Early home development and school

Children carry the ways of home with them to school. These may have been happy enough in themselves but to a young child's mind they must often conflict with those of the school, which can seem to be a frightening, alien place. This is particularly so when the school's national culture is different from the child's own. Here are two instances of a dramatic change of environment, or *culture shock*, one involving a national culture change, the other not:

An Indian girl spent her early years in rural India. She naturally attuned herself to living in the open air and to the easy-going 'timelessness' of her particular village. When she came to England, school life seemed strange, cold and machine-like. Precision and tuning seemed almost to attack her. She made many friends and was well liked. But her school days and class-work were strained and unhappy. Her teacher thought her a slow learner and she became seriously dispirited about her abilities.

An only child was much loved by the many elderly people in his family but most of his time was spent alone. He felt happy in this for, from a very early age, he populated his imagination with the people and things he loved dearly. He was reading at three and this increased the scope of his imaginative loves immeasurably. He normally never played with other children. By the time he went to school he was very well equipped to deal with both teachers and his lessons, but the presence of other children was quite outside his experience. They shook him out of his rich, solitary inner world of imagination. Because of his cleverness and his capacity to charm adults he became a 'teacher's pet', and was thus hated by his schoolfellows who bullied him mercilessly. He never made friends with a child all through his primary-school years.

We can see that this boy was able to carry across his amiability with the adults in his family to good relations with his teachers. But his friendliness could not transfer to finding *comradeship* and *reciprocity* with his peers. This was a terrible price to pay for the teachers' special regard for him and for his scholastic success.

Many parents seriously fail to recognize the importance of differences in habit between home and school. Parents who are strangers to a school's culture must naturally find it difficult to help their children with the change. But many parents without such handicaps display surprising personal lethargy and ignorance. Here are some instances:

Some years ago, a mother was very worried about her son's health, and insisted he wear many layers of clothes throughout the winter when the other boys all wore jeans and a jersey. He was teased about this by the other boys, but dared not go against his mother. Later he found acceptance of a sort by becoming the clown of the class, but he says he never forgave his mother.

A mother said to a friend, 'I'm worried about Jimmy going to school, the teacher won't understand him like I do', to which the friend reposted 'That's why it'll be good for him.'

A 6-year-old girl wisely said in praise of her teacher, 'Ms Patel tells you off in a very nice voice.'

Let us look at this situation of children together at school more closely.

Inside the classroom and out: the society of other children and their teachers

Many children, in urban England at least, will have got used to some of the ways of classrooms from going to a playgroup or nursery school. A young child at 'proper' or 'big' school is confronted with at least five different kinds of personal relationship. These are: the child and his teachers; the child and other children; the child, other children and the teachers; other children and the teachers; then, lastly, other children together. In class, the core aim in all these relationships is formal learning, or *scholarship*. Without this, the essence of school is lost. However, there are other functions of life in school that are just as vital. These are to do with the social and emotional relationships of children together. Let us have a look at them (Holt, 1982, 1983).

The society of other children

As children fundamentally wish to be enjoyed by their teacher nearly as much as by their parents, there must naturally be an underlying competitiveness in any classroom. Poor performance relative to others usually leads to despair and listlessness in a beginner. Doing better than others can be equally disturbing, as we saw in one of the examples above. A child doing well is placed in danger of being envied and ostracized by the less successful. 'Swot', 'bookworm', 'teacher's pet' are sneers designed to distress a clever child. Invective like this could be justified if a child becomes arrogant but it can be meted out to even the most humble child if he or she is clever.

Even with this competition in the classroom, children have the opportunity to find themselves in the special society of others the same age. This is often a crucial turning point for later enjoyment of other people. Previously, companionship with others will have been mainly under the close eye of mother, or another intimate adult; but in the school playground, and afterwards in the streets or fields, a child will be alone with others of his own age.

Children can be frightening because they may be strange, hostile, less controlled and less responsible than ordinary mature adults. They are fundamentally anxious and in fear of shame when they go to school. They will do all sorts of things to alleviate their own sense of inferiority. On the positive side, they will be spurred to learn new skills, both in class and with other children. This creative side of competitiveness must be invaluable, but fear of inferiority often brings less useful defensive manoeuvres into play – like being subversive, or bullying, teasing and scorning others. For example, a child who is upset because he cannot read a passage in a book may feel better, for a time at least, if he sees someone else in greater difficulty. This silent thought itself does not amount to bullying. For example, the thought, or even public comment, 'I can read better than Ann', might have scorn in it, but it is not, by itself, teasing or bullying. However, when a child actively repeats and repeats: 'Ann can't read, Ann can't read', until the little girl is in a paroxysm of humiliation, this is very nasty teasing – verbal bullying. The child is no doubt using a violent *projection* as a defence against feeling inferior. But, more important, it is *sadistic*, intended to hurt, and can be as cruel as inflicting physical pain.

Togetherness *in groups* particularly lends itself to violent projection. Teasing and bullying is then transformed into *scapegoating*, when children gang up, obliterating their own fears and self-doubts in the communal glee of disturbing someone else. For example, an 8-year-old boy heard of a new gang that had started at the other end of the street. 'Can I join you', he shyly asked; but he was told 'Don't be stupid, it's against *you* – that's what it's *for*.'

The fact that the members of a group get together in bullying means that they support each other in *obliterating*, not only their fears of loneliness, shame, powerlessness and inferiority, but also their guilt. In effect 'It's all right because we're all doing it.'

This can, of course, become institutionalized: some teachers are frankly sadistic in the way they systematically set about frightening their classes. Religious, racial and national scapegoating can be common – even teachers can be covertly malicious. However, it is possibly on the wane in many British schools because of stringent new laws against racism, which on the whole are well accepted.

Apart from the dangers of malicious pleasure in incitement to prejudice and bullying, the company of other children is a rich ground for enhancing both intimate friendly *reciprocity* and whole wide networks of new relationships. A child can identify with his companions as fellow-sufferers on equal terms in the treadmill of school. Reciprocity also gives a unique opportunity to develop the sensitivity of a *depressive*, or *self-blaming* aspect of *conscience*. This state of mind is crucially important in being ordinarily *self-responsible*. It goes with being a thoughtful, kindly and honest, communally minded person.

The particular depressive form of conscience was first seriously investigated by Melanie Klein (in Segal, 1973). It is certainly based on feeling sympathy for other human beings. The roots of this must lie in early family experiences but, from going to school onwards, it is well exercised in a wider society. It was Kohlberg (1976) who first emphasized that the development of conscience only solidly begins after going to school, when other children of the same age are around. It is here, perhaps, where *democracy* outside the family is born.

Teachers and formal learning

It is perhaps useful to emphasize two functions of a schoolteacher. One is to introduce the ways of the world outside the family to a child who can often be baffled and anxious. The second is more obvious – to preside over formal learning. The first task has, in fact, been given much thought by infant school teachers in the last half-century, and it is now standard practice for a child's introduction to formal learning to be slow and playful, with many intimate conversations between teacher and child. This is a great leap forward for freedom of thought and self-respect compared to the dreary discipline of an old-fashioned teacher drilling lessons into children.

Even so, parents and teachers can still fail at times to recognize the anxiety a child can feel about the differences between home and school. Young children are simply not able by themselves to resolve these differing ways and *contradictions*. For instance, school may say it's good to be religious whereas home may say it's bad. Or a school may pride itself on its multi-faith practices, while parents may see this as a dilution of their beliefs. Both parents and teachers need to help children with the great transition and the contradictions that are involved.

Teachers and other professionals are sometimes prone to blame home circumstances for a child's distress – often rightly, but sometimes not. Maybe they do it to absolve themselves from shame or guilt about inadequacies. Even so, a child's trepidation must, in part at least, be a product of the convergence between what he or she brings from home and what is being encountered in the new environment. School could be just as unhelpful in attitude as home. At the same time, it is best not to forget that personal consideration for an individual child must only be secondary for a teacher – they will be stretched most of the time attending to the class as a whole. With up to 40 children in front of them, and a main responsibility to *foster formal learning*, individual children must be left more or less alone for long periods (Erikson, 1993; Floyd, 1979; Green, 1968; Hale, 1979).

Unlike home, school learning is *work*. The fundamental aim is to become *disciplined* in thought. Thus a teacher, however kind, must basically be committed to being a disciplinarian.

Incidentally, as class learning is a new discipline for the child, we would expect primitive fantasies and feelings to repeat themselves from earlier disciplinary times. Thus, we can expect fantasies about *anal* discipline to come to the fore. These can often be detected in children's private obsessional worries, and, more lightheartedly, in the lavatorialness of school humour. Perhaps it was for reasons of anal–sadistic excitation – for the teachers at least – that the favourite old schoolmaster's mode of discipline was beating boys with a cane on the bottom – of all places.

Returning to more general thoughts, old-fashioned teachers often used to see themselves as needing to combat the unruliness of self-willed imagination. They set out to crush it early by the imposition of iron discipline and repetitive learning. Then, teachers began to see that the need for freedom of enjoyable, self-willed imagination lies, from childhood onwards, at the core of every person's being. If this is recognized, having fun can even be a true spur towards self-generated discipline. The teacher can thus often happily become an aide to a child's wish to *discipline himself* in order to enjoy a subject freely and thoroughly. However, there must also be a part of any child's mind that loathes any form of constriction, no matter how benign it might be in the long run. To this, the teacher must, somewhere, be antithetical – after all, this is what discipline is for.

Old-fashioned discipline perhaps throttled a child's natural wish to discover things for himself at his own pace. Modern methods do not commit this crime but, when the teacher is unwilling to face open disagreement, a child is left deflated, or with grandiose inflated and unrealistic ideas unchecked. Methods emphasizing freedom are obviously rewarding – and also produce strains. A teacher must steer a difficult path between enjoying the pupil's vital and colourful ideas while at the same time checking wild fantasy (Erikson, 1993; Henry, Osborne, & Wittenberg, 1983).

Conceptual development in the early school days

We are now into the region of education proper. But we have no hope of doing justice to its complexities, or to the emotional and intellectual problems that every teacher has to face. Quite apart from this writer's lack of expert knowledge about early educational techniques, we have no space to do more than brush their surface. However, because it is central to the book, we will go on thinking about *concept formation*.

In the last two chapters we saw that a pre-school child developed *pre-concepts*. With the coming of the ability to signify and symbolize intentionally, he begins to be able to use *general* ideas; but these can be full of inconsistencies and contradictions. For instance, a child of two or so going along the road may see a pillar box; then, a bit further on, another. From the child's conversation it becomes plain that he thinks it is the *same* box in both places. Not even pre-concepts have taken proper shape here yet.

Some time later our child may again see the two pillar boxes, and by this time realizes that they are different but *similar*. This does not mean that he understands the logic of pillar boxes and how they relate to their super-ordinate class 'the Post Office'. Of course, by the time a child is off to school, he will have grown out of such misunderstandings. However, children of this age will tend only to centre attention on *one* attribute or relationship at a time. Logical *contradictions* abound in children's ideas about the vast networks of relationships that make up the real world in front of them. They have not yet put ideas about things together enough or fully worked out the logic of the relations between them, such as checking whether contradictions occur or not. Even so, *puzzlement* is a heartening sign of a child's real intellectual engagement with a question.

We have already seen how, from around 3 or 4 years old, and particularly when going to school, a child comes into a much wider network of people than he has ever known before. Remember here also the importance of *imitation* from earliest infancy onward: we particularly saw it working in *dramatic play* or *make-believe*. We also noted it in the workings of human *sympathy* and identification with others. These are all necessary steps towards the vital skill of imagining the self in new positions. From here, one can begin to imagine generally what things are like from any other person's point of view. In childhood, the wide social network of school fosters many exercises for this *mutuality* in thought. Through others, children have great new vistas of reality at hand with which to exercise their minds. A lively child will be imagining many new positions of the self relative to other things and people. You can often see and hear the excitement in children's quick and expressive gestures. *Self-object networks* are enjoyably growing apace in the imagination.

In the last chapter we saw this broadening of mind was happening with a child imagining himself in the position of their parents. In this chapter we are seeing this extending to being in the many positions of other children and adults – particularly teachers. This is occurring not only in the emotional–social sphere, but also in the intellectual world that conceives of things and their networks of physical relationships. A child at school will now be working out about complex systems of relationships, not just between things, but between *classes* or *sets* of things as well.

Using this new facility to see things *from different points of view at once*, a child begins to be able to *conceptualize systematically*. One can then hear a child exercising the capacity to be *logical*, albeit intuitively. On paper this may sound dull, but it is a beautiful thing to hear. The essence of this is awareness of *contradictions*. Integration of different points of view, and thence a realistic breadth of vision, requires, among other things, a comprehension, and then resolution, of contradictions. This is what *logical* thought essentially grapples with.

Piaget pointed out that, after about 7 years old, a child begins to be concerned about the consistent, non-contradictory *classification* of things into *hierarchies of classes* and *subclasses*. Asked to define a car or horse, say, he will *try* to give the characteristics of each, even though he may not get it quite right. He will be truly concerned with logical consistency in a way that a younger child simply ignores and will, for instance, be able to think about cars as a subclass of higher-order classes, such as wheeled vehicles or means of transport.

This consistency is only partial, of course, but a child goes on trying, applying it to one area after another as he goes through school. However, he thinks in this way only about classes of things that are more or less *directly manifest to the senses*. There is as yet no *active* and intentional thinking about *abstractions* in non-contradictory ways. Because of this, Piaget (1972) called this the stage of *concrete operational thinking*.

The purest simple form of consistent or logical thinking is, perhaps, arithmetic. This is based on the counting, adding and taking away of things. It is strictly logical and also, at base, *directly represents* concrete, touchable and countable things. We can now summarize some of the important thought functions that we have been thinking about:

- First there was *logical thinking* at the *concrete operational level*, which is about the *physically* different structuring and positioning of things.
- Second, there was *emotional sympathy* with different people.

Both kinds of thought involve conceiving of *networks* of the *positions* of things and the *differing relationships* between them. Which of the two comes first in a child's development, the physical–logical or emotional–logical, is a very interesting question. Most probably they go hand in hand; the one enhances the other.

It is also important to note that, even though conceptualization has begun to function logically, it adds to, but never replaces, more primitive pre-conceptual feeling and thinking – at least in the healthy individual. For instance, any *inventiveness* or new idea always involves a leap of *imagination*. This must contain an element of dramatic play or *make-believe*. This must initially *ignore* some of the logical rules of non-contradiction. For instance, in make-believe, things that are *different* in reality must, in imagination, have been seen, for a moment at least, as *the same*. To play at soldiers a child needs to imagine a stick is the same as a gun. This is not logical but it is absolutely vital for some stages of all thought. For example, a teacher may say in an arithmetic lesson, 'Let's say that this plasticine is dough and we're baking bread'. This initiates a make-believe of playing at bakers' shops. For a moment the children *are* bakers. However, the teacher then expects them to continue into a logical, non-contradictory way of thinking within the make-belief. For instance, she or he may say, 'You carefully mix some water in with the flour in a bowl, then put in a little salt and some yeast; then you rub and twist them together to make a quite stiff dough. Put that in a baking tray and then into the oven.' Imagination and reality must go hand in hand in valid thinking, but they must never be confused – if this happens, the thinker has gone a bit crazy.

The development of industriousness

As important as classroom work, is a child's gain in skill and knowledge in playfulness – whether it be alone, or in the company of other children. A moment's reflection upon boys' and girls' games, conversations and hobbies makes us realize that children probably glean as much information about the world from informal conversations with friends and family, and watching TV, as they do in the classroom.

As one grows through the school years, gaining in understanding the logic of concrete operations, skills develop; and with them awareness of *self-efficacy* comes about. As this becomes more solid, the need for make-believe gives way to sheer pleasure in reality-oriented *industry*. We have just noted that make-believe is still an essential first step; but to grow up, it must become subsumed under logically tested, non-contradictory, realistic ideas. Erik Erikson (1993) wrote cogently about this.

Here is a memory that illustrates this transition:

I used to do a lot of tinkering and woodwork. I can remember pretending to be a busy carpenter or engineer with oil-soaked clothes when I was mucking about. It was fun doing it, but of course nothing ever really worked after I had finished. One day the handle of my mother's brush broke and in examining it, I realized I could shape a new one if I selected the right wood from the pile in the garage. I did this, screwed it on, and my mother could use it again. I was very pleased – I didn't have to pretend any more.

The practice of make-believe play perhaps falls away earlier in girls than with boys. Many boys in their early teens are still absorbed in make-believe games and hobbies, such as model aircraft, cars, and so on. Girls of this age probably have as many daydreams as boys, but their skills often seem more oriented to reality. They certainly often tend to be ahead in schoolwork.

This may in part be due to the fact that a girl is of the same sex as her first human model – her mother. What is more, most of her infant and junior schoolteachers, whom she has seen at their tasks every day, will have been female too. It is thus probably easier for her to imitate and identify with them, and thence to develop her skills and sense of efficacy. A boy, on the other hand, is of a different sex from his first model, and probably from most of his early teachers also. He tends to become antipathetic to identifying with them at quite an early age and thus, maybe, learns less from female teachers. A town boy especially will usually have only a transient acquaintance with the tasks of men like his father – apart from the ubiquitous computer, of course – who are likely to be seen only for part of the evenings and at weekends. With less opportunity to learn from the parent of the same sex, he may be less sure of himself than a girl and hence more prone to pure wish-fulfilling, logic-free, make-believe.

The school child and his parents

As a child gains more confidence to be alone, he usually seeks out the company of like-minded children and often tends to turn away from his parents' conversation. It is often emphasized that children no longer want their parents' company much during adolescence, but this progress towards separation certainly starts much earlier. Children itch for the companionship of other children; it has a life of its own, with its many enjoyable secrets hidden from adults. As children get older, at least in Western societies, they often like ganging up together to scorn and giggle at the silliness of their parents and other adults – not to mention having fun bullying other children. This naturally uses the projective mechanisms that are involved in any *scapegoating*, as we mentioned earlier. During early school years this is usually transient towards adults so that a child can be laughing at his parents one minute and crying to them for help the next. It is probably not until adolescence that the persistent perception of faults in adults plays a truly central part in development. This is not always destructive – it is often part of the attempt to develop a rounded and fair opinion of one's parents, 'warts and all' (Green, 1968; Holt, 1982). At the same time as this is happening, there is no doubt that most children still really enjoy the quiet company of a parent, especially if they have an interest in common, like cooking, sewing, doing carpentry or going to football matches.

As the child's tendency towards separateness is only partial, a parent's consideration and attitude is still overwhelmingly import-ant. The conscious focus of a child's mind may be directed away from his family, but fundamental decisions are still mediated through it: he lives where they live, is fed and clothed according to their notions, and goes where they go at weekends and holidays. Both economically and psychologically, they are incapable of independence. Children of this age, by and large, are quite aware of this and accept the ways of their parents without open question or rebellion. This does not mean that the child acquiesces in all their thought and feelings. Much will be kept in the inner world and may even be quite unconscious. At most, negative feelings, if disturbing, will manifest themselves in nervousness or 'difficult behaviour'. Their ego-functioning has not yet developed sufficiently for open, self-determined rebellion. This must wait until adolescence.

Further reading

Barrett, M., & Trevatt, C. (1991) *Attachment Behaviour and the School Child*. London: Routledge.

Berg, I., & Nursten, J. (1996) *Unwillingly to School*. London: Gaskell. A collection about school refusal.

Erikson, E.H. (1993) *A Way of Looking at Things*. New York: Norton. This is particularly useful for the discussion of the development of 'Industry' (pp. 604–605).

Hale, G. (1979) *Attention and Cognitive Development*. London: Plenum Press.

Kohlberg, L. (1976) Moral stages. In: Lickona, R. (ed) *Moral Development*. Chicago: Rand McNally.

Klein, M. (1973) In: Segal, H. *An Introduction to the Work of Melanie Klein*. London: Hogarth.

Piaget, J. (1972) *The Child and Reality*. Harmondsworth: Penguin.

Salzberger-Wittenberg, I., Osborne, E., & Henry, G. (1983) *The Emotional Basis of Learning and Teaching*. London: Karnac.

Sroufe, L. (1996) *Child Development*. New York: McGraw-Hill.

Chapter 9

Adolescence

James Rose

Cast your mind back to your own teens. You might recall moments when it seemed that you or the world would never be quite the same again. Such a realization may have been associated with an ill-defined thrill or a dread – or, maybe, both at the same time. These changes may have centred about senses of physical changes and growth of your body, or your feelings about a girl or a boy of a similar age or a sense of change in how you were recognized and regarded by others important to you.

With memories like these in mind, we can go straight into thinking about the main psychodynamic changes that occur in adolescence and its main developmental tasks. In terms of chronological age, we are talking about the onset of adolescence being around 10–12 years and merging into adulthood in the early twenties.

Paul van Heeswyck (1997) summarizes these tasks as follows:

- The moving away from the close and familiar security of home and school to the wider variety of people and ideas in the world at large.
- Ownership of the body, which was previously held under a kind of leasing arrangement with the parents; this involves integrating into the body image the newly awakened sexual feelings and fantasies, as well as rapid changes in size and strength.
- The attainment of personal autonomy and becoming a separate person; this is usually taken to mean the establishment of a confidence in and a responsibility for one's beliefs and actions.
- The achievement of intimacy with others based on secure personal boundaries and a fixed sexual identity.

- Adaptation to the adult world of work and care of the young, with the twin values of the identification and pursuit of personal and career goals, and commitment to agreements entered into and tasks undertaken.

Why adolescence?

It might be said that adolescence as a process occurs because of a conflict of expectation between developing individuals and the society in which they live. Its onset can be defined by arrival of puberty but its termination is much harder to define objectively. For this reason, it often makes more sense to talk about a process of *adolescing* by coining a new verb to describe something that begins but perhaps never quite finishes until death. The adolescent can feel alone in a quite new way; but his new reactions to this experience will impinge upon all around. All those around him will be affected: family, friends or representatives of authority.

At a societal level, this has given rise to the notion of a 'youth culture' as if this process of adolescing were a new social development and that young people today are pioneers of a new order. This was perhaps the consequence of starting to realize that different cultures managed the process of transition from childhood to adulthood quite differently. While the idea of adolescents being pioneers might be gratifying to some adolescents, we can be pretty sure that the experience that something new happens when puberty 'turns up' is not a new phenomenon.

One of our earliest-known written inscriptions shows that concern about adolescence has been with us for a long time. King Hattusili of the Hittites, in about 1620 BC to his son of thirteen:

> Keep thy father's word and stay away from wine in favour of bread and water while in youth, but when old age is with thee drink to satiety. And then thou may'st set aside thy father's word.

One may pause to ponder on all the hard work that went into preserving these thoughts for posterity. It was clearly important but it quite possibly means that the son was a long way from observing his father's admonitions.

Three thousand years later, Shakespeare, in *A Winter's Tale*, reflected a comparable feeling when he, in the words of the shepherd, described this period thus:

> I would there was no age between ten and three and twenty, or that youth would sleep out the rest; for there is nothing in between but getting wench with child; wronging the ancientry, stealing, fighting.

However, these quotes make it clear that the 'problem' of adolescence is different for the individual adolescent and for society at large. The adolescent may be experienced by the modern 'ancientry' as nothing more than an irritating pain; but the individual teenager, in the middle of his existential ponderings, will sometimes feel that he is the first to confront the serious moral dilemmas of the day. Adolescing is therefore potentially a heated business for all concerned. The word 'crisis' has been often invoked and sometimes this epithet is well deserved.

In this society, the difficulties of going through the adolescing process are to an extent complicated by there being no clear points of conclusion marking the passage into adulthood. In some senses, they are present, e.g. the age of majority and the right to vote, but these do not have the same meaning as in some other cultures where the negotiation of rites of passage impose an obligation from which there is no evasion. We may say that, for the sake of a rough rule of thumb, adolescing is a process that begins with puberty and that by an individual's early twenties, he will have moved from a state of infantile dependency to one in which they are on the way to being able to *live, work and love* beyond the bounds of his immediate family.

In the face of the complexity of a phenomenon, which has a beginning but no clear end, we have to impose some kind of structure. Beginning with the fact of puberty, we can see that this has consequences for the individual and those around him because the arrival of the mature sexual body means that the individual has the power to procreate. To do this, the individual must find a partner. Doctors who offer family planning and contraception services to adolescents and young people have described to me a change in the way that their patients think and talk about their sexuality as they get older. Younger adolescents (aged between 13 and 15) talk about '*having sex*'; those between 16 and 18 commonly talk about '*having intercourse*' but those older than this will typically talk about '*making love*'. Thus, we note that the matter of 'finding a partner' is not simple and mechanical one but embraces the developing capacity for a relationship as the adolescent becomes not just the *master or mistress of their own minds, but also of their own bodies.*

It is also true that at about the arrival of puberty, and without any known causal link,[1] comes a profound change in an individual's cognitive and intellectual capacities. Its potential impact is not solely on the capacity to learn but also to relate to oneself, the family and others. It has been described as a move from egocentricity to formal logical operations (Piaget, 1950). Fonagy and Moran (1991) suggest that essentially this means that the capacity to see oneself in a physical and/or social context has been acquired even if this is not always maintained in moments of strong feeling. It is associated with the capacity for abstract thinking and a change in the structure of moral thinking such that notions of fairness, based on equality for all, are enriched by notions of equitability, which recognize differences between individuals (Piaget, 1935). This introduces the possibility of being able to see the different positions of several people at the same time, which permits the possibility of effective cooperation in a group so that, over time, it can become organized.

Society demands that the period of the dependency of formal education ends and the individual must take his place in adult society in an adult role. There is no evasion of this fact simply because the passage of time requires that the individual becomes an adult in whatever way he can. Given all these changes, occurring at the physiological, psychic and social levels, it is not surprising that the idea of crisis has come to mind. Laufer (1965) suggests that adolescence can be described as a period of narcissistic crisis and that the purpose of our inquiring into this process should enable us to find out how the adolescent deals with this crisis.

Life crises have been defined as personal situations that arise when well-tried structures of adaptation and defence are no longer adequate to assimilate new demands, which may impinge either

---

1 Statistically significant correlations in lower social groups between the age of onset of puberty and measured verbal intelligence have been observed but are thought to be a statistical artefact due to an association between late puberty and large family size (large family size being associated with a lower average level of verbal intelligence. (Westin-Lindgren, 1982).

from within or outside an individual. Loosening up, with at least partial disintegration, of thought and feeling, then occurs. This is accompanied by anxiety and perplexity and often also impulsive action. Regressions, with the re-emergence of gross primitive modes of fantasy, thought and feeling are likely. The likelihood of regressions, in the face of the ongoing developmental progression, emphasizes that the discontinuity wrought by puberty and the loss of ego-centricity produce effects that reverberate during the subsequent decade of life and which echo on throughout an individual's life. It has been said that the pattern of normal adolescence is akin to a kind of see-saw or to-and-fro between progression (going forwards) and regression (clinging on to the past) (Ladame & Catipovic, 1998). This has made it hard to establish a clear behavioural definition of normal development or indeed what might be deemed to be 'normal' disturbance.

As a result, authorities on adolescence have differed on the crucial matter of whether disturbance is an *essential* part of adolescence (Coleman, 1990; Rutter & Smith, 1995). This makes it particularly difficult to comprehend Anna Freud's (1958) observation that an upholding of a steady equilibrium during the adolescent process was in itself abnormal, and therefore not always a sign of health. Parents talking together about their experiences with their early adolescent children will, however, probably recognize the following:

> Whereas the latency child (approximately five to eleven, twelve years) had begun to show definite and well-circumscribed character and personality traits, the pre-adolescent (approximately eleven, twelve to fourteen years) is once more unpredictable. Where the latency child has become modest, reasonable and well-mannered with regard to food, the pre-adolescent reacts with greed and demandingness; insatiableness in pre-adolescence frequently leads to thefts of food and sweets. Similar changes occur in almost all the spheres of the child's life. Pre-adolescent boys in particular are known to be dirty in their lavatory habits and negligent in their clothing. Cruel and bullying actions are regular occurrences; so are mutual masturbation, the seduction of younger children, and sexual compliance towards older playmates; destructive acts, thefts and robberies are carried out alone or in company with others. Within the family the pre-adolescent causes disharmony by his

selfishness and inconsiderateness; in school he is frequently in trouble because of his lack of interest in the school subjects, his inability to concentrate, his irresponsibleness and insubordination. In short, the whole promising process of adaptation to the environment seems to have stopped short. What parents and teachers are confronted with is *once again* [my italics] the full, undiminished impact of the instinctual forces within the child.

(A. Freud, 1949)

This extract, which can read as an immense comfort to assailed parents, giving them the feeling that they are not alone in their sense of total failure, gives an impression of adolescence as a time of storms and doldrums. However, the sociologist John Coleman (Coleman & Hendry, 1990) takes the view that the contention that the psychoanalytic 'storm and stress' conceptualization of adolescence is erroneous and not borne out by any of the major studies of adolescence in recent years. While there is general agreement that, in the teenage years, major adaptation has to occur; the great majority of teenagers seem to cope well and to show no undue signs of turmoil or stress. Similarly, Graham and Rutter (1985), in reviewing adolescent disorders from a psychiatric position, took the view that, in contrast to the expectation of psychoanalytic theorists, 'most adolescents do not *show* [my italics] emotional disturbance'.

Such conclusions raise a great many questions not just about methods of investigation but also about what may be deemed to be 'normal' or 'abnormal'. Nevertheless, at bedrock, the question is whether we are looking to account for the factors that form the adolescent experience or whether we are seeking to make sense of the impact that the adolescent has on those around him. The paradox of adolescence is that, while these two may begin to converge as the individual passes through adolescence, what the adolescent 'shows' or, more accurately, how he is interpreted by adults, will not coincide with his own experience. If we are looking for the factors that form the adolescent experience then we must turn to what we know is unique about the onset of adolescence.

Puberty, physiological changes and sexual behaviour

This refers to the maturation of primary and secondary sexual characteristics. It is the arrival of these changes that announces the onset of adolescence; even though young people may have anticipated them in some way. These 'developmental patterns' are universal in their applicability across different cultural milieu but their *meaning* to the young person and those around him is very culture bound. In addition, there have been significant secular changes over the past century. Adolescents in Western Europe, the United States, and Japan today experience puberty earlier than their counterparts 100 years ago. In addition, they grow taller, weigh more and appear more mature physically than previous generations of adolescents (Leffert & Petersen, 1995; Chumlea, 1982; Frisch, 1990; Tanner, 1989). These changes have been linked with improved nutrition and overall health.

Associated with earlier onset of puberty has been an earlier average age of first intercourse. Thus, Schofield (1965) reported that only 5 per cent of girls had had intercourse by the age of 16, but this had risen to 12 per cent by 1978 (Farrell, 1978) and to 19 per cent by 1990 (Wellings et al., 1994). It was not clear what effect changes in contraceptive technology, availability and use have had; but those having first intercourse at 13 to 14 years were still reported to be twice as unlikely to be unprotected as those having first intercourse in their late teens or early twenties.

Recent surveys of early heterosexual experience (Wellings et al., 2001) suggest that the trend towards earlier heterosexual experience, which had stabilized amongst boys, may also have done so for girls by the mid-1990s. It was also reported that there had been a sustained increase in the use of condoms and a decline in the proportion of men and women reporting no contraceptive use at first intercourse with decreasing age at interview. Pregnancy before the age of 18 was strongly associated with whether a girl had first had intercourse before the age of 16, had left school at 16 and had not lived with both parents to age 16 years. Overall, there is therefore strong evidence to suggest that sexual behaviour is heavily influenced by sociocultural factors.

Changes in girls' ideas about their bodies

The appearance of breasts and the widening of hips are likely to be the first impacts of puberty. Depending on the girl herself, and the cultural climate of family and neighbourhood in which she lives, these experiences can vary from fun in exhibiting her body to fearful shame and ungainliness. The greater sexual openness of the

West at this time must surely be welcomed if only because it allows some simple natural enjoyments at a crucial time of life.

The fundamental shift of puberty comes with menstruation. This means not only 'the curse' with its worries about internal functioning, bleeding and mess but also its consequence – 'I can have a baby'. This, together with the general development of her genitals, means that a girl is likely to be swept with sexual feelings which can, of course, be delicious, disgusting or frightening depending on the girl. She cannot, from her past knowledge, have immediate means to deal with the new feelings, however nice they might be in themselves; they are new, with the result that some form of crisis is upon her.

For instance, in extreme cases, it is quite well known that some girls cannot bear themselves as menstruating women. Some get into competitive slimming and, when a serious level of starvation has been reached, their periods stop. In a pathological way, they have succeeded in returning to what appears to be a pre-pubertal asexuality. Other girls, also worried about their attractiveness, comfort themselves by overeating and succeed in keeping the boys away by being too fat.

A girl who is not worried in these ways usually finds herself fleetingly but powerfully attracted to boys and men. Being unsure of herself she usually resorts, to begin with, to dismissing them. Conversations with best friends may then be full of delight in how silly or ridiculous the boys are, but the fascination remains. As counterparts to these powerful attractions can be 'crushes' upon older girls or school mistresses, who seem to epitomize something *wonderful to be attained*. They are passionately *idealized*. On the other hand, the object of devotion may be a girl who has a child-like, non-sexual, innocence of some sort. It seems here that a girl may be in love with what she feels she is losing forever.

These crushes on females, which may only be fleeting or even virtually non-existent, are likely to be interspersed with bursts of passion for *part-aspects* of men or other boys. A boy is distantly loved 'for his red hair', 'his gentle face' or because of 'his firm voice'. This falling in *love with parts* is most publicly manifest, of course, in feelings about pop stars. In this we can hear the re-emergence of primitive modes of feeling and all-or-nothing emotions, they tend to infinity about simple aspects, parts or even bits of people. A similar sign of opening out into the *benign regression* in the normal crisis of adolescence can be detected, if less obviously, in a re-emergence of fleeting sexual feelings about parents. A father is quickly passionately loved and then equally violently, irritably scorned. A mother is bossily shouted at and then childishly made up to. Thus, we can see that the *very effort* of the strenuous efforts to distance from, and dis-identify with (or be as different as possible from) parents, both as individuals and as a couple, betray the opposing wishes without which the apparently withering hostility to the parents would become meaningless. It is hard to see how these moments can easily be captured and recalled save by living through them. Consequently, we should be not surprised if surveys often do not seem to grasp the emotional infinities of adolescence. Equally, it is hard to persuade a parent of an unruly teenager of the truth of their offspring's devotion. Yet, it appears true that parents' acorns do not fall far from the tree, however improbable this prophecy can appear in the heat, or immediate aftermath, of heated altercation. This, no doubt, is partly why Winnicott (1971) said that, with adolescents, we play for time.

Boys' ideas about their bodies

With boys too, the most marked personal feature of puberty is a genital excitability, which they do not know what to do with. A boy is usually swept away by crushes on part aspects of girls, their breasts, hair, smile or posture. Not knowing what to do with himself, he usually takes to switching to boisterous mucking about with his pals and jeering at girls. Homosexual crushes burst out about part aspects of boys or men. Sexual feelings towards parents come up and, as with girls, are usually brushed aside with embarrassment. His body will probably have grown several inches in a year and he does not quite know what to do with it. He tends to be ungainly and irritably shamefaced.

The body image and others

The consequence of puberty is, of course, a perceptibly changed body; and thus, *subjective body image*. These changes will be judged relative to peers but there seem to be differences between how boys and girls experience and evaluate early maturing of their bodies. Early-maturing boys seem to be more self-confident and popular and have more positive body images. These boys are reported to develop muscle and increased heart and lung capacity (and hence are better able to compete athletically); look more mature and feel more attractive (Simmons & Blyth, 1987). Early-maturing girls, by contrast, are not reported as achieving popularity or leadership amongst their peers (Brookes-Gunn, 1987; Dorn et al., 1988; Simmons et al., 1983) and it is thought that the high cultural evaluation of the pre-pubertal, long-legged thinness in females contributes powerfully to the greater confidence of late-maturing girls and girls' greater vulnerability to eating disorders (Leffert & Petersen, 1995). Most cases of anorexia nervosa, for example, arise during the teens or early twenties (Graham & Smith, 1985) at a time coincident with the phase of increased fat disposition. Whether it can then be concluded that cultural pressures, by themselves, can be assumed to have such powerful and destructive effects on some individuals, but not others, is more questionable unless something of greater relevance to the individual boy or girl, which will also be active, is taken into consideration. The question that we have to answer is why should a cultural value have such a destructive impact on some young people but not others. Something must powerfully differentiate young people and operate at the individual level and not the cultural.

The pubertal and adolescence

'Pubertal' is an unfamiliar word coined to translate the French word 'pubertaire', as distinct from 'puberté', meaning puberty. In Philippe Gutton's (1998) view, puberty is to the body what the pubertal is to the psyche. What does this mean? We have just reviewed the impact of the arrival of the changes of the sexual body at puberty and their apparently differential effects on the boy and girl. Gutton suggests that the meaning of these changes to the boy and girl will not confined to a changed body image or greater feelings of popularity and self-esteem but that there will be a new experience of the newly potent genitalia in relation to (or in phantasy in the presence of) the genitalia of the opposite sex. Thus, he quotes Freud (1923) who says, 'It is not until development has reached its completion at puberty that the sexual polarity coincides with *male* and *female*.' The real impact of what Gutton calls the pubertal is that puberty changes not just one's conception of one's own body but also our conception of the body of the opposite sex and ushers in the idea of the *complementarity* of the sexes. This idea of the complementarity of the sexes creates a discontinuity in the sexual development of the individual because for the first time there is a knowledge that that individual boy *or* girl can create a baby with a member of the opposite sex. The members of the two opposing camps can do something together; indeed, they need each other for that purpose. This is what Freud (1905) meant when he said that sexuality becomes organized under the primacy of the genitals and that it becomes altruistic.

Gutton (1998) continues, 'Pubertal pressure has the aim of separating phallus and penis. Once the penis has been separated from its phallic significance, the female sex is revealed in the place where phallic castration had been expected'. Again, what does Gutton mean by this? What 'phallus' means in this context is that it is the signifier of desire. It is not to be taken simply and concretely as an erect penis. It signifies, both to the owner and others, that *desire is being experienced*. It is easy, therefore, to understand a young adolescent's embarrassment about his erection because he feels it betrays what is in his mind in a manner outside his control. Although boys frequently experience erections and emissions of semen, the developmental task now is to incorporate the sense of their potent sexual bodies into their sense of themselves. The same task confronts girls with their newly arrived capacity to menstruate. Menstruation creates a new positive definition of a girl's identity.

Both sexes, therefore, have not only to incorporate the fact of their sexual bodies into their sense of themselves but also to incorporate *the possibility of a new potential relationship between themselves and a member of the opposite sex*. This is the consequence of *complementarity*. Perhaps it is this that is at the basis of the experience that something happens at, or around, puberty, which means, for the individual, life will never be the same again. This very private experience, which like masturbation probably occurs to most if not all, ushers in a radical change in the developing adolescent's experience of the parental relationship and the experience of peers of the same sex and the opposite sex. All this is experienced within the matrix of the newly arrived sexual body and newly acquired cognitive abilities of the mind. This points to the idea that adolescence represents a *discontinuity* in development in that the individual experiences the possibility and prospect of something new and radically different in their lives.

Evidence for discontinuity

So far, we have considered the impact of the newly mature sexual body and radically different cognitive abilities upon the individual. However, it is also true that various kinds of psychic and behavioural disturbance can be observed that occur with a marked increase of frequency from puberty onwards and which then decrease as adulthood beckons. This rise and fall suggests that something is occurring which is qualitatively different from before and after.

The main forms these disturbances take are in the various conduct disorders; eating disorders and schizophrenia; depression and associated suicide. These are serious disorders with potentially serious consequences for an individual's life (Graham & Rutter, 1985). While the percentage of adolescents developing disturbances requiring psychiatric assistance has been estimated at about 20%, the rise and fall in the frequency of incidence suggests that it cannot be assumed that these disturbances strike randomly within this age group. It seems to be true that they display the extreme end of reactions to the adolescing process that others, of the same age, negotiate without such worrying manifestations.

A developing identity in a new body

The impact of the arrival of the new sexual body has perhaps its most profound impact upon the adolescent's sense of him- or herself. Just as we noted that one of the important effects of the negotiation of the Oedipal phase was the establishment in the child's mind of a sense of morality, there is evidence of a profound modification in this aspect of the adolescent's mind. The latency child has had, given a favourable family setting and social environment, the chance to develop a good enough getting along with his social world to enable 'the age of industry' to unfold fruitfully. But puberty brings a severe jolt to this equilibrium, as we have already noted, which means that the basis of the equilibrium, which was essentially identification with the parents and what they stand for, must change if development is to occur. The tranquillity of latency is thus apparently replaced by tumultuous difference from and indifference to parental values. In the background, the moral agency, which was the legacy of the earlier Oedipal struggle, is also going through a similar recapitulation. This makes possible new states of mind for the adolescent, associated with an inward depressive preoccupation, which can seem quite withdrawn. Such states are not the same as depression, even if they can resemble it.

New-found physical and cognitive strengths, coupled with fresh re-perceptions of parents, siblings and friends, make possible new evaluations of the adolescent's impact on others and their capacity to hurt, both physically and psychically. The awareness that childhood is being left behind, never to return, gives rise to a sense of finitude and the possibility of death. Beckoning adulthood, with its abundant and yet daunting responsibilities and freedoms, is not therefore to be regarded by all adolescents as a totally unmixed blessing. The body, being both the message and the messenger of these changes, is therefore not surprisingly the arena in which the disturbances characteristic of adolescence are often played out.

Impulsive action is now possible as a means of expression in a new way but a failure to contain and control these actions can have implications more serious than before. Partly, this simply reflects the fact that young children cannot be convicted. However, self-report data suggest that there is also a substantial increase during adolescence in the amount and range of delinquent activities, although there is probably less change in the number of individuals engaged in anti-social behaviour (Shapland, 1978). Background factors clearly play a part before adolescence. For example, conduct disorders in childhood are strongly associated with reading difficulties, severe family discord and disruption. However, the correlation with these determining factors is not as strong with conduct disorders or delinquency beginning in adolescence (Robins & Hill, 1966; Rutter et al., 1976), which suggests that something else, not a feature of the adolescent's environment, is having an effect.

Both attempted and completed suicide shows a very marked increase during the mid-teens, having been extremely rare before the age of 12. The affective disorders (depression and mania) show the most dramatic increase over a comparable period. It has been suggested that the greater propensity of adolescent males to be conduct disordered hides the extent to which they experience depressive disturbances. Egeland and Hostetter's (1983) finding that males and females suffered depressive disorders to an equal degree in the Amish community – a community with a very low rate of delinquency – is consistent with this suggestion. Whatever the truth, it does seem that the onset of puberty creates the conditions for the marked rise in depression and suicide. However, it is important not to confuse depression with depressiveness, which is a feature that is more widespread and normal and which reflects a growing capacity for self-awareness.

Finally, the fact that drug addictions, schizophrenic psychosis and eating disorders typically have their onset during the teens and early adulthood, but are rare before puberty, again suggests that puberty creates the conditions for their emergence. The Laufers (1984) have shown that these severe manifestations of psychopathology can be considered as attempts to repudiate or deny the existence of the sexual body. This leads to their notion of developmental breakdown. The severity of these breakdowns reflects the extent to which these disturbances in development represent an adolescent's *psychotic break with the reality of the body*.

Perhaps one of the most difficult aspects to grasp of these young people's behaviour is the idea that when they attempt suicide or self-harm, i.e. they attack their own bodies, it is not necessarily the bodies that the external observer sees that they are, in fantasy, attacking. The lack of sympathy commonly felt by medical staff towards adolescents who attempt suicide repeatedly often reflects the hatred some adolescents can feel towards their own bodies. One very attractive young women made repeated attempts to kill herself as a result of the guilt she felt about having a healthy body while her younger sister was severely physically and mentally disabled and confined to a wheelchair. Her tragedy was that it was very difficult for her to be in touch with her own ordinary feelings of depressive misfortune without comparing herself with her much more unfortunate sister. As a result, she felt she had no right to be happy without feeling deeply unworthy.

Another young woman, who was very overweight, continually cut herself as a means of expressing her anger towards her very overweight and depressed mother, who had suddenly died when the young woman was in her mid-teens. Having had no present father or siblings from birth, this young woman had been left alone by her mother's death. Her very apparent reparative tendencies suggested a deeply unconscious sense of guilt about her mother's death. Thus, the continual self-harming satisfied the need to express hatred towards the abandoning mother and to inflict punishment upon herself for having failed to save her mother. But, to do this and keep her guilty feelings from consciousness, she had to equate her own body with her mother's. Hence, it was extremely difficult to separate and mourn her mother's death or to form a satisfying relationship with a man.

Getting organized

So far, we have seen that a great many factors have a bearing on the course that an individual's adolescing process takes and the overall shape of the individual that emerges into young adulthood in their early twenties. We have contemplated the initial effects of the onset of puberty and examined the hypothesis that this disorganizes the earlier structures developed since the emergence from the Oedipal period into what has been termed latency. We have looked at the ramifications that that this disorganizing has on the relationships with the adolescent's parents and peers. And, finally, we have seen that in normal development there is a continual to and fro between the drive towards adulthood and the mourning for lost childhood with the sense that its passing situates the individual in time and space in a generational way that is quite new to the adolescent.

About one in five find this process deeply troubling in the sense that they need professional help to negotiate these years, but there is good reason to think that most, if not all, will be firmly structured by their experiences in these years. Anna Freud (1958) felt that there was a difficulty in recapturing the experience of adolescence in an analysis, which suggests a kind of amnesia afflicting the direct recall of adolescent discontents. General and systematic surveys of adolescent experience by sociologists and psychiatrists lead them to believe that the psychoanalytic 'storm and fury' theory of adolescent is overdone and creates a distorted view of adolescence, starting from a baseline of pathology. Psychoanalysts will reply that reliance on the conscious recall of experience, coupled with the difficulty that many adolescents have in discussing their experience with anybody – let alone an adult – will achieve only a superficial glimpse of the adolescent experience. This is not to say that all adolescents are at risk of suicide but that all have to face certain tasks of adjustment that each must solve in their own unique way.

However, it can be said that at the emergence into young adulthood during the early twenties, the disorganization and disharmony of the teenage years has settled into something discernibly structured and organized. It often seems now possible to foresee the shape of how the adolescent will engage with the world of work, the kind of partner they will choose and the kind of moral and political stance they will take towards the world. Something organized, therefore, has emerged from the disorganization of the earlier years. Sometimes this seems to happen in a short period of time with the result that the individual concerned just does not seem to be the same person anymore. They have purpose, direction and grasp the means to achieve this purpose with both hands and with a new determination.

One aspect of the adolescent's life that we have not mentioned in great depth is their relationship with peers of the same or opposite sex. We have observed how the early adolescent boy, embarrassed by his new sexual attraction and attractiveness to girls, seeks refuge in a bantering denigration of these new figures of fascination with his former playground mates. They too have changed their function without his or their realization and have becomes allies in the confrontation with the representatives of the other sex. In a very significant way, they are figures to be like and thus *identify with* and a means of coping with the anxieties of confronting the *different other*. In a group, members have their markers of identity in the group 'uniform' (although woe be to s(he) who calls it such). More compliance is demanded by the gang, whose purpose is not just to manage the anxiety of encountering difference but also the envy and denigration of it.

An adolescent's peers play a crucial function in providing a space beyond the confines of the family and home to consider, contemplate and review the rigours of the encounter with the strangers they encounter in the world beyond home. In the UK in the last century, National Service provided this space in an institutionalized manner for most, regardless of class or ability. In some countries now, the same is true. Education is now the main institution providing this opportunity but, sadly, certainly unequally with regard to ability and, probably, also with regard to class. Nevertheless, it is within groups and institutions that adolescents find a way of being and working with others that enable them to transcend the self-conscious agonies and ecstasies arising from the arrival of their sexual bodies. Thus, others gradually recede in importance as being something with which to identify in order to face difference. Others become people *to be with* rather than *with whom to identify and hence to find one's own being*. This sets the stage for adolescents to find their effectiveness in the adult world through working and loving with others in full acceptance and welcome of their difference, as we shall now see.

Further reading

Coleman, J., & Hendry, L. (1990) *The Nature of Adolescence*, 2nd edn. London: Routledge.

Copley, B. (1993) *The World of Adolescence: Literature, Society and Psychoanalytic Psychotherapy*. London: Free Association Books.

Laufer, M., & Laufer, M.E. (1984) *Adolescence and Developmental Breakdown: A Psychoanalytic View*. Norwalk, CT: Yale University Press.

Perret-Catipovic, M., & Ladame, F. (1998) *Adolescence and Psychoanalysis: The Story and the History*. London: Karnac.

Van Heeswyk, P. (1997) *Analysing Adolescence*. London: Sheldon Press.

Chapter 10

Work, identity and love

James Rose

I must create a system or be enslav'd by some other man's
(from *Jerusalem* by William Blake)

We finished the last chapter on the theme of how an adolescent's peers seem to change in his mind from people to be *like* or, in other words, to identify with, to people to be *with* or *with whom to cooperate*. It was suggested that this sets the scene for the next stage in development, which is to move into adult modes of relationships with other people and to engage creatively with the world. Let us now turn to discovering and establishing oneself in the adult world through work and love. In France, Raymond Cahn (1998) uses the word 'subjectivation', which has been translated into English as 'becoming a subject', to try to capture this process of emergence from adolescence into young adulthood. By this he means that, in engaging with the external world, individuals can gather up their internal world of feeling and belief and incorporate it into their sense of themselves. Thus, a subjective sense of being (or an identity) emerges, which enables the individual (or subject) to stand, as it were, with a foot in both the internal and external worlds without one predominating over the other.

Naturally, the sequence of this development of subjective identity starting with adolescent internal crisis, followed by going out to work and then falling in love, often does not take place in this neat order. All three can be concurrent and interweave. Even so, the order has some meaning, for the break-up of childhood patterns of obedience, the acute adolescent crisis, must precede the finding of a solid work identity if the latter is to be felt as freely and deeply satisfying. Likewise, we will argue that people in our culture must have found an assurance about themselves to be alone and self-sufficient (through work particularly) if they are really to esteem themselves as worthy of the lasting commitment of another's love and bringing up children.

If you were to ask how one knows when this been achieved by someone, one way to tell is whether you find that in talking to that person that they seem to have become organized in a way that they weren't before. An impulsiveness of thought and a sense of compliance, or reaction, with or against you seems to have given way to something more balanced allowing the existence of two minds that can exist together effectively and happily rather there being an implicit, but constant, struggle. In short, they seem to talk to you in a different way.

I have used the words 'being' or 'identity' and 'individual' or 'subject' above to try to capture the emerging complexity of the young adult's experience or being and to set it apart from how this will create behaviour that will be experienced by others. Thus, we might say that a young person seems to have a new identity but he himself will say that he just feels different or, perhaps, more real (Winnicott, 1963). One way it is marked in social terms is by the idea of the achievement of the age of majority, which could be called the modern version of the *rite de passage* found in many societies, which marks the transition from childhood to the status of the adult in a given society. So marked can be this change that it suggests *that a new discontinuity has been negotiated.*

The move from school to work

In the main, education in the school system in Western culture as it stands at the moment, makes demands that have much in common for all pupils. But when young people leave school, and if employment is available, each individual finds a place and a kind of work that demands its own specific form of skill and presents its own satisfactions and burdens. Young people find themselves in less homogenous settings than school presented, with new expectations and privileges. But it would be a mistake to think of the individual young person as simply being passively moulded by the employment system. The individual's experience of work will be shaped by the opportunities of the work role and the capacities and inclinations that he brings to it.

Here is one young man describing the way he is received home by his mother now that he has started his apprenticeship. Note that he would have therefore been about 17:

> My tea is always ready when I get home from work – I never have to wait around for it like I did when I was at school. My mother used to say, 'You'll have it when it's ready, my lad' – but now she says 'Come on Roger, your tea's all cooked and ready for you'. And I get a bigger portion, too. (Carter, 1966)

Although this may read like a glimpse of an age now long gone, along with the 'rust belt' industries; testing ourselves in the adult world still takes place through the *effective contributions* we make to others. We can do this in a variety of situations, in friendships, love, hobbies, sport, home, local activities and movements, and in *money-earning work*. Money represents in real terms – not just symbolically, like pocket money – a flexible means of exchange. When a young person enters the economic system, he is in a position to earn money and then spend it. The young person as an economic being is borne; thus creating a youth culture. By this means, we have arrived straightaway at finance, hence inevitably to questions of economic policy. Whether we like it or not, we are in political issues. We are here because political responsibilities are thrust by society upon all individuals whether they want them or not. Some embrace them wholeheartedly; others ignore or reject them as they choose, but their impact cannot be obviated once the age of majority is attained.

I, as I imagine do most of the readers of this book, live in a Western, more or less capitalist and market economy. Here, among other things, people are rewarded *differentially* by *money* for their contributions. These differences in rewards can be grossly biased and hence hateful to many. In a market economy the financial rewards, for any given contribution, depend largely on its scarcity and the demand, or how much of it is wanted by those who have got money to spend. The intrinsic difficulty, danger, pain, responsibility, or cleverness required to do a particular job are not directly rewarded, only the extent to which that service or product is wanted by those with money to pay for it.

How far this system, centrally based on the desire to maximize financial profit, is the best one for people to live in is a very open question. In its pure form, it is a greed system based on paranoid notions of scarcity and demand. However, within this system, is a freedom for individual initiative, which is precious. But it often omits or devalues concern for others, relegating their care to a narrow, ineffective, private responsibility. Does not compassion warrant deep and wide social thought and political action at a community level? It must be of central public importance in close, highly populated nations. Perhaps a culture valuing at least some socialist ideals can be richer and happier than one controlled by a greed morality. But, what of its antithesis – has state socialism created happier cultures?

These are vastly important questions, which are beyond the scope of this book, to be explored in social, economic or political terms. We can only ask, and must go on asking about the psychological impact of these political questions whatever our work. But, even though this is not a political book, its subject still has a central function for political thought. Every human being is subject to a political system. The final measure of a system's justice and effectiveness must be made against the criterion of the personal experiences, happy or otherwise, of individual, conscious human beings. These issues are there to be faced by all young people, regardless of race, creed or culture, whether they consciously do so or not. As young people develop from the infantile ties to their parents, it is inevitable that the cockpit of these conflicts will be in these economic, political and philosophical arenas.

Political decisions can surely only validly be made with better knowledge of what brings individual happinesses and misery: and this book is of course, an elementary essay in this quest. Psychologists have long known that the so-called economic theory of what motivates people within the institution of employment is insufficient to account for all that is observed. Not only do individuals find their effective identities, as social beings, *through working with others*; they also achieve their subjecthood *by working with others* in relation to the exigencies of external reality and their own internal worlds. Money acts as a means, however imperfect, of enabling quite disparate activities to be compared and evaluated. It thus serves to be a crude medium of triangulation by which individuals can place themselves in a social system. However much we resent economic inequality, we are forced into the rigidities of the feudal system without money as a medium of exchange.

We can therefore see why, as things stand at present, *work* is often equated with *money-earning activity*. Money earning is now almost universal in the world in both socialist and capitalist societies. It has the great advantage for every individual in that *self-earned money* gives *freedom to choose* one's satisfactions, and the means to do so. It also permits individuals to stand independent from the family in deciding how some of their desires are to be met. However, money earning is a narrow definition of work because it relates to some of the ends achieved by the individual. If we broaden the definition of it in terms of *intentionally making effective contributions* to others, then conscientious unpaid service to family, friends or the public would be felt as work. This accords well enough with general usage.

What differentiates work from play is that one works for something more than immediate personal pleasure. Conscientious *discipline* is intrinsic to any work. It seems that work must be rewarded, not necessarily by money, but it is hard to conceive of a person going on disciplining himself for no recompense at all. Reward can often be from the knowledge of being useful, people's gratitude, pride of achievement, a little relief from fear of a tyrant, or even neurotic pleasure in suffering. But work without recompense of some kind is inconceivable. To work, therefore, is to be part of a social system. To play is to practice the intertwining of an individual's external and internal reality.

When going out from school or college, a young person is faced with a variety of situations: friendships, hobbies, sport, home, loves and, with luck, paid work itself. He has to assess intuitively his contributions to and satisfactions from all these in shaping the style of his life and finding a satisfactory sense of himself. This is done only half-consciously, probably in a blundering fashion, and is naturally often seriously avoided. But making an assessment of our contributions is centrally important to growing up; it takes *courage*. If he fails, a person is left flirting with self-deception, which results in a very shaky sense of self-esteem and integrity. Furthermore, these contributions involve effects on others, so the scrutiny of *conscience* plays a central part in this process of finding self-satisfaction.

But work also entails loss of freedom, of time if nothing else; to gain some freedoms, with money for instance, *sacrifice* is inevitable. Making *compromises* is essential to working out any adult style of life. Here are a few examples of older people reflecting about this in conversation:

I am a cowman of course, and it's good enough work. But politics is what stirs me. I wouldn't like it as a job, but it and I go well enough together.

In doing social work, I at last found I was happy. It was me. I couldn't imagine doing anything else. I relaxed, I suppose, in the evenings, but the middle of me was being a social worker.

In those days football and motors were my life. I wanted to become a professional, but my dad said I must really help in the shop. Being in a village with no-one else to do it I could see his point, so I said, right I'll do it, but Saturdays must be mine for football, and it was agreed. Later, I ran a taxi from the shop and everyone hereabouts came to me if their cars wouldn't go.

As well as sacrificing time, any kind of work entails varying degrees of skill and differing forms of *discipline* to master anxiety and hence the use of defences. For instance, a dustman has to master his disgust, a steeplejack his vertigo, and a teacher has to master class discipline. A lorry driver must keep anxiety within bounds but maintain enough to be vigilant. And amongst many other controls, a nurse must restrain her fear of causing death while still having it available in her caring; she needs to be friendly but to check her sexiness; must be immaculately clean but not give way to disgust or nausea. You will by yourselves easily be able to specify what disciplines and defences are important in other sorts of job (Smelser & Erikson, 1980; Stevens, 1979; Terkel, 1985; White, 1975). Think of some jobs and try it for yourself. All jobs have their *satisfactions* (their rewards, financial and personal); their *difficulties* (i.e. what makes them hard to do and what you have to learn in order to do them) and their *distastes* (i.e. what it is about them that makes them unpleasant to do). We can see from the quotations above how the speakers' work went toward defining for these people who they think they are and how much what they do is 'them'.

Creativity, responsibility and authority

When the young person enters the workplace, the psyche-soma of their individuality meets the sociotechnical of the external world in a new way. By this I mean that the emerging subject, or a mind in a body, is in a place that can be thought of as a technical, which is also a social, system, whose task it is to transform material of some kind into something else. In a petrol station, for example, empty fuel tanks are changed into full ones and emptied as the petrol is sold to passing trade. In a coalmine, coal is brought to the surface. In schools, pupils enter in state of ignorance and, hopefully, as time passes and given effective teachers and a facilitating learning environment, they learn and eventually pass into the adult world. The technical processes exist in a social system with supervisors, colleagues, management and possibly trade unions. Taken as a whole, the young person enters a complex system of authority and has much to learn. How he copes has much to do with how he has experienced learning in the past and the extent to which he can draw on experience of past achievement.

When a person settles into any job he will find varying degrees of *repetition*, together with opportunities for *creativity and responsibility*. Let us consider some of the personal strains and satisfactions involved in these. We are particularly thinking of paid work now. Although automated processes, resulting from new technology, have replaced much large-scale repetitive work in conveyor belt assembly; all jobs entail much repetition, even the most creative. Even with robots and computers, offices, factories and farms demand millions of man-hours of mechanical boredom allied to the minimum of creative interest. *The essence* of *repetitive* work lies in speed of movements carried out time and again without variation. From the personal point of view, *choice of action* is excluded once the skill has been mastered. This seems to constitute the drudgery of repetitive work more than gross physical toil. Just as a child does, the adult mind seems to need exploration and variety for its satisfaction; when a task cannot be invested with imagination intolerable boredom is likely to set in.

Much work, fortunately, requires a great degree of choice. Thus a fitter has more choice as to how to go about a task than a data-entry clerk. The greater the freedom of invention, the more *skilled* does the individual have to be. This entails self-disciplined sacrifice of idiosyncratic whims. For, like a mother with a newborn child, the worker has to submit himself to the limits of his tools and material. But, after perhaps years of self-discipline, the individual, his body and his materials have formed a sort of unity. Here we see a strange outcome of self-discipline: so that self, tools and materials become almost the same. This gives rise to the possibility of creativity and a sense of personal authority.

A person's skill will, then, be a pleasure to perform and a beauty to watch, and his products of high quality. *Art* requires skill and more besides, it starts with a person becoming 'at one' with or the same as his object and materials. To be good he must lose himself in them. This recalls the loosening of the boundaries of the self, referred to frequently in previous chapters. And then, as also mentioned, the creative artist tries to allow a personal abstract vision to arise, which he reproduces. It is usually only after years of devoted practice, when he is master of himself and at one with his materials, that this is possible (Milner, 1957).

Skill and art can, of course, be present in anyone's everyday work, paid or not. It will be tainted, however, when one cannot be bothered, or have not the time to develop mastery, so one has to make do with unsatisfactory, botched-up jobs. It is of interest to note that skill and truthfulness have much in common because learning involves taking careful account of feedback. If our pride prevents us from recognizing the truth of our ignorance and mistakes, then our learning will be impaired. A skilled worker knows truthfully about his materials and their functions. A bodger makes much *pretence* of knowledge. In the end, his deceit can then, of course, be towards himself as much as to any customer. He is being irresponsible towards his customer and undermining his ability to find his own authority.

Both repetition and creativity were exercised in school, so they will not be new to the working adult. But full *responsibility* for a task upon which other people depend will be relatively new. Responsibility for a task means being entrusted with its successful completion. You will remember how the infant first needed to trust his environment and then began to trust himself. With this he began to be responsible for his own functioning. By adulthood, however, other people will expect to put their *trust in* him. They will become like infants, as it were, in his hands during the period of the task he has to perform for them. Thus passengers need to trust their driver, house owners their plumber, and patients their nurse. The experience of being trusted in this way contributes to the individual finding their authority.

The individual's sense of responsibility involves knowledge of the task to be carried out. It also requires other *foundations*. His *conscience* must be operating so that he recognizes the existence of others and feels *concern* about his effect on their well-being. This operates to inhibit impulsiveness or withdrawal from the reality of the task. It requires *continuity*, sticking at the task no matter what personal impulses arise. Lastly, it involves *anticipation* of possible trouble and disasters. The responsible person must be able to tolerate anxiety about possible *faults*, both in themselves and in the situation at hand. Only then can he realistically watch over it. The exercise of responsibility has great satisfactions.

The individual is master of the situation and is also being *parental in the sense of accepting responsibility for the conduct of affairs in that sphere on behalf of others*. This involves burdens of personal anxiety and guilt. To be responsible, a person must use his feelings without being overwhelmed by them or being carried away into egocentric fantasy. Each task provokes its own particular anxieties, which some people can bear while others cannot. For instance, an individual may find that anxiety about heights is too much to contain, so he would not make a good airline pilot. On the other hand, his anxiety about vomiting, death and damaging others may easily be under control, so that being a doctor would be quite tolerable. Many tasks involve no direct responsibility for other people's well-being. But all jobs involve it indirectly.

To quote from a study of the transition from school to work by Bazelgette (1978):

> The patterns of work in all the firms studied involved young employees in collaborative relationships with colleagues and supervisors. That is to say, in work, a person joined a team, which was usually striving to achieve something. The young person's part might be small in itself, but the goal for the team called for something from everyone. In the school 'work' was an individual activity and one's success was assumed to be principally a function of one's own effort, though some feeling of teacher's efforts having some influence on the pupils was common and understandable. There was also a feeling that the product of working in employment was tangible: one could see a stud completed, recognise an assembled relay, appreciate a completed sale. More than this, it did not take a great feat of imagination to envisage how some of the parts fitted together to make an intelligible whole: as the operator said at Reliable Engineering 'if it were not for what we make, cars would fall to bits on the road'.

This description of the growth of responsibility will probably take away some of its possibly pedantic and dull connotations. Its essence does carry a necessary solemnity. It entails conserving and is thus, as it were, conservative. And in many ways it is antithetical to romantic exploration and personal creativity. It is perhaps the loss of romantic freedom that makes responsibility loathsome to many people, young and old; they seem to associate it with dullness and hence deadness. Perhaps they are frightened too, not only of depression, but also of possible guilt. Balanced against this is the sense of being part of an essential whole in the external world ('if it weren't for us the cars would fall to bits') and this perception of being in a structure reflects a capacity for internal structuring which is taking place in the young person's mind. *Hence we see something being organized internally and externally at the same time.*

Being responsible is also burdensome because one often has to direct other people who are likely to be oppositional and revolt against orders. It is perhaps these factors that make some people carrying heavy responsibilities feel that they deserve high recompense, both in large salaries and luxurious perks. In addition, a person apparently weighed by responsibility can also, often quite unconsciously, gratify his yearning for omnipotence by playing covert ruthless games. For responsibility does carry with it power over other people's lives. Politicians, particularly, are notoriously prone to indulge in ruthless power games even though they frown with the burden of their immense responsibilities.

But some people can carry responsibility with a quiet naturalness. It need not be flashy but can be deeply enjoyable. Its steady working, with self-scrutiny to watch out for insidious ruthless games, is essential to the good working of our, or any, society. It is a must in parenthood, unless we are unconcerned about shattering the growth of those we have brought into the world. Self-scrutinizing responsibility is the keystone of helping professions: here it needs cherishing because it can so easily be swamped by histrionic or paranoid game playing. Perhaps these professions could more forthrightly lead in responsibly cultivating a climate of understanding of individual predicaments in life.

The sense of the dull conservatism of responsibility may arise if there is a belief that responsibility is so directed to meeting others' needs that fulfilling one's own needs are obviated. However, if creativity, with its regression, romance, and madness, is not kept alive throughout our lives then we neither have the means to change ourselves nor can we provide the environment for others to change. We become either very dull, shrunken people unable to face crisis, or arthritic martinets, self-satisfied with power and unable to be either humble or flexible. We become committed to be conservative without thinking and we fail to look inward as a means to respond to the challenges of the external.

If responsibility has negative connotations, so too does the notion of authority with its inevitable association with authoritarianism. However, it seems to me that to be authoritarian is essentially an abuse of one's authority because it suggests that authority is being confused with power and being used to dominate others. The authoritarian personality (Adorno et al., 1982) essentially uses his social position to project his own despised parts into others who can then be victimized, as the Nazis persecuted the Jews. A person who acts with authority is someone quite other than this because he can act creatively and appropriately as the situation demands in relation to others. To do this effectively requires a consciousness of one's own skills, temperament and limitations in the context of an awareness of the exigencies of the situation and the needs of others.

The study by Bazelgette (1978), referred to above, of the transition from school to work carried out in the early 1970s pointed to the unconscious hostility expressed by adults to young people. Bazelgette suggested that this hostility can be quite covert. 'Few adults are angry towards the young to their faces. What we do is to construct situations which effectively imprison them and impede their transition to full autonomy and responsibility.' He pointed out the profound difference in the nature of the role of being a pupil and being an employee. A school pupil is not expected to make any contribution to the survival of the school by his individual effort, in contrast to the contribution, however minimal, that the young employee makes. It is also obvious that the ratio of adults to young people is far smaller in school than in working life. The opportunity for young people to learn from adults about authority and responsibility was consequently far smaller at school. With a large proportion of young people passing from the non-adult world of school to the similarly non-adult world of unemployment, we should perhaps not be surprised at the growing occurrence of the so called psycho-social disorders.

Identity

We have just been considering the young person, if he is lucky, facing the situations of paid work, friends, family and leisure. Here each specific activity can be considered as a *role*. At any one time a person has a multiplicity of these. When, and if, he has found a *personal patterning of these roles*, and where the emotionally charged contradictions between them have been more or less disentangled, which then *together give him inner satisfactions, he then usually experiences a sense of wholeness and well-being*. This integration is often referred to as *adult identity*. It emerges as a result of repeated experiences of the effective exercise of personal authority in meeting responsibility, which gives rise to this sense of wholeness and well-being. Because this learning necessarily takes place over time, an individual, through the exercise of authority in relation to the responsibility for others, becomes rooted as a temporal being. Hence, an intrinsic element of the notion of identity is its continuity over time.

This identity, although delimited by forces of one's culture, as well as inheritance, is essentially idiosyncratic and private to each individual (Erikson, 1963, 1968; Lichtenstein, 1977; Lynd, 1958; Smelser & Erikson, 1980). We have been slowly leading up to this concept of identity, particularly when we have been stressing that the honest scrutiny of our conscience is essential in finding *integrity*. For it is by self-scrutiny that we assess and balance the enjoyments of our own life with those of others. We have stressed many times that this conscience seems to be born in the experiences of infancy and is readily shattered, distorted, and impoverished. It is for this reason, perhaps beyond all others, that psychoanalytic therapists are often so concerned about the early years of life.

In previous chapters we have also stressed the importance of intellect, particularly its logical activity, in emotional development. We have, for instance, suggested that *emotions may be viewed as thoughts that are not yet fully formed*. We can now see that the desire to be logical with stress on non-contradiction and hence consistency, plays its part in the integration of the self's identity. We may always have to negotiate conflicts and contradictions in our life roles but, without a truthful awareness of them, we cannot realistically feel we have integrity.

Erikson's idea of identity, although of quite recent origin in systematic thought, has now become part of our everyday language. We thus hear of work identity, sexual identity, class identity, racial identity and national identity. Because these concepts have entered into everyday thought so quickly and powerfully, they must reach deeply into us and must deserve serious consideration, argument and books of their own. We can only draw attention to them here and point out that they are slightly different from the overall individual self-identity we have just introduced. Sexual, racial, national, class, and work identities refer to the individual's feeling of belonging to certain groups as distinct from others. A person must experience a multiplicity of such identities for he belongs to several of these groups at once. They are, as it were, sub-identities of a person's overall feeling of being himself, his self-identity.

Residues of childhood

Even though a person assumes the responsibilities of being an adult, and his childhood-dependent attitudes slip into the background, this does not mean that they have died within him. The childish parts of himself must remain active, often unconsciously. When unassimilated into one's present life their insistent repetition may make one prone to *neurotic symptoms* of one kind or another. We cannot discuss this fully here but a little introspection will probably make it plain to the reader that there are urges in himself which continue more or less unchanged from his own childhood. Here are a couple of illustrations:

A young boy was brought up in the country. His father ran a progressive boarding school, which was regarded with some suspicion by the local people. The boy's mother cared little about this, and ran her family with a back-to-nature philosophy. Her pigs, goats, hand-loom weaving and homemade pots were unusual and were laughed about in the neighbourhood. The young boy grew up isolated from the local children, though he went to school with them. He was baffled by them and envied their conventional toys and games, so that he rarely felt at ease to join them. When he grew up he became a schoolmaster like his parents. His resemblance to them seemed to end there, for he went to work in a city and was more conventional in his ways. He was respected and very well liked, so that he quickly became head of a department. However, as soon as he cast off his professional mantle he was crippled with shyness. He could not bring himself to be at all intimate with others in the neighbourhood. When not at work, people outside his family seemed like a race apart. They were experienced as looking askance at him just as they had done years before.

We can see in this example how childhood and early adolescent relationships with peers were repeated as this man sought to find a way of both identifying and disidentifying with his parents. It seems that the lack of contact with peers interfered with his capacity to find his identity beyond the parental model in the occupational sense and profoundly affected his ability to form social relationships in his adult life.

In this next example, we can only, in truth, speculate on the forces that propelled the boy out of the home at a comparatively young age and why the prospect of failure brought him close to suicide. However, this example is given to illustrate how we might think how an individual's history is incorporated into a developing idea of an occupational role, which gives powerful expression to that person's idea of himself as an adult. This organization of a young person's history replicates the organization of the instincts discussed in the last chapter:

Another boy, many years ago, was one of the elder of many children. He was very fond of his mother, but each year brought another birth, so that he had but little of her company. He took this stoically, and in fact became particularly admired by his family for his bravery both at home and in childhood exploits. His mother died when he was 10 and his father struggled on alone to bring up the family. Two years later the young boy said he wanted to relieve his father of one mouth to feed and was determined to join the Navy. His father gratefully accepted this further demonstration of bravery.

When he was 18, after six years at sea he fell ill and was invalided home from the East. In the ship on the way back he seems to have gone through an acute adolescent crisis. He became aware that he had no future in the Navy, and could see no way of life that would fulfil him. He wondered whether to throw himself overboard and finish it all. Then a 'radiant orb was suspended in his mind's eye'. He exclaimed, 'I will be a hero and, confiding in providence, will brave every danger'.

Later in adult life this is just what he did. As Lord Nelson, he became the brave hero not only to his family, but to England at large and to succeeding generations of schoolboys.

In both these examples, which are both from the past, we can see elements of adult identity. These are both creative and neurotic at the same time but, nevertheless, organized into a subjective identity. Perhaps Nelson, in leaving home to go to sea, was unconsciously searching for his dead mother as well as making room for others at home. When illness catastrophically threatened to sever him from the Navy, suicide seemed to be an option. But then the idea of 'confiding in providence' was a new avenue to his mother, which incorporated the fact of his mother's death. Later on, Nelson's heroism was close to suicide but it was inspiring heroism none-theless. We might say that providence, or kismet, had its final word at Trafalgar because of his insistence of effectively offering himself as a target to the French snipers. However, it is possible to suggest that Nelson had found a way of incorporating his devotion for his beloved mother and compensating for his resentment of his siblings in the manner of his life and the manner of his death.

Compromise and adult identity

Throughout adult life, demands to *conform* to other people's requirements are continually impressing themselves upon the individual. At the same time, he has his own inner wishes, so that conflict becomes inevitable. If a person is to maintain an integrity of his personality, he has to make *compromises* between his own wishes, his conscience, and demands of the outside world. It seems that integrity is lost when chronic *splitting* with denial of emotions occurs, so that one set of interests obliterate others. Fanaticism is one instance of this, and a person preoccupied only with himself is another. So, too, would be someone who surrenders himself totally to others' demands. For example, compare these two men, both bank managers:

Mr A. was highly esteemed by his superiors and customers. However, his whole life was consumed by his bank. He had no hobbies. People were invited to supper on the basis of their business connections, His family life was invaded by ideas and strictures about the bank, He would say to his wife, 'You mustn't wear trousers in the front garden because customers pass'. Or, 'You should order your groceries from Jones's because they bank with us', and so on. In submitting to the bank he was unable to enjoy either his own bodily functioning or the inner lives of his wife and family. He repeatedly fell sick and his wife, failing to make an impression on him by ordinary means, soon found herself turning into a chronically hysterical individual. Although esteemed by many, he had failed to go through the agony of making an integrating compromise between the various demands of his situation.

Mr B. was actively interested in athletics, music and literature when young, but went into the bank to earn a living. When quite an old man he said, 'I often thought I would leave the bank and do something that directly interested me more, but I fell in love and decided that getting married was the more worthwhile. And to do this I had to stay in the bank.' However, he did not forget the expression of his inner life. He continued to be a reader, talker and musician in his leisure time. 'The bank was satisfactory in a way. It was secure, and looking after people's affairs was interesting. But everyone knew my heart was in other places as well, and because I wasn't married to the bank, I didn't get far up the ladder.' Here we see evidence of making compromises, but not of losing self-integrity.

We see in Mr A. a common form of fanaticism, although it is not usually graced by this term; he was obsessed by ambition and conformity to banking. Mr B. on the other hand, tried to evaluate the various aspects of his life and sought to compromise between them. Because of this, he may have suffered the fate of being thought ordinary, but no-one would say he was a nonentity and many were glad to have known him. Mr A. *compromised himself*, he lost his integrity by denying so many parts of himself. Mr B., on the other hand, *made compromises*. The course through adult life seems to be a continuous compromise between conflicting issues. As new situations arise, so the individual is called upon to develop new patterns of thought, to find new compromises, which will maintain his own and others' integrity. It seems that many people muddle these two meanings of compromise. They think a person who makes compromises is a weak or flawed character. This is plain foolishness, of course, and tacitly gives assent to fanaticism.

Is adult identity continuous ?

Some writers seem to think that once an adult identity has been founded, in the mid-twenties say, this should remain set through life. Even Erikson, to whom we are indebted for introducing the concept, often seemed to imply it. It may have been true when life was short and societies relatively static. But even a cursory glance at lives today points to the many shifts or roles, often of a funda- mental kind, that individuals have to develop through life. A woman, for instance may leave school, genuinely find her indepen- dence through being a secretary, then fall in love, marry and forget all about her previous work in engrossing herself in mothering. When the children go to school and grow away from her, she may find herself dissatisfied with married dependency and seek a new, paying career which offers more personal creative satisfactions than a secretarial office. So she becomes a student again, trains and gives herself a pattern of responsibilities she has not known before.

All these require change and development of adult identity, and each change is likely to be a life crisis of greater, or less propor- tions. This being so, the individual must expect to proceed through a break-up of old patterns, loosening into regression and testing new modes of competence of a similar form to that of 'adolescing'. Cahn's concept of 'becoming a subject' differs from Erikson's concept of identity in that it suggests that the individual's capacity or sense of his subjectivity is developing throughout his life. It may be said *to be felt by the individual* as beginning in adolescence because of the gradual loosening of the infantile ties in early adolescence. But later crises can often be even more searching than the teenage shifts. It is for this reason that so much time is spent during adolescence around the second individuation process required by puberty; but the process of becoming a subject will, hopefully, be repeated, with modifications, at any time of life.

A young man, who was treated in psychotherapy for several years, started his therapy when in his late teens at the recommendation of the counsellor at the sixth form college he had been attending. He said that he was lacking in confidence and felt very anxious in the presence of other people. He had been living with his maternal grandmother for the past 5 years. The significant facts of his family history were that his mother had suddenly left the family home when he was 8. He and his brother had lived with his father for a while. Their father then remarried and they all tried to live together until the situation broke down. The young man moved to his grandmother's flat when he was 13. This was experienced as very difficult and consciously he had little but contempt for his step-family, seeing them as superficial. It was this contempt, of course, that he saw in others towards him. The dominant features of the therapy were the extreme sensitivity he felt about the ends of sessions and holiday breaks and his yearning for male figure with good authority.

When this young man began his treatment he had been unemployed. He soon obtained work as a delivery boy for a manufacturing company. In the first year of therapy he re-established contact with his father, from whom he had been estranged for 5 or more years. Then he moved from delivery to a more creative job in the company employing him, which was accompanied by a quantum shift in his perception of himself. He had now, he thought, a chance of becoming normal and adult. One of the most significant features of this period was that he claimed to give up smoking cannabis, to which he had been apparently quite habituated.

This paved the way for him to find and visit his mother again, whom he discovered not to be the violent heartless bully of his fantasies, but actually depressed herself. This was a shock to him because it upset all the fantasies he had built up to rationalize what had happened to him. This new mother did not fit the violent mother who had left him and whom he felt hated him. It put in question his fear of women and then it began to be revealed that he often watched pornographic cable TV and visited massage parlours for 'relief'. He could now see that his fear of women arose from his hatred of women, and in particular of his mother. What was especially interesting was the belief that developed in him that he needed to stay in contact with his mother to enable him to have a relationship with a woman. The relationship with his mother went through many ups and downs. In any event, the gradual repair of this relationship indeed enabled him to think instead about having a relationship with a girl, which he successfully achieved. At the conclusion of our work, this relationship was firmly established, as was his continued occupational success.

We can see in this account the complex interweaving of the young man's developing sense of his creativity as he progressed occupationally and through his developing sense of himself as an adult. We also see how the untangling of his relationship with his mother enabled him to develop an adult sexual relationship. This paves the way for our next topic. So, now let us turn to the other fundamental of young adulthood, in our culture in the late twentieth century at least; the development of sexual orientation and falling in love.

Falling in love

In our society, when the subject of sexual love arises, the issue of marriage and parenthood is not far away. Turning our minds back to previous chapters, the whole sequence of the history of erotic development through life will be recalled. First came the baby's erotic love with his mother and the necessity for harmony and synchrony between them for healthy physical and mental growth. Then came frustrations of this love, easily evoking experiences of extreme distress and hence mad rage. At this time, also, intellectual events were readily accompanied by gross physical reactions. Thus the whole complex web of meaningful enjoyment, puzzlements, frustrations, rage and despair that a child felt, with his mother in particular, was interwoven with his eroticism.

In other words, meaningful adult love and eroticism have roots in the mother–child relationship and their bodies together. This was continued in conflicts over social and bodily control in the second year of life. Then, though less obviously, the joys and conflicts of the child about his parents seemed to be sensitively focused upon genital urges and fantasy, which was epitomized by the Oedipus complex. With growth into relative independence and going out into the company of other children, the child seemed to be less erotically attached to his parents and assumed a certain detached dignity; latency had set in. Although he was easily aroused and sexually curious, there were probably few major changes of sexual feeling until puberty. At this point the arousal of the genitals and body growth insist that a child is a sexual being like his parents.

This acted as the trigger to the adolescent sequence, which, if successful, culminated in the ending of dependent expectations about parents. We have noted that the first directly sexual feature of an adolescent's turning away from parents is crushes on other people. These tend to have a disconnected and primitive all-or-nothing quality about them. They are passions for *parts of people* or *abstracted* physical characteristics: for instance, firm mouth, mellow lips, copious breasts, or the way a head is held. These are physical attributes, but they usually also symbolize *personal characteristics.* For instance, a firm mouth reminds the adoring one of 'determination', mellow lips suggest 'sensuousness', copious breasts evoke ideas of 'generosity', and so on. They are *physical metaphors*, rather like *dream symbols* in which physical attributes also stand for more psychological functions. This contention is supported by the fact that physical attributes are not the only things adolescents fall in love with. Psychological characteristics of a person are often quite explicitly felt as objects of passion. Although the form that this can take is apparently subject to almost infinite variation, it seems to be a key fact that, by the time an individual has reached his early twenties, sexual orientation becomes largely fixed.

If so, we have encountered another discontinuity, which is now thought to be influenced by psychic and biological factors (Friedman & Downey, 1993). However, the experience of this process of unfolding object choice is one of the most significant in any person's life. Whatever its determinants, each individual's experience of the process is unique and must be respectfully treated as such if we are to gain access to its secret mysteries. The fact is that, for some, object choice is for someone of the opposite sex (heterosexual) and, for others, the choice is for someone of the same sex (homosexual). Why this should be is far from clear – all we can really be sure of is that it is the case. Here are one or two examples of young people's reflections about their loves:

> I am in love with Jacques more than anyone, it is I think because he, like I, is half in love with death (15-year-old)

> I love Dean, he is nothing but pure kindness (14-year old)

> I only fall for hard men. I think it is because they are the only ones who could stand my violent temper (17-year-old)

Why are these *abstracted parts of a person's character* fallen for with such deep personal meaningfulness? The girl who gave the last example gives a clue. She sensed she needed someone to control the rages she could not manage herself. She *fell in love with a characteristic* she felt *deficient in herself*. This tallies well with the age-old saying of, *'Falling in love with your other half'*. This stems from Greek mythology, which held that man had originally been happily whole but, later, one-half of the soul had become separated from the other. Thus mortal men were always incomplete, searching for their other half.

If at least one aspect of falling in love is towards a characteristic we feel deficient in, then we would expect that a person would feel extremely humble compared to his adored one. Idealization would be a facet of love. This is certainly the case. You will remember how love and idealization loosens one's conscious experience of emotions so that awareness of limits or boundaries between things become emotionally blurred. One feels towards infinity. The loved one is all goodness and beauty and the world itself is infused with beauty too. So the loved one *is* beauty, which at the same time is *in* all the world. It is, of course 'quite mad', this 'infinitizing' of things. But if one has, in some sense, experienced it, if only once, life seems to have been worth living.

However, this sort of level of loving is experienced in an all-or-nothing way. This being so, we would expect even slight misunderstandings to lead a humble lover to switch to violent hatred at being betrayed. This is certainly likely to happen with immature crushes. They are *unstable*, what is more, since idealization of the loved one tends to *deplete* self-esteem, a lover readily becomes explosively envious. Obviously this is not a complete unravelling or understanding of the crush. The girl quoted above who was in love with Jacques, for instance, said she loved him because he was *like herself* 'half in love with death'. Here she had found a comrade in her suffering, the two, alienated from the rest of humanity as they saw it, could understand and comfort each other like babes in the wood. Only when the *idealization is reciprocated* does this self-depletion receive a counterbalance of idealization of the self. But this state of affairs does not create an enduring stability. In thinking about object choice, we have to distinguish between a choice based on finding something missing or lost to the self in someone else from one in which the choice is based on finding something that not only complements the self but makes possible the achievement of something that cannot be done by the self alone. The obvious example is given by a man needing a woman to create a child *and vice versa*. Each cannot, alone, achieve this but together they can.

These motives for attachment give positive lines of inquiry into the riddle of why one person falls in love with another. There is, of course, another aspect to the riddle, which concerns why some people fall in love with someone of the opposite sex whereas others fall in love with someone of the same sex. These lines of enquiry are not exhaustive but are, I hope, at least a start.

At this stage we have simply discriminated some types of characteristics that can be fallen in love with, and of course they could belong to a person of either sex. In 'adolescing', apart from social pressures, movement of love for a person of one sex to love for the other is usually fluid, at least at the level of fantasy. But we have so far described only the crush, the first stage of being in love. Let us proceed to the second where the fantasy crush generates a real two-person relationship. An indisputable fact of sexual development is that some arrive at a homosexual choice and others a heterosexual one. This fact is, however, particularly hard to explain. There is equally no doubt that the homosexual object choice has aroused strong condemnation in some societies, whereas others seem quite tolerant and accepting.

We shall consider homosexual choice first (Chasseguet-Smirgel, 1980; Riutenbeck, 1973; Rosen, 1979; Tieffer, 1983; West, 1960), and then heterosexuality (Geer et al., 1984; Masters & Johnson,

1966; Scharff, 1982; Schofield, 1973, 1976; Shor & Sanville, 1978; Tiefer, 1983; Tunnadine, 1983).

Gay or male homosexual love

According to some people, homosexuality falls into the category of a perversion. That is because the man's genital does not find orgasm within the genital of a female partner; a part of another man's body is used instead. The genital act cannot then be thought of as being in the pursuit of reproduction and thus the instincts have not moved from being auto-erotic to being altruistic. This was essentially Freud's (1905) definition of what is perverse. These days, however, the medical (or psychopathological) view of homosexuality is no longer seen as being as liberal as it once was when it sought to replace the religious judgement that homosexuality was evil. Today, there is little consensus about homosexuality; it is being reassessed, partly in political terms because of gay liberation, partly in sophisticated interdisciplinary analyses of the development of gender, heterosexuality and homosexuality. Some say that it makes more sense to talk about the homosexualities rather than homosexuality as a specific condition. However, this new 'liberalism', which seeks the 'modernisation of sex' (Robinson, 1989), often avoids in its turn certain difficult questions: the prevalence or meaning of leather, sado-masochism, prostitution and other forms of hustling, cross-dressing, effeminacy or hypermasculinity, and drag balls in the male homosexual sub-culture. One will, of course, find aspects of heterosexual behaviour that is similarly 'perverse' in flavour.

If we take a purely biological stance, we may assume that humans have biological urges to reproduce like all other animals. Thus we could be said to have biologically determined urges to have heterosexual reproductive intercourse. Those who argue from this to say that it is inconceivable that homosexuality could have any genetic aetiology will find their position undermined in two ways. First, genetic determinants do not always function in a way that obeys what is apparently common sense. Second, it is not true that homosexual couples avoid taking responsibility for children and seek to establish family units. They do. The new technologies of pregnancy make viable what would have been inconceivable even two decades ago.

What seems apparent in homosexuality, whether male or female, is a *revulsion* against the heterosexual act and this seems profound. What is more, the revolt, either in terror or disgust, must be primarily against the idea of the penis in relation to a woman's genitals. Usually, almost any physical contact with a woman is avoided in homosexuality, but the main dislike is the idea of the penis within a vagina. We must note, however, that women *as people* are not necessarily disliked by homosexual men; it is the *sexual arousal in relation to them* that is. Here, however, there are usually fears of the most fantastic kind. We cannot go into this in detail but it is worth noting that *paranoid anxieties* are usually not far away. Consequently, something psychologically very intense must be happening.

In the last chapter, I referred to the growing awareness of the complementarity of male and female genitals that develops in early adolescence and the new relationship to the parent's sexuality that results. It could be said that something about this complementarity is fiercely avoided. Close to the revulsion against 'penis in vagina' very often goes an *idealization of the penis*. This may involve a desire for a man to admire his own penis or it may be to adore another's. It is not universal, but penis adoration is an important aspect of many 'gay' cultures. 'My dear, whole lives have been wasted chasing dick', says a character in Holleran's (1983) *Dancer from the dance*, summing up the loss of life that can follow upon this preoccupation. Close to this is often a profound enjoyment of physical make-believe. This involves the playing of 'male' and 'female' roles in sexual partnerships with the anus standing in for the vagina as often as not. This, again, is not universal in homosexuality but it does point the way to the importance of anal excitement and fantasy in much male homosexuality. If we remember how discipline and control are intimately related to primitive anal fantasies, then we can wonder whether homosexuality also seems to involve a revolt against certain levels of discipline. This seems to be implicit in Foucault's (1983) position, which seems to suggest that apparently deviant forms of sexual behaviour represent efforts by some to establish their identity against the prevailing 'norm'. This can look to be supported by the observation that the behaviour itself is a revolt against ordinary biological ways. Whatever the facts are about the aetiology of homosexuality, we can readily see that sexuality, like money, takes us into the political. Let us therefore consider an example of the experience of homosexual love.

To get the flavour of a homosexual love, here is a brief description of such a choice. It is anecdotal and can do no more than create further lines of enquiry. However, a feature to note is the gathering sexual organization directed at finding an object to achieve the satisfaction of the sexual drives. But we should not assume that the structure of these drives, because they must be conceptualized partly as being physiological, must be directed solely in the service of reproduction – to become altruistic, as Freud said. The particular form the organization takes will reflect the individual's sexual history from birth. The fact that some individuals make same-sex object choices and others choose the opposite sex makes the assessment of what is 'normal' very problematic. This can be seen from this example of a young man's sexual development:

A young man had, since earliest childhood, been preoccupied with the necessity of pleasing people. His father said he seemed very happy and very clever when a little boy. If there was anything wrong it was that he was too good! He got on well with his father, who was sensible and quiet. He doted on his mother, who histrionically lavished adoration on him. The company of many old ladies, whom his mother also looked after, matched this adoration. He was precocious intellectually and hence quickly became something of a teacher's pet at school. Perhaps because of this he tended to be very frightened of the jealousy of the other children and, being small, had no means to assert himself physically. He yearned to please them. Going into his teens he became readily acceptable as a clever boy, but was still obsessed with the need to please. At this time he began to consciously dislike his mother, feeling that she overwhelmed or ate him up. He also began to be aware of how ruthless he could be and noticed that he often dreamt of being a despot, like Caligula for instance. But he was in fact effectively unassertive, and awareness of his ruthlessness doubled his wish to be nice and liked.

In his late teens he tried a lightning affair with a girl but was thrown into chaos by her flighty histrionics and discreetly retired from the encounter. He went on liking women, and had many as friends, but sexually he kept his distance. Then he fell passionately in love with a brash, ruthless young bisexual man who was apparently socially more outstanding and successful than he was. The Caligula of his dreams had been found, in actuality. The young man was enthralled. The ruthless man seemed to find kindly innocence appealing, so they fell into a passionate affair. The ruthless man, however, soon tired of this and found another *amour*, leaving the young man hurt and bereft, determined to give himself to a gentler lover next time.

In this we see many elements. Not only is there a *revolt* against 'good' practices, together with a dread of being *overwhelmed* by a woman's excitability, but also a *hunger for the character of the loved one*. In overt homosexuality this hunger for another's character often seems to take a physical form. It is wanted physically, even to incorporating the loved one's body, and penis in particular. This is the *idealization of the penis*, which we have just mentioned. It may be wanted inside and this can be achieved in oral or anal intercourse. Or it may be wanted as something to fondle and worship in mutual masturbation. All of these are, of course, common in homosexual intercourse. This single example cannot validly be extended to make general conclusions about homosexuality but I think you will find the features mentioned here are quite common.

Lastly, remember that not all love between men is homosexual. Men can love each other as people very passionately, there may often be sexual feelings involved, without there being any exclusion of each other's heterosexual loves. Thus, two happily married men can be deeply fond of each other without any loss of love for their wives. Although every one, no doubt, has some homosexual urges, the noun homosexuality, or adjective 'gay', is perhaps best confined to refer to a man's sexual desire for another man to the exclusion of women. It is thought these days more conceptually correct to speak of the 'homosexualities' and, further, to assume that heterosexuality is just as much the object of our scrutiny and curiosity.

We have not yet mentioned *bisexuality* except of course to suggest that everyone probably has sexual feelings about both sexes. Bisexuality proper refers to those who enjoy actual sexual intercourse with members of either sex. We will not go into this in detail here. We can point out, however, that bisexuality does seem to instance how some people can *split* their lives into mutually exclusive, contradictory even, roles. They can at one time be passionately homosexual and put this aside quite quickly to turn to a woman. Whether this entails falsity must remain an open question here.

Lesbian or female homosexual love

Lesbian loves usually have, it appears, rather different psychodynamics. There must be a similar revulsion against genital arousal. This time, of course, it is against the penis relating to a woman's vagina. Some lesbian women get on well with men, some enjoy 'being a man' in male company. Their love of women seems often to be with themselves in the role of a man. The function of physical make-believe is clear enough here. Many other women profoundly loathe not only penises but other aspects of maleness as well. Here the penis seems to be a physical symbol of all 'macho' qualities against which women must cling together in mutual love for protection. Here the paranoid elements are applying not only to genital arousal but to masculinity as an abstract idea. However, as we have noted, there are many women who can like men as people and whose loathing of maleness is apparently confined to the genitals and physical contact. Another common feature is the positive desire to be mothered sexually. Men as such are not so much loathed but objects of active indifference.

When a woman loves another sexually she often also hates her. This hatred can be denied and projected violently onto the idea of men so that the woman can say to another as it were: 'We don't hate each other, it is men we loathe.' We are then close to the anti-macho relationship mentioned in the first paragraph. Here is one brief description of some aspects of a lesbian woman's life:

A young woman had been brushed off, when a little girl, by her mother who inordinately doted on her older brother. He was a rather soppy cry-baby, bitterly envied and yet held in contempt by his sister. Her father was rather distant but loved by the little girl, however he was careless about the home and was denigrated by her mother. When grown up, she liked and was liked by both men and women. But when close to men she found herself overwhelmed by hate and contempt for them. Being unsure of herself in intimate relations she began to feel very lonely and yearned to be fussed over by a woman, as her mother positively had not. She met a colleague who was openly contemptuous of men but warm and affectionate to women and also wanted to be soothed by female affection. They naturally fell for each other and lived together for a long time. However, it was not entirely satisfactory. One young woman loved children and wanted a baby, the other was hungry for the company of women with strength, definiteness and power so that neither was completely fulfilled.

Here we have a pattern that is different from the male homosexual; there is *envy and contempt* for *sexual men* and yearning to be *fussed over in a motherly way* by women. This again is only an anecdote, but it shows themes that can be quite common in lesbianism (Cameron, 1963; Rosen, 1979; West, 1960).

Remember also that, as with men, not all women's love for each other is lesbian. Passionate affection can continue between them without the exclusion of heterosexual loves.

Values and difficulties in gay and lesbian homosexual relationships

At this point it must be emphasized that we have described only a few of the vast multiplicity of feelings and fantasy that are set loose in sexual arousal of any sort. Many involve projections of the self into another, or fusions of another into the self. Others involve, as we have noted, fantasies of being of the opposite sex to what one physically is. These fantasies are thought of as repugnant by many people and hence to be condemned. Such condemnation, often of a vehement kind, seems to be driven by the protesters' own hidden fears of perversity and usually has little real substance.

Freud (1905) noted that for heterosexuals the gender of the sexual object changed for women whereas it remained the same for men. By contrast, in homosexual object choice the reverse is true in that it changes in men but remains the same for women. The means by which this occurs for the heterosexual is said by Freud to be via the identification with the parent of the same sex. If we consider the two examples given above, the young man's life seemed to be constructed around the pleasure and gratifications of pleasing his mother to the point that he was 'too good'. He was fond of his father but there did not seem to be any evidence that he had struggled to dis-identify (ruthlessly) with his parents during his early adolescence. He seemed left with a sense of having to disavow being aware of his 'ruthless' self, which he then sought in a 'ruthless' partner. This left him defenceless against his partner's ruthlessness towards him. The young woman, on the other hand, had been faced with a mother who seemed not to value her and a father who seemed to be uninterested in her or the family. She yearned to be mothered and found a partner who could fulfil this role of the interested mother. In both these cases, the choice of partner seems determined by the search for something perceived as *missing* in the self. The implication of this search for something missing to be found in someone of the *same* sex is that it is intrinsically unstable and comes at the price of obliterating one's heterosexuality. It is unstable because the perception of this longed-for something in another must be based on projection and be, therefore, imaginary. Furthermore, the strength of the anxieties about this missing part of the self can be so strong that its 'discovery' in the other is experienced as something concrete. If the relationship ends, the inevitable agonized sense of loss is experienced as if something real has been cut away from the self.

This instability, at least when held in fantasy and not acted upon, has great value; the shifting of identification of self from one sex to another in imagination, for instance, is essential for sympathy with the other sex and for creative breadth of vision. It is also intrinsic to certain areas of learning and work. For instance, if a man is to learn how to nurse babies, or if a woman is to model herself on male teachers to develop competence in her work, both need to enjoy identifications with the opposite sex. It is, I think, one of the major social achievements of recent years that prejudice against this cross-sex identification has begun to relax. Among other things, cross-sex identification enriches heterosexuality. A woman, for instance, can enjoy identifying with a man when she has a real man's penis inside her and vice versa.

However, when actual homosexual or lesbian relationships occur, certain *impoverishments* do seem to be inevitable. This because the biological heterosexual relationship is obliterated, denied or otherwise revolted against. The young man discussed above, for instance, did not find a relaxed use of those feelings that made up his ruthlessness when he fell for a ruthless young man, he simply got hurt. He was excluded from using his ruthlessness *mixed* with warmer feelings to give him firm thrustfulness, either in a sexual relationship or in other affairs. A large part of him had to play the innocent. And the young woman could not satisfy her yearning to be engrossed with a baby by lesbian intercourse. This raises the question as to how heterosexuality compares, so let us now turn to this to continue the argument.

Heterosexual love

As in homosexuality, perverse fantasy is usually embedded in heterosexual love, but there is something else as well. We have just noted that in both male and female homosexuality there seem to be severe persecutory and paranoid feelings about arousal with the *opposite* sex. These persecutory feelings of fear and hate are strong enough to swamp and then freeze heterosexual urges. A person who can turn to heterosexuality is not ruled in this way by paranoid fears about sexual arousal. The fears must be either milder or strongly defended against. Remember, heterosexual performance is no guarantee of health at all.

Whether it be a homosexual or heterosexual love, a young person, taking the momentous step from pubertal crush to an actual approach to a boy- or girlfriend, opens up the possibility of sexual reciprocity. We referred to reciprocity in the early chapters when describing those mutual contributions to each other's self-esteem, which can occur between parent and child. In these younger days such reciprocity was in a one-sided context, the parent really held power, now it can be more equal. As we noted earlier, the idealizing lover can be loved back so that he not only feels humble but, by being idealized in return, he is made to feel wonderful as well. He probably comes to feel, and be, more vital and colourful than he was before.

Where this reciprocity takes place with someone of the opposite sex the two, obviously enough, physically fit like jigsaw-puzzle pieces. The man's physical ecstasy, centred on his penis with its particular form, fits with and affirms the woman's ecstasy, centred on her vagina with its different shape. As their body shapes complement each other, so too does much of their fantasy, which is closely tied to body shape and impulse. And, since thought patterns are fed by fantasy, so there is the likelihood that more intellectual functions can work in harmony too.

It is this mutual body acceptance that can give a blessed inner stability and peaceful harmony to young lovers. At best, unlike homosexuality, there are no loose ends. There are, as it were, no penises with nowhere to go, no unused vaginas or breasts that will never give milk. This is important, if only because it is neglect of these parts of the body that can give rise to violent, painful, even uncontrollable paranoia and destructiveness. These neglected parts are somewhere felt as belonging to the self, even if unconsciously, and when a self feels neglected it is hurt and easily becomes destructive. It is the harmony or synchrony between two people of the opposite sex, rooted in physical intimacy without loose ends, that homosexuality and lesbianism seem to miss. Having said this, it is as well to recognize that heterosexuality can itself become a chronically defensive trick. For instance, it may be used as a flight from depression while at the same time being swanked about as the 'height of normality' to less fortunate creatures. Naturally this is a subtle but unpleasant form of cruelty. It can be a make-believe against fears of homosexuality, passivity, impotence or frigidity, and all sorts of other anxieties.

Remember, too, that many homosexual or lesbian partners are happier, fruitful and creative with their partners than with none at all or with an incompatible member of the opposite sex. Heterosexual lovers are usually not satisfied to rest with physical harmony, which, even though it may give rise to intellectual enjoyment as well, is often transient unless there is a deep, reciprocal appreciation of character as well. When this appreciation occurs, for instance, a person may have some ability, which he believes in but is unsure of, and deeply wishes for it to be affirmed by a lover. If it is not noticed a person can feel just as hurt as if his whole soul and body has been spurned. The 'chemistry' of *whole characters in interaction* is as important in love as that of bodies. This interaction starts with idealizing crushes, which, as mentioned, seem to involve a falling in love with aspects of character. This idealization by itself can be full of contradictions and very instable. But for lasting enjoyment something of the following process must also, perhaps, take place. A lover may idealize and want some characteristics for himself but then sense that if he had them they would be antipathetic to him as a whole person. When this occurs, he may be glad of a partner with these ideal attributes, so that he can possess them at one remove.

Here is a simple example. The characteristic used is a part of the body, but it could apply to any characteristic of bodily or mental functioning. A man may particularly idealize and dote upon his girlfriend's delicate, expressive hands. It might be that he simply wants expressive hands like hers for himself. He may yearn to be a beautiful musician, but feels he could never be one because of lack of dexterity. In such a case he might simply feel his own lack, and his loving idealization may turn to corrosive envy. In another case the young man might equally like to have such delicate hands. But, at the same time, he is proud of his own heavy, muscular hands, and delicate and heavy hands just cannot go together in the same person. So as *a whole person* he does not want delicate hands. But he is very glad that he can possess them at one step removed in his loved one. Likewise, his girlfriend might want in part of herself to have strong hands, and yet be proud of her own delicate ones. She reciprocally will thus dote upon his strong hands, while being pleased by her lover's appreciation of hers. Both partners are happy.

This might seem a trivial example but the notion can be applied to many more complex characteristics. The example is intended as a concrete metaphor for complementarity.

We have argued here that, because of complementary sexual body shapes, heterosexuality is *potentially* the most satisfying, stable and harmonious form of love. Remember, too, that heterosexual loves themselves can also be full of perversities and paranoias. We are not trying here to extol the healthy virtues of heterosexuality, but we should not especially plead for the unquestioned 'health' of homosexuality either. *We seem to arrive at the idea that the form that an individual's sexual life ultimately takes will reflect the full spectrum of that person's emotional history, in its most intimate detail,* which becomes organized into a sexual identity.

It is this structure that is referred to as the central masturbation fantasy (Laufer & Laufer, 1984). Sexual identity reflects that the same blend of responsibility, authority, and temporality that we observed earlier but this time in the context of a deep emotional intimacy with another person. This structure is created out of an individual's sexual history and becomes organized out of the child's 'polymorphous perversity' into a coherent whole. Hence we see the creation of organization as the central feature of the individual's relation to the external world through work and sexual life with partners being reflected in that individual's internal world as their sexual history is bound together into a form that satisfies ancient and modern desire. All this must be created by the individual because of the risk of 'being enslav'd by some other man's'.

Lastly, something of very little recognized importance. Although kindly heterosexuality is of inestimable value in a couple's intimate life, it is vital in a much wider way as well. Inhibited genital sexual feelings underlie the ordinary conversation of men and women everywhere, in work as well as in leisure. I am not referring to trivial flirtatiousness, which can be full of innuendo, but to dignified, respectful *charm*. With this, in a quiet way, men and women, married or single, can enjoy each other fully as human beings, including their sex. There need be no suggestion of physical lust or indecency. It is sanity at its simplest and best. It is perhaps the surest of guards against madness of any kind, and relies on the full recognition of the differences essential to complementarity of parts to the whole. However, I must add that heterosexual falling in love may be necessary in harmonious love, but it is not sufficient. Simple liking and respect for each other seems to be just as, even more, important in the long term than the more romantic aspects of loving. But let us continue with this in the next chapter.

In conclusion, it will have been noted that an adolescent passing into young adulthood can be recognized as such by his finding personal authority and his readiness to accept responsibility. This cannot ever be a simple process. Winnicott (1968) summed up in the following words the need for adults to be aware of their own authority in their dealings with adolescents and to be capable of acting authoritatively in the face of being accused of being authoritarian:

What I am stating (dogmatically in order to be brief) is that the adolescent is immature. Immaturity is an essential element of health at adolescence. There is only one cure for immaturity and that is the passage of time and the growth into maturity that time may bring. Immaturity is a precious part of the adolescent scene. In this is contained the most exciting features of creative thought, new and fresh feeling, ideas for new living. Society needs to be shaken by the aspirations of those who are not responsible. If the adults abdicate, the adolescent becomes prematurely, and by false process, adult. Advice to society should be: for the sake of adolescents, and of their immaturity, do not allow them to step and attain a false maturity by handing over responsibility that is not yet theirs, even though they may fight for it.

Organizing as the task of adolescence

In this chapter, we have seen processes of organizing taking place as the adolescent finds a place in the adult working world and finds a partner. The significance of these processes is underlined by the fact that we have reached into the political debates of the economic world and sexual politics. The fact that these issues create such potential for strong feeling and will, no doubt, continue to do so, suggests that these issues can create conflict and turmoil for most as they negotiate their way out of adolescent dependency on their parents and into the adult world. It is hard to remain in a state of adult dispassionate detachment when buffeted by young people. To hope for any understanding, a tolerance of these disturbances must, it seems, be accepted. For, as Winnicott suggests, each individual creates his own system – whether he or we like it or not – and we seek to usurp this process at our peril. The best we representatives of the adult world can do is to examine our own relationship to our own authority because ultimately the developing adolescent will be asking us, in his idiosyncratic way, how we did it and go on doing it.

Further reading

Baruch, G. (ed.) (2001) *Community-based Psychotherapy with Young People*. London: Brunner-Routledge.

Bazelgette, J. (1978) *School Life and Work Life: A Study of Transition in the Inner City*. London: Hutchinson.

Erikson, E.H. (1963) *Childhood and Society*. London: Paladin.

Lanyardo. M., & Horne, A. (1999) *The Handbook of Child and Adolescent Psychotherapy: Psychoanalytic Approaches*. London: Routledge.

Rutter, M. (1995) *Psychosocial Disturbances in Young People*. Cambridge: Cambridge University Press.

Chapter 11

Partnership and marriage

Christopher Clulow

It might seem rather odd to include a chapter on marriage in a book on human development, even when the title is prefaced by the less formal term 'partnership'. After all, the social institution of marriage has been criticized for impeding the development of women. It has been charged with obstructing social change by representing values and practices that belong to another age. Most tellingly, it can seem to have questionable relevance when people are increasingly choosing not to marry, and to divorce when they do marry. It's as if we echo Mae West's sentiment that marriage might be a great institution for other people (and those who do marry tend to celebrate in style by spending a fortune on weddings), but we ourselves are not yet ready for an institution and may never be.

So does the term 'partnership' fit the bill better? Certainly it reflects the prevalent view that the nature of the 'glue' holding couples together is of a less formal and more private nature than traditional marriage. And it captures how people are currently living their lives. More than three in five women who do choose to marry for the first time are already living with their husband to be. Two thirds of their weddings will be civil rather than religious events, a quarter of which will take place in 'approved premises' other than registry offices (hotels, stately homes, and so on). Around half of all conceptions take place outside marriage and in excess of one in three births are to unmarried women, although, tellingly, nearly two-thirds of these are registered by both parents living at the same address (The Stationery Office, 2003). Yet, ironically, as the deregulation of marriage becomes more marked there is a counterbalancing movement to regulate cohabiting partnerships, and that goes for opposite as well as same sex partners.

Some of this is for good, old-fashioned economic reasons (to ensure justice with regard to children, property and pensions once the relationship ends). But there will usually also be a wish to symbolize within the partnership, and for others outside it, the nature of the commitment that is being entered into or consolidated. That commitment will have important emotional and psychological dimensions, as well as the evident legal, social, and economic ones.

It is here that the concerns of this chapter link with those of preceding chapters. When committing ourselves to our partners, to whom are we really making a commitment? To the community to which we belong, which depends on couples to provide an environment in which individuals can contribute to society by raising children, producing goods and services and caring for dependent relatives? To our partners as the people they actually are, rather than the ones we would like them to be? Or to ourselves? This last possibility frames a vital question for the psychology of partnerships: when we fall in love and choose the person we want to be with, are we choosing an actual other person or a reflection of ourselves? Are we seeking an internal object of our own in our choice of partner – the quest of Narcissus searching for the elusive Echo that turns out to be no more than a reflection of himself. Or are we committing ourselves to forging a real relationship, the condition that Nora describes at the end of Ibsen's classic play *The doll's house* in response to her husband, Torveld's, pleading to be something more to her than a stranger: 'You and I would have to change so much . . . that life between us two could become a marriage.' This is the commitment to development, for every partnership is a journey from narcissistic object relating to 'marriage'. No wonder partnerships are capable of evoking intense ambivalence, an ambivalence that can resonate at public and private levels.

The tension between the personal aspirations of people in their love relations and the social buttressing of an institution in which the public has a vested interest is nothing new, nor are the strategies they deploy to manage the dilemmas associated with making a commitment. Samuel Johnson diagnosed the ineptitude of people as the root cause of marital unhappiness and prescribed arrangement as the solution:

> I believe marriages would in general be as happy, and often more so, if they were all made by the lord chancellor, upon due

consideration of characters and circumstances, without the parties having any choice in the matter. (Boswell, 1791/1990)

Just over 60 years later John Stuart Mill, who wanted to live with Harriet Taylor but realized it would be socially impossible outside marriage, saw the institution as the problem and wrote the following disclaimer:

> . . . the whole character of the marriage relation as constituted by law [is] such as both she and I conscientiously disapprove, for this amongst other reasons, that it confers upon one of the parties to the contract, legal power and control over the person, property and freedom of action of the other party, independent of her own wishes and will. (Mill, 1873/1989)

Such tension is the stuff of some of our greatest literature and drama, in which the struggles of individuals torn between the dictates of their hearts and the constraints of social obligation are tracked in the minutest of detail, both of them interacting in complex ways to shape the outcome. Take, for example, Elizabeth's struggle to recognize her feelings about Darcy in Jane Austen's *Pride and Prejudice*. Marriage was not simply the consequence of love, nor were the impediments to it just of an external nature. On the contrary, love and marriage followed from a change in consciousness:

> Had I been in love I could not have been more wretchedly blind. But vanity, not love has been my folly . . . I have courted prepossession and ignorance and driven reason away . . . Till this moment I never knew myself. (Austen, 1813/1985, pp. 236–237)

Or again, Noel Coward's heroine in *Brief Encounter* is caught in the bitter-sweet conundrum of love and loss. Laura and Alec long for an ideal, unordinary love. But the power of the film lies not in the consummation of the ideal but in its renunciation. True, the conventions of the time would have judged their affair harshly, but Laura's renunciation was based not on fear of censure but on her own self-respect. She did not succumb to the pressures of others but arrived at her own position.

Development arises from struggling with the competing commitments of partnership: the partners to themselves as individuals, to each other as a couple, to the families they create as a result of their union and to the wider communities of which they are a part. It also arises from the capacity of adult partnerships to engage individuals at an unconscious level, reactivating conflicts associated with past love relationships and their legacies of separation, loss and trauma. It is here that the potential for development lies. But how do we make the right choice of partner. And is there such a thing as a 'right' choice?

Choice of partner

Making a 'good match' is what everyone wants in choosing a life partner. The criteria for such a match have social, economic, religious and psychological dimensions. Different cultures, periods of history and individual preferences determine the relative emphasis accorded to these dimensions, and much turns on perceptions of what marriage and partnership is for.

From a societal perspective, traditional marriage is primarily a social contract which has been (and perhaps in some quarters continues to be) relied upon to provide institutionalized answers to key questions that every community and their elected representatives must answer: Who will provide economically, and who will care for dependents? As befits a patriarchal society the answers to these questions have been very gender-specific over the past three centuries, perhaps best summarized by the late-Victorian poet Alfred Lord Tennyson in the lines: 'man for the field, woman for the hearth . . . all else confusion.' Men dominated the public domain of political and economic activities; women dominated the private domain of domesticity and home life (the titular 'head of the family' role reserved for men was some compensation for their often having little place at home apart from siring children and paying the bills). The law defined the relationship between men and women in marriage in terms of ownership: the woman was the man's property; her children were his heirs; sexual infidelity constituted theft by another man; her identity was defined by that of her husband.

So, the contract was primarily between provider and homemaker. Evaluation of what made for a 'good' marriage – even as late as the mid-twentieth century – was primarily in terms of these roles and how well they were performed. Wars and pestilence might temporarily disturb the established order – and result in a rate of re-marriage as high as ours today – but the established order was conceived, in some sense, as being 'natural' if not pre-ordained.

The picture is no longer the same. Changes in education, contraception, economic structures, employment opportunities, welfare entitlements, transport, public attitudes and a myriad of other factors have freed women of many aspects of their dependence on men. Culturally there is a wish to replace the old patriarchy with an egalitarian order that is inclusive, non-discriminatory and sexually emancipated. Attitude surveys over the past 40 years confirm this change of values, although changes in behaviour have proved harder to achieve. Nevertheless, the social position afforded by marriage, valuing men as providers and women as homemakers, has given ground to an emphasis on companionate qualities – mutual respect, friendship, tolerance, sexual compatibility, fidelity and so on, and there is a broad measure of support for this to be provided outside marriage. So the freedom and range of partner choice has grown immeasurably in the past 40 years. Commitments have become looser, more personally defined and less certain.

The sociologist Anthony Giddens (1992) writes about the emergence of the 'pure relationship', entered into for its own sake rather than any associated benefits, and continued for only so long as it continues to deliver enough satisfaction for the parties concerned. No longer are obligations to family and kin simply based on blood ties; they are increasingly negotiated as the essence of family life is defined in terms of social and psychological factors. A new set of opportunities and constraints surround us in pursuing Freud's twin life purposes of loving and working – *lieben und arbeiten* – managing the home/work balance in attending to our personal and collective needs for care and productivity. And there is less anxiety about the instinctual drives that led Freud to postulate in *Civilization and its discontents* that monogamy was part of a social contract to contain sexual love and transform it into a wider platonic love that could bind larger social units together. Sexual activity outside marriage is no longer surrounded by guilt as it once was, except when one or both partners are already in a committed relationship.

It has been proposed that underlying the traditional structuring of gender roles in marriage is an even more deep-seated, but concealed, emotional contract concerned with the dynamics of dependency. The unconscious agreement here is that women will protect men from an awareness of their dependency needs by being the dependent partner. Reciprocally, men will protect women from the discomfort associated with competitive assertiveness by being the independent partner (Orbach, 1993). The origins of the pain associated with this unconscious contract are said to be located in child-rearing patterns that perpetuate traditional gender role differences. What psychologists have described as the 'male wound' (Hudson and Jacob, 1991) is seen as resulting from a socially enforced separation of boys from their mothers to make an identification with the man's world as represented by father, and it is said to act as a spur for men to protect themselves against the possibility of future hurt. No such journey has to be made by girls, who must differentiate and separate themselves from their mothers without the psycho-socio-cultural imperatives to which boys are subject. Indeed, the unconscious message from mothers to daughters may be that to be cared for you must care for others – a message of merger rather than differentiation. The unconscious gender agreement can be seen as underpinning an established social order and protecting against an unconscious anxiety that to change the relations between men and women will have catastrophic psychological as well as social consequences. As the social order changes so must the psychological contract (or perhaps the process works more powerfully in reverse?). So whereas the last century started with a campaign for educational literacy for women, it ended with one for emotional literacy for men.

The stage is now set for internal qualities rather than external structures to be the defining features of the good marriage. Or, rather, the boundary of the external world that is deemed relevant to the quality of a relationship extends only to one's partner, with children and work assuming prominence at different stages of the partnership. In these circumstances, relationship parameters become the focus of marital research, resulting in claims that factors like facial expression, states of physiological arousal and the emotional accessibility of partners to each other in high-conflict situations are the key predictors of divorce, or that a key factor determining the impact of divorce on children is the capacity of parents to manage conflict appropriately. No longer are we just looking at socio-economic disadvantage to predict the likely outcome of marriage (although the statistical correlation is well-established). The focus of attention is on the couple, and the individuals who make up the couple, rather than on the environment in which they live out their lives together. Most couples concur with this shift, believing that marriages break down because of matters like conflict, infidelity, betrayal, isolation, emptiness, violence and the loss of a sense of self, or of sharing something in common – personal explanations rather than public causes.

In these circumstances the function of partnership is increasingly considered in affective terms. Partners expect emotional support from each other, and expect their partnerships to be robust enough to withstand the expression of feelings generated by circumstances internal and external to their relationship. The expectation of partnership is for social and emotional stimulus, a still point in a turbulent world and a platform from which to create a meaningful existence. In attachment terms, adult partnerships are expected to provide both a haven to which to retreat and a secure base from which to explore – oneself, one's partner and the wider world. The balance that is struck between protection and development will vary between couples and within the life course of the partnership.

A 'good match' must therefore encompass something more than coming out of the same social drawer, or being drawn together by similar interests. There needs to be some psychological resonance between the partners which, despite its often unrecognized nature, has the capacity to spur partners on in terms of their own development. When partnerships founder and help is sought, therapists need to understand something about the unconscious choices that have been made by the partners, and the unconscious contract that binds them together. For in making a commitment to another person we are also making a commitment to ourselves, and there is no greater spur to personal development than having to tangle with uncomfortable issues within a relationship that is vital to our sense of felt security. So, to get the most out of partnerships in developmental terms we need, in some respects, to 'marry our problem'.

Another way of saying this is that, in our choice of love relationships, we are deeply influenced by the assumptions about ourselves in relation to others that we all unconsciously make on the basis of what we have experienced in growing up. As we have seen in earlier chapters, we live out in current relationships aspects of what we believe we have experienced in former relationships, and nowhere is this more likely to be true than in relation to the people who matter most to us. Intimate adult partnerships are transference relationships par excellence. They recapture the bodily pleasures, rapturous gaze and passions of infancy in ways that cut through personal cautions and social convention. Like the fairy tales of old, the passions of the mind are capable of transforming frogs into princes and angels into devils. And always there is the quest to be made whole, to put right something that has gone wrong, to be reunited with something that we feel might have been lost to us, or to find someone who awaits us if only we can find the magic key. In all of this there is an underlying question of whether we are living in the realms of fantasy or reality, whether we are passively 'in love' with an experience or actively 'loving' another person as she or he actually is.

A renowned American couple therapist, Milton Erickson, interviewed about what made for a good marriage talked about there being four states of love (Haley, 1985). The first he described as infantile love: 'I love me'. Then came the state of loving 'me in you' – loving someone because they are 'my' brother, sister, parent, dog and so forth. Adolescent love was depicted as loving another for what they do for you – basking in the glow of their attractiveness, talents and other kinds of reflected glory. Finally there was mature love: cherishing someone out of concern for them, and finding enjoyment in the other person's enjoyment. Usually, this is a reciprocal process. While Erickson's language implies a linear developmental process of growing up, it might be more accurate to depict the capacity to love in different ways as different states of mind, all of which may be found in the same person at different times. For example, the idealization that accompanies young love is unlikely to persist for long (although there are moments when this can return). Perhaps this is just as well, because the experience of being 'in love', while heady for the recipient, can also be accompanied by a sense of fragility: 'Will he or she continue to love me when they know what I'm really like?' Again, partners and parents, who are usually compassionate and considerate, may behave in self-absorbed and demanding ways when going through stressful periods in their lives. This is, perhaps, most evident during separation and divorce. The capacity for mature love is partly a consequence of what has been internalized from earlier love relationships and partly a product of current circumstances. Either way, the power of relationships to influence relationships is unquestionable: there can be no more transformative experience than to be known and loved for whom one is.

Intimacy and isolation

Every love relationship has a developmental and defensive potential. Partnerships are based on a mixture of identification and
difference, and people vary in the balance they find most comfortable at different stages in their partnership. The early stages of a
relationship will often be characterized by an exclusive sense of
identification between the partners, where similarities will be high-
lighted over differences as they establish in their own eyes, and in
those of others, a sense of 'us' as a couple. But if the sense of 'us' is
fixed over time it will inhibit the acceptance and discovery of
differences between the partners. The 'you and me against the
world' mentality locates everything potentially threatening outside
the relationship, and the voyage of partnership becomes a Hansel
and Gretel-type excursion into the dark woods where endless
threats to survival weld the partners together. It is then as if the
partnership must be preserved at all costs, and sometimes the cost
is the inhibition of development.

Equally, the discovery of differences in a relationship can be
challenging, interesting and open new pathways. But sometimes
differences are clung to as a protection against fears that intimacy
– developing a sense of 'us' in the relationship – will threaten to
obliterate separateness and override any distinctive sense of there
being a 'me'. Some couples fight tooth and nail to ward off the
belief that intimacy will expose their soft underbelly and render
them fatally vulnerable. Edward Albee's portrait of George and
Martha's marriage in *Who's afraid of Virginia Woolf?* is a vivid
depiction of the different psychological games that can be played to
protect partners against the fear of intimacy, and of the unconscious recruitment process that goes on to perpetuate past patterns
of relating that extends beyond the couple to those who come
within their orbit (Clulow, 2001). In these circumstances the closest
the partners can come to creativity is in the world of fantasy, and
then enormous effort must be expended on preserving the fantasy
from the harsh glare of reality that constantly threatens to expose it
for what it is. Difference must be preserved at all costs, and sometimes the cost is isolation.

Most relationships contain a degree of complementarity, enjoying both the otherness of the other and a sense of identification
with what she or he can represent of and for oneself. The definition
of the optimist as a person with a depressed friend captures

something of the unconscious agreement that can hold partners together in ways that complement each other. It also suggests the power of relationships to evoke experiences in others that don't necessarily belong to them. Everyone knows how depressing it can be to be in the company of an eternal optimist except, perhaps, those for whom there is some unconscious satisfaction and sense of 'fit' in having their part in the relationship clearly delineated in these terms. Unconscious agreements for managing anxiety through projective identification can take almost any form. Role differences may be in terms of going out and staying in, or caring for and being cared for, or feeling passionately and thinking reasonably. Providing there is a fit between the partners that sustains the unconscious agreement to manage differences in a complementary way all may go well. It is when these patterns become rigid and inflexible, or when they are tested by events (for example, when the carer is him- or herself in need of care) that the system becomes destabilized and challenged to adapt. This can often be the point at which couples ask for help, because what is happening to them feels insurmountable as it is outside their conscious awareness. Conscious awareness is focused on being uncomfortably exposed to a problem, and the problem is usually located in the partner.

It will be becoming apparent that implicit in this view of part-nership are certain assumptions that cast light on why couples are so different, and why they behave in the ways they do. One is that marriages and partnerships can be construed as psychological as well as social institutions. There is a kind of membrane surround-ing the couple that sustains an unconscious contract between them about how they will manage shared conflicts surrounding the vicissitudes of intimacy, isolation, and autonomy. This is some-times referred to as a shared defensive system, a system constructed to manage shared unconscious fantasies about the implications of becoming intimately involved with another human being. It is as if partners recognize their own and each other's ways of managing pain, feelings and anxiety, and implicitly sign up to an agreement to join forces in finding a comfortable balance that sustains them as a couple and as individuals. From this perspective, one partner's experience cannot be thought about in isolation from their other half. When things go wrong it is not sufficient to treat the depres-sion, anger, or withdrawal of one partner without taking account of what this might mean for the other and the relationship between them. As couple therapists are prone to ask: 'Whose anger is it anyway?' The couple is a system, albeit one that reflects the internal worlds of each partner and the external worlds in which they live out their lives together. The key assumption is that these worlds are shared between the partners in a fundamental way that relates to their security as individuals as well as to that of their partnership.

Another assumption is the significance of boundaries as the site where developmental work goes on in adult partnerships. This is implicit in the earlier assumption that couples are surrounded by a psychic 'skin'; that partnerships are psychological entities. However, within each entity there are boundary matters affecting the space between the partners and the process of regulating distance in their relationship, so that neither feels too 'hot' (emotionally close) nor too 'cold' (emotionally distant) for comfort. The dilemma that Schopenhauer posed for his company of porcupines facing freezing conditions captures a task facing every couple. If they huddle too closely together for warmth the experience may be uncomfortably prickly. If they withdraw too far from each other they may freeze to death. Here we are back to the ambivalence about commitment with which this chapter opened, and the task facing couples of finding a balance between being together and being apart that is sufficiently flexible to respond to the changing needs and demands they face. In negotiating this balance, ambivalent feelings may be separated out between the partners, so that one pushes for togetherness while the other maintains a degree of separateness. This pursuer-pursued dynamic can fuel many conflicts, and often masks fears that the partners share about fusion and isolation associated with intimacy.

Anxiety about psychological space may be reflected in the organization of physical space. Britton, a psychoanalyst practising in London, has described the architectural solution of the French sixteenth century essayist, Montaigne, to protecting and defining mental space in his marriage. Montaigne built himself a separate tower adjoining the chateau he shared with his wife, at the top of which was his study, there being a narrow exposed parapet connecting this with his wife's bedroom. In contrast, Edward Hopper, the American painter of more recent times, shared an open plan studio with his wife. But in order to stay together they eventually resorted to painting a line across the studio floor which neither was permitted to cross. Britton writes:

If we choose to live with someone in an intimate relationship, whether they are of the opposite or the same sex, whether they are legal spouses or not, we are confronted with the problems of sharing space; physical and mental. In these days of informal sexual arrangements, some, prompted by a claustrophobia of marital space, imagine they can avoid the spousal living room by inhabiting, indefinitely, the ante-room. However, they are already operating in just the same way that they would on the other side of that threshold. (Britton, 2000)

Drawing an analogy with psychoanalysis, he goes on to say:

They are like those who continue well into middle age to imagine that they are living on the threshold of life. In analysis they regard what is taking place as the dress rehearsal and not the performance, not realizing that this is their own particular way of having an analysis. Similarly, it is their own particular way of being married. (Britton, 2000, p. 12)

Boundaries also operate to define roles and relationships linked with temporal as well as spatial anxieties. The prospect of physical and emotional proximity to the object of one's heart's desire can stir longing and terror in equal measure when an emotional equivalence is drawn between what's happening now and what has happened in the past (as it always is). Families evoke the familiar, so when we set out to start a new family the process is always accompanied by echoes of the families we have known most intimately – the families we have grown up in. It is here that we learn most of what we know and believe about family life, an education that is all the more powerful for having operated at a subliminal level. It is absorbed knowledge, acquired through lived experience and therefore highly resistant to disconfirmation. Whether we replicate or repudiate what we believe to have been our experience, these beliefs powerfully mould our patterns of relating in later life.

Mother-son and father-daughter partnerships are part of our common folk-awareness. But it is not only the child's relationship with one or other parent that moulds the relationship template for later life. Other family members also exert an influence. So it is that the eldest child in one family and the youngest child in another may choose each other and play out a rivalry for affection and attention that characterized life in their respective family homes. Or they may agree that one will be the parent to the other and either affirm each other in their care-giving and care-receiving roles, or vie with each other to be looked after and to do the looking after. Sometimes these unconscious sibling connections may raise incestuous anxieties that are played out in the couple's sexual relationship, making it difficult for them to be passionately involved with each other.

The legacy of the past for the couple's sexual relationship is most often thought about from a psychoanalytic perspective in connection with Oedipal anxieties and traumatic abuse. The former refers to difficulties relinquishing parental love objects and the persisting aspiration to be first in the affections of the opposite sex parent, which can leave little room for a real lover in later life or may result in replaying the family drama by casting the lover in the role of parental love object to be won at any expense from potential rivals. The latter refers to the wound inflicted when childhood vulnerability has been exploited, leaving a residue for the survivor in later life that may associate all sexual encounters with the experience of being intruded upon, or of being violated.

Less traumatically, reworkings of the Oedipal myth can be especially helpful in illuminating the processes involved in developing boundaries in the course of ordinary human development. Contemporary thinking about the Oedipal situation highlights the potential significance of the parental couple for healthy child development. Put very briefly, psychoanalytic theory asserts that the process of individuation begins with an infant's recognition of self in the responses of his or her mother, a phase that is increasingly accompanied by the dawning and uncomfortable recognition that she exists as other than an extension of the infant's self. Tolerating the loss of the illusion of having sole and permanent rights over mother is the result of an emotionally painful process and represents a substantial psychological achievement. So the first stage of developing a capacity for self-reflection comes through the infant imagining him- or herself being observed by mother. Taking a third person into account, like father, changes this constellation. Occupying a position outside the primary pair of mother and infant, fathers create the conditions for a second stage in the development of a reflective self (and I am using the words 'mother' and 'father' here as social roles capable of being filled by either gender). The child now has an experience of there being a couple from which she or he is excluded.

Children, then, occupy a third position, on the outside of the parental couple, and if things go well they will not be filled up with anxiety about being excluded. They will then be free both to observe and absorb the workings of the parental couple, and they can imagine themselves being the object of observation. As observers they learn how partnerships operate, how intimacy is handled and how differences are managed without being central to the drama (even though they might try and join in); they can enjoy the liveliness of the partnership without feeling diminished, threatened, excluded or impelled to intrude. As the ones observed, they develop a capacity for self-observation, for entertaining another point of view, and for independent thought and activity. The Oedipal situation then becomes the crucible in which the capacity to be both alone and intimately involved with others – a central ingredient of successful partnerships – is developed.

Structures, events, meanings, and processes

Secure partnerships, then, are those in which partners have a capacity to be alone and involved, as well as an ability to move between these positions. Behind the diversity of conditions and circumstances that shape the nature of individual partnerships are common themes and dilemmas. There is the push for change and the pull of security, the longing for intimacy and the fear of being engulfed, the wish to be the same as others and the drive to be different. It is as if couples are engaged in a kind of dance, ensuring, in the poetic words of Kahlil Gibran, that there are 'spaces in [their] togetherness . . . even as the strings of a lute are alone though they quiver with the same music' and that they 'stand together, yet not too near together: for the pillars of the temple stand apart, and the oak tree and the cypress grow not in each other's shadow' (Gibran, 1926).

The nature of their 'dance' is not just of their choosing, but will be affected by events that occur outside the partnership. Predictable changes (for example, setting up home, starting a family, children leaving home, ailing parents) and unexpected events (such as illness, infidelity, redundancy) can constitute a shock to the system, destabilizing an established balance and requiring work to recover equilibrium. While it is unwise to lay claim to there being a natural rhythm in the life course of partnerships, since the points of divergence and diversity are many, there are discernible ebbs and flows in the tide of a couple's life together, which can form a pattern. There is the process of two individuals coming together to create something new, often personified by children. In order for this to happen, other relationships and pastimes must end and be let go of. As time passes, these new creations may be superseded, requiring a re-ordering of the partners' relationship to each other and their wider family and social group.

Change, however welcome, is usually associated with a degree of stress. Leaving home, becoming an 'item', going on holiday, promotion at work, starting a family, all require certain familiar routines and rhythms to be given up to make the most of the new situation. As relationships change, those in them are perceived differently and related to differently. In consequence, they begin to view themselves differently and become, in some respects, different people. Every transition involves a mourning process, however pleasurable the change might be considered to be. Although mourning might seem an extreme word to use to describe the process of adapting to new circumstances, it is appropriate to apply it to the many minor deaths that occur in the lifetime of a couple's relationship. As well as celebrating the new, partners must be able to let go of those parts of their past selves and lives that have become redundant.

It used to be thought that the degree of stress associated with change stemmed directly from the size and number of changes that people faced at any one time in their lives. It was as if a totting-up system could be applied to predict the likelihood of going down with a stress-related illness. But then it became apparent that events impacted on individuals in different ways. Some seemed able to survive major catastrophes relatively unscathed, while others were sunk by the proverbial storm in a teacup. In examining why this should be it was evident that social supports of different kinds make a difference, as does the degree of forewarning people have of what is involved in changes they are facing. But perhaps most importantly, it is clear that events interact with personal meanings in ways that affect how exposed and protected individuals are to destructive aspects of change. Couple relationships have been shown to be very significant buffers against stress when they work well. But they also may not be allowed to offer this protection when events are interpreted in the light of paranoid assumptions. For example, if an offer of help made to a new mother is read by her as an attempt to take her baby away, or as a coded criticism of her ability as a mother, a potentially important lifeline may no longer be available to her. And if the new father who made the offer is feeling excluded by the baby, his partner's response may compound the feeling that he has been rejected and betrayed. Every couple therapist knows how difficult the concept of reality is, when the subjective realities of each partner move apart from each other. As the late Anthony Powell (1972) said, 'it's not what happens to people that is significant, it's what they think happens to them'. And people often need to talk about their experience before they know what they think is happening to them.

In the same way that individual partnerships change over time, responding to different needs and circumstances, so too do public institutions. Marriage is not the destination for couples that it used to be. It is no longer needed to legitimize sex, or to provide a route into the world of adulthood or to confer social status. If it is embarked on at all, it is as a point of departure, and one that may come within an already existing history of commitment between the partners. Partnerships are not tableaux depicting a static condition, but dynamic institution-cum-relationships that occupy a space between internal and external realities. At a public level, the institution of marriage bridges the couple and their rapidly changing socioeconomic, legislative, cultural, and religious environment. At a private level, it bridges his inner world and hers, and represents their jointly constructed reality as a couple. Partnerships are open systems, susceptible to and mediating between different levels of reality in public and private domains. They operate in the space between these domains; small wonder, then, that they are constantly repositioning and redefining themselves during the lifetime of a couple and the history of a community.

So does a chapter on partnership and marriage fit within a book on human development, as we queried at the beginning of this chapter? It is clear that some dimensions of marriage are no longer relevant to our concerns, but that others remain vital. Because humans are social beings there is, throughout life, a need to be connected with others at an emotional level, to be known by them and to know them. From an evolutionary perspective our survival might depend on it. Partnerships provide a basis for our individual life projects because they offer opportunities for us to know ourselves, and to be known and accepted for whom we really are, without having to assume the mantles that go with many other social roles and relationships. They also provide a spur for change. In that sense they have a developmental 'people-making' role, offering opportunities for emotional and social development.

This 'people-making' function extends to the next generation when couples produce children. The quality of the parental relationship has been shown to be very important for healthy child development, in the same way that it has been linked with the health and well-being of the adults. This is not to say that two parents are always necessary to ensure the best chances for the next generation. In psychological terms, one parent may be able to embody enough of an 'internal couple' to provide children with the experience that allows them to develop a balanced sense of themselves in relation to others, just as two parents who operate in fused or separate ways may deny children the opportunity to develop in this way. What is important is the quality of relationships as distinct from the form they take. Partnerships can enhance the capacity of adults to act as parents *and* they can diminish those capacities. They can check the impulses of children to 'divide and rule' in their dealings with others *and* they can encourage patterns of relating that are deceptive, manipulative, and exploitative. They can provide an environment within which children and partners are free to test themselves and develop new strengths, *and* they can confirm the worst that people fear about themselves, so inhibiting further exploration. The subtle interplay between form and process allows no absolute judgement about the relative merits of two-parent families, but serves to emphasize the relevance of what goes on in relationships to shaping the social ecology of the next generation.

Further reading

Clulow, C. (ed.) (1995) *Women, Men and Marriage*. London: Sheldon.

Clulow, C. (ed.) (2001) *Adult Attachment and Couple Psychotherapy. The 'Secure Base' in Practice and Research*. London: Brunner-Routledge.

Cowan, C.P., & Cowan, P.A. (2000) *When Partners Become Parents: The Big Life Change for Couples*. Mattwah, NJ: Lawrence Erlbaum Associates.

D'Ardenne, P., & Morrod, D. (2003) *The Counselling of Couples in Healthcare Settings*. London: Whurr.

Fisher, J. (1999) *The Uninvited Guest. Emerging from Narcissism towards Marriage*. London: Karnac.

Macfarlane, A. (1987) *Marriage and Love in England: Modes of Reproduction*. Oxford: Blackwell.

Martin-Sperry, C. (2003) *Couples and Sex*. Oxford: Radcliffe Press.

Reibstein, J., & Richards, M. (1992) *Sexual Arrangements. Marriage, Monogamy and Affairs*. London: Heinemann.

Ruszczynski, S. (ed.) (1993) *Psychotherapy with Couples: Theory and Practice at the Tavistock Institute of Marital Studies*. London: Karnac.

Chapter 12

Parenthood

Eric Rayner

Being a parent seen as a developmental sequence

We have come a full circle since the start of the book. This will be a long chapter about a complex subject. We return to pregnancy and the early years of childhood, but this time we will be mainly identifying with the parents. Of course, grown-ups still carry their childhood with them in memory; but they are now due to be *responsible* for bringing up a new generation. It might be useful to browse through this book's early chapters to recall what is involved in parental responsibility. A central theme here is that: as a child grows, so a parent needs to grow in *sympathetic responsiveness*, or *attunement* with their child – remember Stern's (1995) pioneering work about this. This requires not only being intuitively aware of oneself at the *same* ages as one's child; but also, vitally, the recognition that our children's lives are different from our own, and that they will have different problems.

It seems to be only through being *sympathetic yet separate* that parents can help their child – who cannot yet act alone – while at the same time letting them be free when it is safe. If parents fail here, they are either neglectful or they care so intensely that they choke initiative; both can be detrimental to development. Parents are, in a way, called upon to *develop in parallel* with their children. Their job is to help them towards adulthood. This is the point of view of many writers about childhood (Anthony & Benedek, 1970; Brazelton & Cramer, 1991; Byng-Hall, 1995; Carter & McGoldrich, 1980).

Naturally, everyone fails to live up to the criteria of a good parent in some ways. Parents have their own lives to lead and cannot notice everything about their children. What is more, a child cannot develop independence if parental scrutiny is perfect and thus intrusive. Some ordinary neglect and *getting it wrong* is not only inevitable but also *necessary* for a child to be happy and unspoilt. Even so, if childhood is to be enjoyed by both sides, then parents do have to be serious about their responsibilities. It is only through being responsible that parents can really enjoy themselves as parents. But it is exhausting, and cuts out many other enjoyable things.

Parents in society

In countries where there is little technology, cheap medicine and trained staff will not be available, and high fertility will be balanced by high mortality. It was like this in Britain until about a century ago; death was common and a child could only hope, but not expect, to live until old age. People tended to be fatalistic – life lay in the hands of God. Although many parents loved their children just as much as they do today. There is evidence that neglect, exploitation and cruelty also flourished. On the other hand, with rural living and extended families, children could explore and wander safely to the homes of friends and relatives nearby. Responsibilities of care could then be spread easily beyond the nuclear family.

Modern urban families are often hemmed in by lethal motor traffic – even when not cooped up in high-rise flats. Parents are under continuous stress to be vigilant. Being a long way from relatives gives freedom from interference, but parents usually have to cope alone. They will have very few hours to relax – and to let themselves be ill.

With modern medical and dietary knowledge giving a longer life expectancy, parents can be more optimistic and throw themselves into enjoying bringing up their children. But there is a price to pay in heavier guilt when something goes wrong. The predicament of parenthood is epitomized by birth control itself. There is greater freedom to choose about having children, but with this parents have to bear more responsibility for their sexual pleasures.

In our society, it is mothers who carry the brunt of these worries most directly. Mothering is a high-risk occupation for anxiety and depression; but is often devalued. Mothers do not usually expect to be honoured but will bashfully apologize for themselves: 'Oh, I'm just a mother'. Yet it is largely upon mothers that the future vitality of any society rests (Daws, 1989; Oakley, 1974, 1979; Parker, 1995).

Our conditions of life are much fairer than they used to be. But it has justifiably been argued that much remains to be done to lighten mothers' often lonely burdens. On the other hand, many fathers' habits have changed in recent years: they are more engaged within their families, and partners are usually fundamentally more democratic together. Mothers can be freer than at any time in known history. So while some employers still need to re-think their practices over working hours if the isolation of mothers is to end, it also needs to be said that the modern nuclear family does provide vital conditions for the care of children; it is too precious not to preserve.

It is only mothers, not fathers, who get pregnant and lactate – it is they who can go enjoyably into what Winnicott (1964) called *primary maternal preoccupation*. So there is a good chance nowadays that a mother can really enjoy herself – and her child too. She still has to expect to lay aside some career ambitions, but not indefinitely. Let us look at mothering more closely (Daws, 1993; Fraiberg, 1977; Stern, 1995).

Fantasy and reality in having a child

Primary maternal preoccupation is a *life crisis*, where old ways of adaptation and defence are loosened to allow changes to happen. A mother at this time cannot be as vigilant about all things around as she had been before. She needs to relax, withdraw from many things and even regress, and for this she has to become more dependent upon others.

The baby inside a mother's womb is likely to become the focus of vivid bodily feelings and imaginings – fantasies – about the future. She can become prone to dream of things for her child that she missed – or to dread that her own bad experiences, and unwanted characteristics, will recur in the new life. As the baby is inside and part of her, it becomes part of her own inner world of emotion-laden ideas. But he or she is a new creation, a real physical and mental person – not just a fantasy in mother's mind. The two mental functions, fantasy and the reality sense, continuously interplay all through life, but they are especially vivid at this time.

The closeness of a baby to his mother's inner world of feeling and fantasy, both in the womb and after, means that her thoughtful exchanges with her child are especially warm and deep. For things to go well, however, she also needs, continuously if subconsciously, to test her fantasies out against what the baby is really like. For instance, a mother might be ruminatively looking at her baby and catch a glimmer of resemblance to her own father. The baby is likely then to be endowed with a web of feelings about her father. But soon the baby might turn and look like her mother-in-law, and this could then arouse its own particular imagery. After this, the child might chuckle in his own special way and make it obvious that he is both ordinary and a unique living person all of his own. The mother's fantasies will of course come up time and again, and each will be altered slightly by new memories and new realistic perceptions. Active and deeply felt living representations of the baby then slowly integrate (Parker, 1995).

Such a close interplay between inner and outer worlds needs a delicate mental to and fro by a mother, and this can easily be thrown into disorder. Thus maternal anxieties when the baby is young are not uncommon, maybe even leading to breakdown. Sometimes this takes the form of a gross breakdown of the differentiation between what is externally real and what is imagined – as in a *puerperal psychosis*. Much more frequent are post-natal depressions. Here a mother usually experiences a miserable flatness of feeling and an inability enjoyably to endow her child with a flow of emotion and imagining. Mothers can then feel dreadfully worthless. A baby may be dimly aware of trouble in mother and, with nothing else to engage with, he can become badly disturbed too. Ordinary wafts of maternal depression, in transient form at least, seem to be almost inevitable and must be accepted as one of the normal crises of early mothering. Even so, when depressive moods become chronic, it is worth looking for skilled help. In Britain, talking about it to a health visitor or GP is a useful way to start. Some mothers do not break down, but unself-consciously turn their children into playthings of their fantasy in a tyrannical and chronic way so that it becomes a life-style – this must often be pathogenic for the child. Here are a couple of extreme examples:

A woman had a mother who had got pregnant again 2 months after she herself was born, and after having her next baby went on to be rather neglectful. Years later, the woman herself produced several children and tried to keep them all as babies as long as she could. She seemed, through them, to be having the gratification of one long babyhood, which she herself had in many ways missed. She appeared to lose interest in each new child as soon as they began to walk.

A married couple lost their five children in a fire. They then had five more children, each of whom bizarrely turned out to be of the same sex as their counterparts in the first set. The children were given the same names as those who had died. When the fifth was born, the whole family, with great sounds of rejoicing, emigrated, just as the parents had been planning to do just before the disastrous fire of many years previously.

The psychiatric literature is full of instances of repetition like this. It must be stressed, however, that the nature of any parent's fantasy is not just a question for psychiatrists. Every child that comes into the world is, in some measure, 'the sport of their mother's madness'. This is probably part of the fate, happy or dreadful, of any ordinary dependent child. When a mother continues to enjoy having her fantasies, but still keeps sensitively aware of the real states of herself and her children, then the experience can be rich for all the family. It is awareness and enjoyment of reality that matters most for mental health.

Multiple responsibilities in mothering

Mothering is a continuous to and fro between the mother and all her children. It is acting and reacting in complex ways from dawn to dusk. Both she and her child can deeply enjoy each other, yet still be naturally self-willed, tired, and cross. If a mother loses this precious to and fro awareness and enjoyment, her child is left alone. Children are glad of being alone in small doses, but it is unbearably disturbing if prolonged. As a child grows older, the areas of activity where the 'to and fro' is needed become perhaps less intense but wider and more various. This calls for more and more maternal flexibility.

Perhaps the most stereotyped idea of a mother's functioning is simply of cuddling and nursing a young baby. This is one of the most precious things in life; but many young women are so cosily and erotically aroused by it that they think of little else. Then, when the children grow out of being babies, they find themselves at a loss and often become irritable, bored, depressed, and neglectful. The children are then left under-stimulated, drifting about lonely, puzzled, disillusioned, and disturbed. Such miserable conditions are often reported by health visitors, GPs, and social workers. Fathers also may tend to limit their ideas to a cuddly fantasy of infancy. Then, being unable to envisage the other, later responsibilities of a mother, they can be prone to dismiss their wives' other work with the children as trivial.

Years after their infancy, many young people complain bitterly that their mothers can still only see them as babies, and not as they really are. It seems to be endemic and is often a source of children's chronic indignation.

Depressed mothers often find the stage where a baby moves away to explore very hard indeed. It feels as if the children are losing interest in them. Then, in her withdrawn gloom, a mother does not make it feel safe for them to explore. It has been noted that *hyperactive* children, with an *attention deficit disorder*, frequently have had seriously depressed mothers – although it must often be an open question which trouble came first.

One mother epitomized the essential quality of mothering as being one of *multiplicity*. Casting back to previous chapters, it becomes clear just how complex is the patterning of activities between everyone in the family in those years. A mother is called upon to watch over all these complex happenings, and to respond to them as her conscience and sense of reality dictate. This is the *responsibility* of mothering – it is utterly exhausting and wonderful.

A mother's changing responsibility with growing children

As a child grows up, a mother is called upon to develop her responsiveness to match. This needs continuous new intellectual and emotional articulations and learning. Let us look back at the earlier chapters to clarify this (Hollway & Featherstone, 1997; Parker, 1995).

The first months of a baby's life see a mother preoccupied with *attuning* her thought and body to a new human being. After a few weeks, a baby is noticeably recognizing the mother as a separate being. He then wants to discover his own boundaries by playing with her. Towards the end of the first year, or even before, a baby will be crawling and walking. He will be getting into breakable things and dangerous places, so an ordinary conscientious mother finds her will clashing with his. Discipline has become a crucial issue. The time has come for a mother to take the initiative and, often forcefully, help her child into this next stage. This sort of tussle will probably go on until adolescence and beyond – much of it really enjoyably, so long as mothers are not 'tussle-phobic'.

As time passes, the baby, now a toddler, develops talking and exploring. When mother has time and inclination, she can spend enjoyable hours in helping with investigation and explanation. If she is not interested, she will easily lapse into irritated boredom. Then, if this continues, the little child can feel neglected, become lethargic, depressed, and seriously disturbed.

After a year or so a mother may be having another baby. She will then need to relax into her pregnant preoccupations; but at the same time she still needs to keep in tune with, discipline, provide for, and enjoy her toddler. After the second birth, she will have broken nights of feeding and tired days with both children. On top of this, she has their jealousies, which are often violent, to negotiate – and then find ways for all to be pals together again.

By the age of two or so, a child will probably want neighbouring children to play with. A mother needs then to broaden her horizons – to befriend other mothers and to be liked and trusted by their children as well. For this to happen she has to extend her ways of thought to be able to talk to several children and their mothers, probably from different backgrounds, all at once. The breadth of response needs to become even wider if a mother has several children of different ages. A glance at a tea party with a dozen children of different ages and backgrounds, all talking and gesticulating at the same time, is enough to show how exhausting mothering can be.

Coming out of infancy, the child begins, in a not very definable but omnipresent way, to become a *sexual* person. A girl or boy will enjoyably be cuddling, wriggling and charming their mother or father in noticeably different ways. The parents' sexual feelings towards their children will be less obvious and little talked about; but most will be privately aware of their stirrings and will readily discipline themselves against impulsive erotic expressions. However, some parents do not bother to check their own, or their friends', eroticisms, and then, catastrophically, child abuse can arrive.

Mothers often find that they have no self-consciousness or trouble in enjoying cuddling and kissing their children, of both sexes alike, until they are about 3 years old. Their sons' cuddles and kisses may then feel a bit more sexy than their daughters', but it usually feels all right. In fact, it feels all right to most modern parents to be a bit sexy – although too much is arousing and even seriously disturbing, too little is depleting. However, if it goes on too long, or is too exciting, most mothers will ordinarily find it natural that they must call a halt. Fathers usually have similar reactions, but obviously the other way around, feeling sexier with their daughters. Children of both sexes want caresses, and can feel deeply hurt if peremptorily rebuffed. One ordinarily happy mother, equally fond of all her children, said she found herself rather guiltily cuddling her son in secret when her daughters were in another room. The incidence of *sexual abuse* is mostly by fathers and other male relatives, but can be by mothers as well. It demonstrates how hard it is for some people to keep their incestuous, sexual, and aggressive arousals in check.

Five years old means school age in Britain, and with it comes the need to follow the child's intellectual progress, and to find friendly working relationships with teachers. Soon after going to school, a child tends to turn more and more towards the company of his friends. Children are often ashamed of showing that they are still much involved with their parents. Sexual feelings and play with parents and siblings begin to feel acutely embarrassing. This marks a beginning of *latency*, with its long, gradual process of mothers and fathers losing physical intimacy with their children as they grow towards puberty. On the other hand, this is usually well compensated for by interest in the widening activities and social networks of the children.

When puberty and adolescence arrive, all of a parent's old ways of doing things are likely to be called noisily and sometimes stormily into question. It becomes a 'time of judgement'. Mothers, and fathers, can be torn with guilty worries about their earlier failures. They can also feel full of shame and indignation in the face of the arrogance of their teenage children, who can so easily talk as if their parents are fools. At the same time, parents will go on worrying whether the children will turn out all right. Even so, most parents also look back on these years as deeply satisfying, when an *equality* of wisdom and friendship between parents and children begins to take shape.

Mothers going to work

When technology was limited and life expectancy short, a young woman could expect that the rest of her life would be taken up by nursing children and domestic economy, so long as her husband earned enough for the whole family. A great deal of intelligence as well as heavy physical labour was needed at home. Modern technology, with sophisticated domestic machinery available to millions, has given mothers more time to enjoy their children. This has made the burden of motherhood less obvious than it used to be. However, many mothers are now torn between their family and work, from pregnancy onwards.

To enjoy herself thoroughly, a mother needs to put aside most other work, from some time before birth until her child is a few months old at least. Optimally, this would continue with a mother seeing herself as the central figure until her child has begun to grasp the idea of self-control – both bodily and socially. When mothers *have* to work, for financial or other reasons, it seems that a child can realize from quite early on when their mother is genuinely doing her best, as distinct from fobbing her young children off on others. Some women seem to be protected from post-natal depression by working, while for others it may be a cause. Brazelton (1988) warns us that the *prospect* of returning to work early may damage the emerging attachment of both parents to their expected baby. He points out that the unusual amount of illness in mothers returning to work in the first few months is not just due to exhaustion, but that a disruption of attachment affects the immune system. If mothers and babies are able to enjoy the timelessness of being together for much of the first year, then a mother's return to work may coincide more naturally with the baby's own process of separation and individuation.

Mothers of older children may continue to feel very conflicted about whether, and how much, to work. It seems that overall satisfaction in families is greatest when mothers do work, so long as all-consuming hours do not leave them too exhausted to enjoy the 'reunion' with their children in the evening. It does seem that the role model of a working mother is productive for children and, as they get older, protects them from the guilt of being too large a part of their mother's emotional investment. If their mother has other strong interests in her life, it leaves them freer to work out their own independence.

Fathering in modern society

As with women, modern times have seen striking transformations in what is expected of fathers. These have not been very dramatic, for men are usually still expected to continue in full-time employment, so a father's career and work identity can still progress steadily when he has a family. However, machines have diminished the male's age-old assumption of ascendancy over women, based upon his greater muscular strength, which had lasted for thousands of years. It was the Industrial Revolution, over 200 years ago, which provided the solid beginning of women's liberation from patriarchal tyranny. Men still tend to excel more often than women in agriculture, the heavy industries, engineering, construction work, ships, planes, lorries and trains and perhaps in some other technologies. But in administrative and office work, and in many professions centrally demanding *intellectual competence* and *wisdom* – such as teaching, medicine, the law, politics, much academic work, journalism and writing – it is now more or less accepted that women can do most jobs as competently as men, and often more so. Male dominance has cracked, and in most Western countries, men and women are usually expected to be basically *equal* in work and marriage. It is democracy at its widest and best, but it is clearly not yet fully established in many cultures.

With this great 'gender-democratic' revolution in our culture, males have often experienced, for three-quarters of a century and more, an underlying uncertainty about their functioning, especially in fathering. However, there are some signs that this is on the wane – that their confidence is perhaps coming back – but without their supremacist pretensions.

Comments like the following are now common:

I think we men fall over backwards to avoid being authoritarian like our fathers, but when we try to be democratic and discuss things with our wives, they often complain that we are being soft and wet.

My grandfather was certain of himself in his narrow confines. But my father had the whole of his world crash about him when he was a young man in the Second World War. I don't think he ever got over it. The only thing he could talk about with pride was that war. I am a bit luckier, but I do wonder where we men go from here.

The problem of fathering is perhaps reflected in recent psychological literature. The first decades of this century were full of psychoanalytic discussions about the significance for the pathology of the individual of childhood ideas about *boys'* revolt against their *fathers*. This is very clearly emphasized in the crucial description of the *Oedipus complex* by Freud, who was born over a century and a half ago and was himself a natural patriarch, albeit a benign one. Then, about 50 years ago, after the Second World War, things moved on and there developed a great deal of interest in the vital importance of *mothering*. After this, for many years, few writers thought it necessary to think about fathering much at all. However, the turn of the twenty-first century sees an emphasis, despite its continuing importance, on the *uncertainty about fatherly identity*.

Technology and modern understanding have exposed the delusions and tricks of male dominance. Thus the extremes of patriarchal attitudes are hardly working in modern Western families – except perhaps in some religious sects, in some right-wing ideologies, and with some backward-looking aristocrats. In many families, the working together of husband and wife as equals in a *democratic team* is now an unwritten and easily enjoyable rule. Perhaps this is not emphasized enough, so that some men can still be little tyrants or unsure ditherers (Carter & McGoldrick, 1980).

The circumstances of a family in early childhood: a father's part

It is a familiar point that mothers do need support from someone. A woman who has, say, three children spaced two years apart, will probably be centrally dependent on others' help for up to 10 years of her life. Either an individual, a husband or partner, or an institution like social security, must finance her, or she has to find others to care for her children while at work. If she is dependent upon an institution like a social security agency, she and her children are unlikely to have the benefit of quick communication with someone intimate. This grows only in friendship, marriage, and long-term partnerships. So, we must conclude that if a mother wants to enjoy full-time mothering, she needs a wage-earner to provide for the family (Borstein, 1995; Parker, 1983).

Of course, this helping partner does not have to be a man – a woman will do as well. However, a child would then not have an intimate male to learn from, identify with or relate to. The importance of this need is obvious for little boys and only slightly less so for girls. If the two women happen to be lesbian lovers, the child will have the puzzle of their sexual intimacy, as well as the absence of a father or other male carer, to contend with as well. However, this is obviously far less disturbing for a child than a violent or untrustworthy father – or neglect all round.

In summary, we can conclude that it still seems valuable, especially during the early child-rearing years, if a trustworthy man 'stands at the door of the cave', just as has been expected through the ages. So while the period of time during which the man's breadwinning is crucial has been much reduced in recent decades, the burden of a *father's* responsibility rests, if anything, more heavily nowadays, in the era of the mobile nuclear family, than it did in past, more static, times. In those days it would be very likely that others of the extended family were close by to give support.

One only has to talk with fathers for a short time to realize how deeply most of them feel about their families. In fact, it is perhaps useful to conceive of a variant of Winnicott's idea and use the concept of primary *paternal* preoccupation as well as the maternal kind. This, of course, would not be rooted in pregnancy and lactation, as maternal preoccupation is; but so long as fatherly concern is not shattered or avoided, it can be a long-lasting and important enjoyment. It can have many different shapes.

A father must look two ways at once: outward towards the world of work and inward to the family. If his wife is to relax, his money earning must, in a sense, be primary. When a man will not, or cannot work, then the family loses its autonomy, together with much of its freedom. Other agencies must be called in to provide the money-earning side of fathering, and this can shame and debilitate the whole family. If, on the other hand, a father takes no interest in his family, apart from financially providing for it through his work, then at least the family remains an autonomous unit. Its members can still respect themselves, however unhappily.

Some men are undoubtedly ill equipped for family life. Their zest often lies in activities outside the home. They may be geared to sporting competitiveness, together with 'old boy' mutual praise and support from their friends, in ways that often seem absurd to women. What is more, very many of the skills demanded of men concern mechanistic technology needing high-grade physical thinking with large networks of colleagues. There will be little need for interpersonal reflection and intimacy. Then, when the men return to their families, quite different qualities are demanded. A father will usually have had no formal education at all about family matters. And, in contrast to a woman, he is unlikely to have learnt very much about such things from male conversation or literature. For instance, women's magazines are full of articles about personal problems and family matters in ways that are hardly seen in men's magazines. In short, pressures conspire to take a man's interest away from intimate family matters. Yet these problems will be present for a father for many years

It must be added here that times are definitely changing now, at around the beginning of the twenty-first century. Men's activity within the family is now not only written about but also publicly encouraged. For instance, there is now statutory provision for men to take up to two weeks paid paternity leave at and after a child's birth. Let us now go into family matters in a bit more detail.

The family environment

The place where a family settles will often be determined by where the husband's work is and what his earnings are. This is something that deeply affects his wife and children, and so a man will almost inevitably be held, or feel, responsible for any unhappiness or shortcomings.

The predicaments of work and housing are seen most poignantly with migrant families, who will have moved to an alien place for work or to escape persecution. It is equally difficult for people who are unemployed. Often, the only accommodation available imprisons the wife and stunts the children – some of Britain's city tower-block estates are notorious.

Even if a family can afford to choose where to live, housing can be the source of a woman's misery and resentment, especially if the man is a tyrant – of course, it can be the other way around if the woman is undemocratic and dominant. The actual house or flat itself is only one consideration. Also vital are the social climate of a neighbourhood and the availability of schools. Yet these are often difficult to estimate without living in the district first.

Looking after a mother

When a father turns in towards intimacy with his family, he will probably be ill prepared if he has learnt about life mostly from men's company. Within the family he will first have been a husband, so our earlier thinking about love and marriage still applies. But, when his wife's pregnancy and her maternal preoccupations arrive, he needs to widen his vigilance as his wife slackens hers. Just as she mothers their baby, so he needs to look after her. He is, in effect, being *maternal*, and will probably be emotionally identifying with his first carer – his mother. When a father fails to develop this care, his wife is left profoundly alone. In an extended family she would probably have female relatives to turn to; but in modern mobile nuclear families, there is often only her husband to help.

A mother often needs to be *held*, as Winnicott put it, both physically and psychologically. This conception is akin to Bion's commonly used technical term 'acting as a container' – both are useful, evocative metaphors, but they only hint at the complex activities involved. *Emotional conversations* between a couple are vital. Here a father would listen with sympathy to his partner, while reflecting more widely on other perspectives including his own point of view. Then he may realize there are things he ought to do for her, as well as simply being a discussant and arguer. Holding like this will be needed, not only in fraught situations, but also almost every day when the mother wants another opinion about herself or the children on routine things. Very often these could be gleaned from other women during the day. But when crucial questions arise, a father will be involved with the family situation more intimately than friends or neighbours. Likewise, of course, a wife is needed by her husband – to hold, contain or look after him.

The usual time for these second-opinion conversations is after the children have gone to bed. Husband and wife can then relax and off-load their feelings on to each other without hindrance. This is one very good reason for the routine of packing young children off to bed as early in the evening as possible.

There is no doubt that far more men are proud to be domesticated and useful about the house than was the norm half a century ago; we can honour ourselves that male-female democracy in the family has come to stay in most parts of these islands.

Moving to less happy things, a husband's failure to keep thoughtfully calm and 'hold' his wife's anxiety is a frequent cause of chronic bitterness in a family. For instance, you will often hear such words as: 'Oh, him, no sooner is he home than he's out in that garden of his', or 'When it suits him he'll be as sweet as pie to the children, but help me with them? Never!' Or she may say 'He has no idea what I have to cope with at home, he just comes in and criticizes'.

Fathers likewise often react to their wives' anxieties according to their own characteristic modes of defence built up over the years. Some husbands, for instance, tend to be scornful by nature. If they really care about their wives, they will probably adopt a mode of chiding that can be both appreciative and fault-finding. But scorn can easily be a nasty, pleasurably sadistic way of ridding the self of feelings of failure while humiliating others. Most people will know at least one martinet husband and mouse wife.

There are many other ways a husband can fail to hold his wife well. A common pattern is to fall into being henpecked. He may be very attentive to her but frightened into a jelly in awe of her. Then, having no independent vitality of his own, he will fail to contain his wife's impulsiveness, which can leave her in a state of chronic anxiety and exasperation. The hidden bitterness within a weak husband like this is epitomized by the man who said with dubious admiration, 'My wife and I are of one mind – hers'.

A father in direct relation to his children

We have seen how a mother needs to attune and keep in touch with her children through each stage of development. The same naturally applies to a father, and if he fails here he loses some of the deepest pleasures of fathering. In past years a father, usually being out all day, was most unlikely to be as intimately involved with looking after the children as his wife. Things have now often changed, and although a mother is usually still the most intimate centre for very young children, a father is often also deeply wanted for his own particular style of living and differences from her. As children grow older, the relative importance of father and mother often evens out, so that he is sometimes more sought after than his wife. But if he has not been in tune with them from the beginning, he will inevitably be ill at ease and something of a stranger. He and his children will have missed a very deep pleasure. Even the ambivalence and quarrels are part of the fun, which can be unforgettably marvellous. Freud probably did not emphasize this fun enough when he introduced his great concept of the Oedipus complex.

Having two parents makes it easier for a child to integrate his ambivalent feelings. Thus, quite early in life a father becomes important as a separate person in his own right. He is of a different gender from his wife, so that boys and girls can find their own sexual identity both by watching and learning from father and mother together; and by the subtle ways in which each parent separately relates to them. A father is also likely to be a *prime representative of the outside world*, while still being an intimate family person. Parents vary, but it is often a father who first explains and demonstrates the geography and differing ways of the more distant world to children.

Modern urban society presents one special problem about this learning from fathers. In the past, children could often go to be with their father in the fields or workshop. But this opportunity is rare today. He leaves home at 8 a.m., say, to do something incomprehensible until 6 or 7 p.m. A man can easily say he works in an office, workshop, school, or factory, but such verbal reports are nearly meaningless to a small child. One has only to see a boy working on a farm with his father to recognize that such an experience is often lost in urban life. A farmer's son of seven or eight can go with his father, watch him and then do things to help, so he can actually do really useful work himself when on holiday or after school.

Children of a father who is an office worker can copy him only from imagination, or by looking at him working at a computer, driving the car, gardening, or when doing DIY around the house. They cannot *see* his primary fathering function of money-earning work. It has sometimes been suggested that this gap in learning has contributed towards the devaluing of fathering in Western society. Another problem is that paternal models will be nearly useless if the child feels personally *unrecognized* by his father, as can happen especially when he is away a lot. A child will probably then be so consumed with hurt, pain, and anger at being unnoticed that he will destroy the example his father presents, however useful it might potentially be. A father needs to attune himself to his children, and get to know and be known, just as a mother is.

Some men still assume that they can safely ignore their children in early infancy – and here they are probably badly mistaken. A father who has mingled in with his children from babyhood will not only have the pleasure of seeing their growth and contributing to it, but will also know them intimately in all their idiosyncrasies. When he intuitively knows their modes of thought, he will not only enjoy it, but also be able to be a 'tuned-in teacher' for them when he needs to impart new knowledge. If he has not known them in their early days he comes in as a relative foreigner, speaking in ways that are unfamiliar, and his disciplines seem arbitrary. Many people report bitterly about this when they look back on their childhoods, while others look back with happy gratitude at their fathers who were close to them.

Just as mothers have difficulties at different stages because of the intrusion of their own fantasies, so also do fathers. Some avoid infancy; others can be reluctant to participate in toilet training, say. It is now getting to be more or less a tradition that mothers and fathers share the nappy and potty work together – and usually thoroughly enjoy it. But some fathers still shy away. This may not matter much, except that a mother will not feel happily backed up in her very important efforts.

Some fathers find disciplining work at home easy and are invaluable backstops for a tired mother. Others find it nerve-racking and impossible to apply consistently. For instance, it is often reported that a father has identified himself too exclusively with his children against their disciplinary mother; he then connives in undermining her authority. Other fathers can, of course, be tyrants, assuming authority without understanding the job.

As we have seen, fathers, like mothers, often find themselves troubled by sexual impulses and fantasies about their children. Having enjoyed cuddling and kissing their children until they are 2 or 3 years old, they then shy off, probably because things feel too sexy. This withdrawal is sometimes particularly noticeable with their sons – probably because fears of homosexuality will have secretly worried most men.

A father is also likely to have his own personal patterns of fantasy about children, just as happens with a mother. When these ideas are flexible, and allow room for him to recognize his children as they really are, they give vividness to him and his children's lives. On the other hand, when a father's fantasy remains entrenched, it can stunt the growth of a child – or embitter them. Here are a few examples:

A father was brought up in a severe religious faith. After many rebellions he saw the light and became strictly religious himself. However, his ambivalent feelings about it seemed to get attached to and affect his two sons. The elder was a lively and rather naughty boy, so that the father became convinced he had no good in him. The younger son, on the other hand, was seen as a shining light of innocent virtue. The two boys then reacted in character. The eldest espoused unconventional causes and became a militant atheist, taking every opportunity to torment his narrow-minded father, whom he loathed. The younger son was obedient and tied to his parents. He was quite talented as a musician but could only play religious music. By his twenties he had few friends of his own, and had never taken a girl out.

A girl bore a strong resemblance to her mother, who died when she was quite young. Her father doted on her, but seemed fixed upon the image of his dead wife. When the girl had grown into her teens he would still take her on his knee and say, 'Your mother will never be dead while you are alive'. As a woman she was often invaded by feelings of being like her dead mother, and was overcome with bouts of depression.

A father felt himself to be a failure, just as his own father had been. He was determined that his son should escape this fate, so he saw to it that he was well educated, and encouraged him to choose a career that he could throw his heart into. This in itself created few difficulties, but the father also felt a failure with his wife, and encouraged his son to take his place with her, just as he had done over careers. Thus he would ask the boy to mediate between him and his wife, and also to care for her in ways in which he had failed. The boy felt proud and rather arrogantly triumphant, but also very disturbed. He remained tied to his parents for many years, at least in part because he felt guiltily responsible for both of them, and unable to leave them to their own devices.

These are just a few examples. Others will readily spring to mind. Because a father's functions are very diverse and lack the consuming unions of motherhood, it is rare that a man breaks down mentally with the complaint that he is unable to father his children. Our society at present seems to make it easier for a father to opt out of his responsibilities towards his children than it is for his wife. This means, not only that a greater burden tends to be placed on a mother, but also that many serious problems between fathers and children might continue unattended indefinitely.

Mothering functions in being a father

It was noted earlier that, traditionally, men were unlikely to get much information about the intimate personal aspects of family life from other men. But times have changed, and this intimate knowledge is often really called for in the modem family – certainly more than at any time in the past. The young man will have had his first and most important experiences of intimacy from his own mother in infancy and after. He will have learnt about life literally at his mother's knee. For instance, a young father taking his baby out in a pushchair and chatting to it will have done it all before, but the other way round – from when he was in a pushchair. He will in all likelihood have have copied his mother as a toddler by trundling a trolley about with dolls or teddy bears. Boys, when very young at least, identify just as strongly with their mothers as do girls; but for boys these identifications with mother are with someone of the opposite sex. We have already noted how children are vehemently conscious of their sexual identity. Thus, by school age, boys are usually prone to be embarrassed and reject the ways of their mother and sisters. They see them as being 'sissy' or 'wet'. This is enshrined somewhat in our society – at least in some single-sex schools and in the attitudes of men talking together. On the other hand, girls can feel just as embarrassed if they are thought of as too much as like their fathers.

We could summarize by saying that there is a tendency to feel anxious about and even reject *cross-sex identifications.* This seems to be particularly so with boys and men. But it is also noticeable in women when they often shy away from doing things they feel are not in accord with their sex. Some women avoid DIY about the house, or heavy vegetable gardening. Many women used to be reluctant to drive a car, it being 'boyish', but this has largely disappeared, in Western Europe at least. Such chronic prejudices in both men and women probably serve to do little but stultify their own and others' lives.

When a man comes to marriage and fatherhood, he often does not realize that many of the functions he learnt directly from his mother will be called upon to the full. It might even be an advantage to have had little education from other men about such matters in youth. A man can then be free of indoctrination and make his own discoveries about caring and intimacy. However, it also means that, depending on the friends he has, he might have little male support, leaving him lonely and unsure when faced with family problems.

Cross-sex identification creates its own problems. A father can one-sidedly turn into something of an 'old woman'. He can get fussy, so that his wife could be deprived of his male determination and romanticism towards her. She is then likely to become depressed and disgruntled because her femininity is left unappreciated.

Mothers and fathers together

Most of this chapter has been about parents individually relating to their children. But we saw earlier, particularly when discussing the Oedipus complex, that children need to integrate their ideas and feelings about their parents in their minds. A child, who has nothing much to go on except memories of the violent splits and rows between his parents, can feel deeply disturbed inside. He will fear for his home's safety and security. As well as this, the mental representations of his parents will not 'marry' or function together in the mind, but will contradict each other, so it is hard to use them in everyday thought.

Some parents seem to be so sensitive to this that they vow never to disagree in front of the children. It is probably a good rule not to indulge thoughtlessly in rows in front of children – they can be especially frightening and confusing. But children are often very sensitive to parental moods – they can often weave wild, anxious solitary fantasies if nothing is said about them. So openly expressed disagreements, recognizing different points of view and phrased in terms that a child can understand, are more likely to calm a child than is a false appearance of solidarity. Fiery arguments can even be fun, even for the children listening nearby, so long as a basic undertone of fond mutuality still clearly remains. Furthermore, when an appearance of agreement is carried on chronically, to the length of falsehood, fundamentally it is *lying*.

Perhaps worse than differences between parents can be the neglect imposed on children by some couples who continue indulging in a self-absorbed, romanticized 'chronic love affair' with each other. By being interested only in showing utter devotion to each other, the two parents often set up a barrier of indifference to their children, who then grow up hurt and bitter, with a deep feeling of 'being a nuisance'. Romantic love may be a prerequisite in providing the impetus and stability to rear children today. But 'great lovers' often fail to make good parents. Romantic love is necessary, but never sufficient.

Parents separating out

Throughout any marriage, with stresses at work, changes in home, bringing up children and getting older, both parents will have been torn in many different directions. Each will have been through a multitude of crises by the time the children are into school age. By then a mother will probably have had to find a new *work identity* for herself, or wilt at home. A father, on the other hand, with his work often to the forefront throughout, may be differently stressed but also have to make his own particular changes. It would seem to be mere chance if both parents find easy harmony together all the time. However devoted and kind a couple may be, it seems inevitable that, in some ways at least, they must assert themselves and thence *separate out* to re-find their own *core ways of being*, or *identities*. This does not mean that they must 'separate' or live apart. It might come to this, but this would be because they could not separate out while still being together.

It has been said, 'Everyone should marry three times – preferably to the same person!' This leads to thinking about the value for parents of sharing the 'growing up and away' of their children. First, it is useful to recognize the importance for children of knowing they have parents who can be happy together without the children around, yet who are available to come home to. Such knowledge gives a deep and precious freedom. With this in mind, perhaps marriage for life is still worth striving for.

Many couples who lose intimacy with each other can find invaluable help in marital counselling and psychotherapy. However, there are many others who really do find life more fruitful and less stressful after they divorce. Yet others plod on, often torturing each other, in a gloomy 'holy deadlock', when they might have both been better off apart. So we must now address the question of divorce.

Divorce

The last chapter on marriage noted that it is not surprising that many people, basing their choice of partner upon youthful, idolizing romantic love alone, later find themselves incompatible. Human beings are limited in how much they can happily attune to each other. Every couple that stays together, let alone those who part, has to manage incompatibilities with each other's characters. It needs hard work, with an emphasis on *unselfishness* (Byng-Hall, 1995; Parker, 1995; Trowell & Bower, 1995).

It could be said that divorce is due not simply to elements of incompatibility, but to intolerance of it, perhaps by both, or at least by one partner. It only needs one determined partner to be intolerant of the marriage for a divorce to start developing. One partner may then leave the marital home, or drive the other out, and may even appear to be the innocent party. Remember that intolerance could have arisen for very good reasons. The other spouse may have been self-centredly promiscuous and insisted that it didn't matter. Or they may have been sadistic, dishonest, or insatiably demanding, grossly perverse, or psychotic. Very often, but not always, a partner's intolerance may be driven by greed, cruelty, promiscuity or other forms of gross *selfishness* of their own. The term selfishness is little used as a psychoanalytic or psychological concept. Something sounding less moralistic and more technical, like '*narcissism*', is usually preferred. But this is snobbishly theoretical, and frankly means no more nor less than selfishness.

Peaceful, amicably agreed divorces may take place, but nearly all would have been along the downward path in rage, torment, and bitterness. The early stages of divorce always seem to involve violent splitting and projection of feelings about the partner, which amount to the paranoid hatred that we saw in the unhappy marriages of the last chapter. However hard a couple tries to be considerate – and many succeed, especially when their children are involved – there is probably always a core of loathing in any separation, at least in the early stages. Looking after each other, tolerance of idiosyncrasy, mutual containment, the keeping of each other sane – all these efforts come to an end. In this light, simple incompatibility is usually a bland euphemism.

Children and divorce

Divorce within a childless couple will still be hurtful but the partners are free to find happier lives. The issues are, of course, much more serious where children are concerned, especially when young. Some partners become so engrossed in justifying themselves that they malignantly charm their children to take sides against their other parent. When one realizes that this may be against a parent that a child has loved and needed, it becomes obvious how nastily distorting of profound feelings this can be. Some parents can be so taken up with their indignation that they ignore the lonely plight of their children caught in the middle. Family courts have to strive every day to combat this sort of neglect. Even so, probably most parents really do go on caring for their children, and they do try to be fair with them about the other partner. This undoubtedly mitigates the terrible disturbance that divorce can create for many children. On the other hand, many children will testify that it is far better to have two separated parents who are happy than two fighting miseries who are piously sticking together.

Let us look at some of the issues that a child must contend with on divorce, starting with the end results that need to be prepared for. Any child coming to adulthood needs to find their own *integrity* as a person apart from his parents. To do this, he must be able to *use* the emotionally felt *representations* of all his family within himself. Thus, a person's own parents may be long dead, but memory of them can continue to live in the mind by identifications with them. These parental, and also sibling, identifications will inevitably involve conflicts and contradictions between them, however happy the family has been. The identifications within a person whose parents divorced are likely to be more conflicted and full of contradictions. But marital counsellors will testify that, if the parents themselves acted with fair-minded concern, the task of bringing these identifications together within the mind need not be impossible to negotiate.

In summary: any child growing up needs to coalesce the mental representations of all his family, and to use these ideas of them together within the self. How can this be facilitated even when parents separate?

First, let us look at the bad side. When a divorce occurs, one parent must leave the children, if they are still young, so that they must all be hurt and depleted by the absence from each other. The parent who remains is usually then overburdened, subject to quiet blame from the children and with solitary responsibilities. There are often fewer opportunities for fun and the parent can shrink into martyrdom. As well as this, divorce is often more apparent than real – whether they like it or not, parents are still tied. Even if they have opted out of everything else, they can still be tied together by mutual loathing and guilt. It is they who brought their children into the world and then upset them. So while divorce must very often be ultimately beneficial to the children, they must still, if nothing else, suffer the daily loss of opportunity to enjoy and add to their identifications with at least one of their parents.

Most optimal alternatives involve exploring ways for both parents to find a freedom from each other that is compatible with both going on having enjoyable contact with their children. This would occur when the children can be at home with either parent separately, and yet still be close to their own friends. Children usually find that visiting a parent in a strange environment is a lonely business. They can even sometimes feel they have no real home with either parent. There may be many different combinations that would make a solution that can be thought about. However, probably all are painful, at least in the early stages. Very often, either mother or father, or both, partner-up with someone else and the children and their step-parents must then try to attune with each other. In fact, some fathers lose touch with their children; others can slip into sexual abuse with them.

Broken homes where the parents have new partners are hardly easy places to make a happy place for the children, However, there is a positive side, for it can mean another set, or even two sets, of people become relatives, and this can be deeply enriching and thus happy. Whatever new patterns are found, it is surely better to work things out with agonized care than to act on impulse and risk ignoring vital issues, however 'spontaneous' 'natural', or 'honest' this may seem.

When parents are trying to work out what to do, they might find this, admittedly oversimplified, list of priorities for children useful. As an ideal, and not more than an ideal, it can be said that any ordinary child needs to be: (1) happy with mother; (2) happy with father; (3) able to see that both parents can each enjoy themselves alone; (4) able to enjoy them when they are being happy together; (5) able to be happy with his own friends.

This ideal would probably require staying with both mother and father in a familiar environment until adolescence at least, and that mother and father can go on enjoying each other. But it is this, the third requirement, that parents go on enjoying each other, that often breaks down and becomes impossible and then is more or less finally ruptured with separation and divorce. However, if the other four requirements are well met, while disturbingly sad for a child, things need not necessarily be catastrophically so. What is more, it is frequently reported that parents can still, even if divorced, enjoy themselves together, at least for short times when thinking *about* their children. Thus our list of priorities points up that labelling divorce as a single simple causal entity, for good or bad, is too crude where children are concerned. Rather, one has to evaluate and then mitigate the many ruptures that may occur.

This list of priorities also makes plain that, under some circumstances, it may well be better for a child to enjoy being with each of their parents divorced, if they are separate, contented people, than to be burdened with two stressed people who keep miserably together because they can't work out alternatives. Fundamentally, it must be the responsibility of each parent to decide the way that seems best for themselves, their spouse and their children – all are certainly important.

Single parent families

The last few pages, which have emphasized the values of a nuclear family, must seem unfair on the many single parents who manage to bring up really happy children. It must first be emphasized that it is one thing to set about making a good job of bringing up a family alone because of death or desertion; it is quite another matter to *actively decide* to have a child without the father being known to the child. A woman who consciously decides to get pregnant in these circumstances could be taken up by fantasies that can militate against thoughtful mothering. We have already seen what a great multiplicity of needs a young child has, and that these require continuing care from a very few devoted and intimate people. From this we must wonder whether only a woman of inordinate grandiosity and conceit would consciously set about mothering alone with equanimity. However, there are usually other considerations; for instance, it has been noted that women brought up in sexually abusive families often want to be all alone in having a child. They have obvious and justifiable fears that their partner might turn out like their father. Even so, a resolve to be a single mother would probably arise only in someone who is desperate, and who, to some degree, denies the reality of all that is involved in bringing up a child. This may not always be the case, but it is surely best to think about it.

Having said this, let us think about people who suddenly find themselves, because of death or separation, as single parents of either sex. Someone living alone with young children is often so busy that they are able to keep going only by staying on a 'high', or in a slightly *manic* mood. In time, this can crack into utter exhaustion and often illness, which is all the worse because there may be little other help available for the children. Naturally it is vital to keep going for the children, but there is a wise woman's saying: 'Your first job as a parent is to *look after yourself* – a broken parent is no use to anyone.'

Quite frequently, a lonely parent can break into a state of serious *depression*, which needs psychotherapeutic or psychiatric help. With luck, the dead numbness of loss will melt away in time. It is perhaps important then, as part of self-care, to let oneself *feel*, to be sad, alone, glad – whatever comes. We will say more about mourning in a later chapter; but remember here that marital loss and loneliness is a *death* of a sort. It is thus an essential occasion for letting oneself mourn. No one has physically died, but the loss of a partner is just as real. People who are left alone may be glad of the relief from a useless, cold, cruel or mad partner; but the aloneness itself means there has been a great loss. Depression is more or less inevitable, and it is surely best to recognize it.

A single parent will probably feel guilty, even remorseful, that the children are growing up without their other parent. One cannot get rid of such feelings, but it is best to keep such guilt in check. Guilt is invaluable to us humans, but it is like a faithful fierce guard dog – best kept in a kennel most of the time. One's conscience is an inner 'good friend'; but it can often be seriously stupid in its fierceness. It then needs one's *conscious self* to tell it firmly to get back into its kennel. The growling and snapping of guilt can easily sap a parent's clarity of resolve when a forthright and firm approach would serve the children best. Without the intimacy of a partner, a parent must have, almost more than anything else, other friends to refer to – to feel with, to be respected, cared about, and argued with. This can only be done by getting out of the house and positively, quite self-consciously, making friends. Often this will be with people in a similar situation who might also need help themselves at times; so that the friendship can then be enjoyably reciprocal. With lots of good friends the burden of parenting can become a joy again. Many single parents have emphasized that *getting into the outside world* is essential to sanity – often more appreciated by the children than are hours of solitary devotion and a tidy house. Children can certainly use a parent who is fun to be with more easily than a solitary, depressed one, who stirs up a multitude of anxieties.

This need for a parent to be out in the world needs to be remembered when thinking of going out to work. When children are very young, the extra money this would bring in is probably not worth the exhaustion and discontinuity that come with it. But when a child is old enough to enjoy nursery school, it is probably better for a parent to have the confidence and refreshment of working than to remain solitarily devoted to the children. Lastly, it is worth remembering that many single parents will have their own original family; and also that their ex-partners may be glad to be available. Children themselves need relatives to belong to and identify with – especially the parent who has left them. This parent may be a long way off but glad to have their children for long holidays. This can be valuable for the children and will give the main looking-after parent a necessary break.

This is a brief and rather inadequate coverage of a vitally important subject, but it can at least serve as a beginning.

Further reading

Byng-Hall, J. (1995) *Re-writing Family Scripts*. London: Guilford.
Daws, D. (1989) *Through the Night*. London: Free Association. Standard text about infant sleep problems and parent–infant relationships.

Dunn, J. (1984), *Sisters and Brothers*. London: Fontana. Brief and simple, about siblings growing up together.

Gorrell-Barnes, G., & Dowling, A. (2000) *Working with Children and Parents through Separation and Divorce: the Changing Lives of Children*. London: Palgrave Macmillan.

Murray, L., & Cooper, P. (1997) *Post-Partum Depression*. New York: Guilford.

Parke, R.D. (1981) *Fathering*. London: Fontana. Brief and straightforward.

Parker, R. (1995) *Torn in Two: Motherhood and Ambivalence*. London: Virago.

Ruszczynski, S., & Fisher, J. (eds) (1995) *Intrusiveness in the Couple*. London: Karnac.

Stern, D. (1995) *The Motherhood Constellation*. New York: Basic Books.

Trowell, J., & Etchegoyen, A. (2002) *The Importance of Fathers*. London: Routledge.

Chapter 13

Being alone

Mary Twyman

It is worth considering what being alone at various stages in the development of human beings can signify. This must encompass discussing whether being alone is a chosen state, deciding one needs to walk along the shore alone to gather one's thoughts, or whether the being alone is imposed by circumstances, a spouse left alone after the death of a partner or by divorce. It might be useful to distinguish the capacity to be alone, as Winnicott has defined it, from the dread of aloneness, which carries with it the often desperate needs of the person for a kind of frantic sociability thought to be essential to ward off the essential experiencing of the self and its fantasies. For to be alone offers the opportunity to follow the pathway of one's own thought. This may be the mature individual's use of time alone, a time of reflection, where thought can proceed associatively and connections previously unremarked can be formed. Nor is this experience purely intellectual or indeed wholly conscious; it does not leave out sensuous experience. Think of a baby, spending time alone in his cot or pushchair, seeing, watching patterns of light in a room, or outdoors, learning visually about the world around him, and taking in the sounds and smells of the household or the garden or the street. This time alone provides space for a vital learning and integrating mental and emotional process to take place, in which gradual recognition of the nature of the baby's environment is built up. Indeed, the provision of quiet time – 'being alone' – is vital, because we cannot in infancy experience and make sense of our experience simultaneously. Therefore there is a need for the quiet time alone to, as we might say, catch up with ourselves, allow for the experience to be made sense of. Winnicott also proposed that one of the primary maternal functions a mother provides for her baby is that of a protective shield, regulating the amount and intensity of stimulation to which the baby is exposed, including from his own emotional state, so that the baby is not faced with more than his immature mind and body can handle. It may be that for most adults, too, there is an equivalent protective shield that needs to be in place in some form or another so that experience, not necessarily particularly traumatic experience, but the everyday ebb and flow of ordinary life and relationships, can be digested. So it is that many of us need to withdraw for a while to think our own thoughts, to muse on what has happened to us recently or what we imagine might be about to confront us in the future. Of course, there is the ultimate being alone of sleep that everyone retreats into, and within that state, the particular form of being alone with our own thoughts that dreaming constitutes.

Being alone in the presence of another, again a concept delineated by Winnicott (1969), describes a state represented by a child playing imaginatively on his own in the house where mother is present, getting on with her own things, while he can be, in his imagination, driving his truck around the building site. Sometimes he will include his mother as a point of reference, someone to share a discovery with, then going off to resume his activity safe in the knowledge that she is unobtrusively present, but that he can safely go back to being alone in his world of imagination. What are the adult equivalents of this particular constellation of internal/ external relationships? One thinks of students or scholars studying alongside each other in a library; artists at a life drawing class, each engaged in their creative endeavour, concentrated but aware of their fellow painters also at work in the same studio; partners doing gardening or household tasks separately but within the overall orbit of each other's presence. At best this being alone in the presence of the other can be the source of fruitful discoveries made by the one individual which are then to be shared with the other, just as the small child shares his discoveries with his mother.

The other very particular form of being alone in the presence of another is the situation offered to an analysand in the psychoanalytic therapeutic situation. Here the analyst/psychotherapist sits behind the analysand, who lies on the couch, out of sight but not out of hearing, and the analysand is invited to put into words whatever thoughts enter his mind. So that what is proposed to the analysand is that he make an exploration of his thoughts and feelings both so that he can discover them for himself, and also that he may communicate them to the listening analyst who is attuned to the analysand's reverie. This, from the outsider's view, quite strange formal setting for a dialogue nevertheless yields a relationship of peculiar intimacy, carefully guarded by the boundaries that maintain uninterrupted time during the session, and confidentiality as to the analysand's utterances. We encounter a paradox here, for the state of being alone in this context carries with it the potential for an especially close kind of relating. It may be that this also reveals the need that many adults have for an oscillation between periods of solitude and periods of genuinely close contact with others. The psychoanalytic therapist will be able to deduce from the way the analysand relates to him in the sessions, or resists relating to him, the characteristic fashion in which the analysand regulates his relating to others. This may be marked by periods of trustful confiding, alternating with periods of withdrawal in a defensive manner. And it will be the task of the analyst to sense from the affective charge that these various states carry how the analysand's anxieties and hostilities are in relationship. His comments on his perceptions – his interpretations – offer the analysand a new viewpoint from which to see his own familiar, taken-for-granted-as-normal way of relating, and how its rigidity might mirror problems of past relating, which are no longer appropriate. Over a long period in a psychoanalytic therapy, such problems will gradually come to be recognized by the analysand, and in a good outcome real psychic change at the unconscious level will take place and new ways of seeing himself in relation to others will emerge. It may also be that a new development from the experience of being in the psychoanalytic therapy arises as the analysand discerns a deeper capacity in himself to benefit from being alone. This may betoken a richer ability to make use of his own emotional resources, to respond to thought, feeling, perception, including aesthetic perceptions in a more profound and meaningful way.

The benefits of freely chosen solitude and the pains of enforced solitude have been richly explored by Anthony Storr in his book *The school of genius* (1988). This extended study cites many examples of the individual's search for the experience of solitude, sometimes in order to undertake creative work – he cites many authors, poets, artists, composers and philosophers, but also scientists and men of action, explorers and politicians who have sought sometimes extended periods of solitude to pursue a particular kind of self-experiencing. Reports back from these experiences frequently include the description of states of feeling not previously experienced. These take the form of accounts of feeling in harmony with the world, a sense of unity with creation, sometimes ecstatic, something contributing to a sense of the appreciation of the beauty of the world, the marvel of creation and a gratitude for the simple fact of being alive. Some see this as closely related to some form of religious experience and one might see the contemplative practices of many religions as analogous, in an internal manner, to the withdrawal from sociability which the withdrawal into solitude for more active people out in the world provides. The term for this in some Christian practices is to go on a retreat, a term in ordinary usage associated with a defeated yielding, but in its religious context indicating a purposeful withdrawal from the hurly-burly of everyday life to allow time and space for prayer and contemplation usually accompanied by an extended period of silence.

While describing these quests for solitude in a benign context, it is important to remember that some individuals' search for solitude can carry more serious and damaging elements. One thinks of the remote cut-off mental states of schizophrenic patients at crucial times in their illness, when the external world and relations with real people are severed and the patient is overwhelmed by the powerful fantasies of the inner world. Perhaps less extreme but no less carrying the potential for danger is the person who in a state of denial subjects themselves to perilous solitary enterprises. A man in psychotherapy told his therapist that he frequently went mountaineering alone, and also sailed alone. His confidence in his abilities bordered on the omnipotent but even had he been expert, as he presumably was, what was alarming in his discourse was the revelation of his conviction that the mountains and the seas were personified by him as uniquely benignly disposed towards him. He could envisage no circumstances in which he would be in any peril; the mountains would 'care' for him, the sea would always carry him safely home to harbour. This evidence of an illusory idealization of the environment as totally safe, specifically for him, derived in part from his history of having lost his mother to an early death in his childhood. To cover over the huge loss, which at the age it occurred could not properly be mourned by the young boy, he had summoned up in his mind the image of a uniquely ever-present totally protective mother and had invested the natural world in which he undertook his solitary climbs and voyages with all the attributes he associated with such a maternal figure. Through his therapy it was possible for him to recognize that ordinary caution was necessary and that his delusional trust in the environment he adventured into bore a close relationship to the image of his lost mother who had left him to deal with growing-up substantially alone. His therapist held the view that his solitary journeys were quasi-suicidal in unconscious intent, pursuing a near fatal path in an attempt to join up with his lost mother.

The enforced being alone that Storr examines in some detail, the predicament of a prisoner in solitary confinement, is not part of most people's usual experience in their development. But those bereaved or abandoned by hitherto close partners, parents, siblings or companions often refer to the state of loneliness that ensues as like being in a prison. They describe the loss of a close relationship in terms of being confined in a way of life from which there is no deliverance, and frequently suffer states of feeling marked by anger, despair and a certain dislocation or disintegration as the realization of their aloneness is borne in upon them. If a process of mourning can be entered into and allowed to run its course, such a feeling of alienation may yield to a subsequent feeling of resolution so that the person can resume activities and relationships that sustain, albeit they do not replace what has been lost. The achievement of mourning for losses, for that is what it is, testifies to the healthy mature state of development that is characterized by a capacity to adapt internally to the reality of what has happened while being able to employ memory and reverie to maintain contact with the lost good. Perhaps the final product of the state of being alone is the capacity to hold on to the good of what is past and to allow for its transformation in the movement towards what lies ahead.

Further reading

Storr, A. (1988) *The School of Genius.* London: Andre Deutsch.
Winnicott, D.W. (1969) The capacity to be alone. In: *The Maturational Processes and the Facilitating Environment.* London: Hogarth Press.

Chapter 14

Mid-life

Mary Twyman

> In the middle of the journey of our life, I came to myself within a dark wood where the straight way was lost. Ah, how hard it is to tell of that wood, savage and harsh and dense, the thought of which renews my fear. So bitter is it that death is hardly more.
>
> (from Dante, *The divine comedy*)

The term 'mid-life', and particularly the idea of the so-called 'mid-life crisis' has entered the popular everyday currency of speech; not always used in its proper sense, but nevertheless testifying to the nature of people's interest and concern with this important phase of human development. The two vast seminal contributions on this phase come from Eric Erikson (1968) and from Eliot Jaques (1970), both of whom delineated the features which are specific to this period of life in man and woman. Jaques' essay *Death and the mid-life crisis* really set the style for an examination of the predicament of the human being in our culture, living longer than his or her forebears had any prospect of doing, and therefore facing a long slow passage from the height of adult achievement – of career, of partnership, of parenthood – to the decline into old age and towards death.

Jaques, writing as a psychoanalyst but being readily accessible to general readers, actually places the mid-life crisis earlier than the ordinary sense of the term as it is now used. He was especially examining the crises in the lives of people of artistic achievement, who seemed to have succeeded early in their lives and to be facing, in their mid-thirties, the dilemma of what direction their work and life was to take from there on. For some artists, it seemed, a new direction could be found and the work went on to fresh achievements, marked usually by a deepening and further maturing. For others, if the crisis could not be negotiated, stagnation, stalemate, often involving physical or psychological illness supervened, and in the most extreme cases a premature death followed.

Certainly a major factor in considering mid-life is the question of where it starts. Is it to be placed at around 35, the mid-point if one is thinking of the life span as the traditional three score years and ten? For most of us in the Western industrialized world, life expectancy goes beyond this. Especially, for instance, when one recognizes that women are delaying child-bearing until their late thirties and even forties, the notion of mid-life seems to be shifting to later decades. Advances in medical science, the contraceptive pill to give safe control of fertility, and the development of hormone replacement therapy for women suffering from symptoms at the time of the menopause, are powerful agents that have affected the general health and well-being of women in their fertile and post-childbearing years; and these two examples will have contributed substantially both qualitatively and quantitatively to women's life expectancy. In our culture, to be worn out by childbearing from the teens onwards is no longer the common fate of most women. For men too, advances in health care mean that they can look forward to a relatively fit and healthy middle age and approach to old age. Except for those perhaps in hazardous occupations, families are unlikely to be faced with the loss of a father before late middle-age or even later, the fate of many a family in the early part of the last century.

The conquering of the major infectious diseases for children and adults in our Western culture has ensured not only that the majority of children survive from childhood to adulthood, but that adults survive to enjoy a longer period of middle and old age. Nowadays, for the first time, men and women can look forward to 30 or 50 years of productive life after their children have reached adulthood. Compare this with the fact that until the end of the nineteenth century no more than 8 per cent survived to the age of 60. Nearly 30 years ago, Neugatan and Hagestad (1976) could write 'We live today in a society . . . that is becoming accustomed to 70-year-old students, 30-year-old college presidents, 22-year-old mayors, 35-year-old grandmothers, 50-year-old retirees, 65-year-old fathers of pre-schoolers, 60-year-olds and 30-year-olds wearing the same clothing styles and 85-year-old parents caring for 65-year-old offspring.' So what are the psychological features that mark these years of mid-life and beyond?

Whatever else there is to say about mid-life, and there is much, what has to be said is that it encompasses change. This is not to say that change is not characteristic of other earlier phases of human development, but these have been mapped out and worked over extensively in the literature of infant and child development, adolescents, partners, parenthood, and definable trends can be teased out. However, the very concept of the mid-life crisis means that the unitary concept of adulthood beginning at 18 to 21 with the 'key of the door' and lasting until death is no longer reflective of reality; whether objective or psychological. Colarusso and Nemiroff (1985) developed Erikson's idea of three stages of adulthood – early, middle and late. This implied two periods of transition; the first being a mid-life transition and the second, occurring between 60 and 65, being a transition into late adulthood.

Hildebrand (1995) suggests that to outward appearances the period between thirty and forty may seem conformist and some-thing of a plateau. Certain major life decisions can be made and represent commitments that have life-long implications. For example, the decision whether to have a family or the decision as to how to earn a living, be these decisions consciously articulated or not, become the stuff of a kind of personal audit during the first transitional period. If the individual decides that changes are to be made, then there is no time to waste. Hence, it seems that one pressure causing this initial review is the realisation of the finitude of life. As the quotation from Dante's *The divine comedy* above suggests, this is scarcely new, but the extension of the life span brings choices undreamt of even by our grandparents.

The detailed scrutiny and research that goes into the formulation of theories about normal development in infants, children, adolescents and the achievement of adult status, lapses when the later stages of adulthood are reached. This may well be because, from mid-adulthood onwards, the emphasis is on the varieties of individual development. This is perhaps the strength and the curious paradox of the mid-life period. For the infant and the child the stages of development are marked, and we know that there are critical periods within which certain milestones are reached. The changes in later adulthood are more widely spaced; menopause can occur anytime between the mid-forties and mid-fifties, except in those unfortunate cases where it arrives exceptionally in the thirties. For men, potency may remain unaffected by ageing, but anxieties about the ageing process itself may affect sexual matters. But for both men and women the central fact dominating the need for change at mid-life is the awareness of the time limit on life. Their future is not infinite.

The individual's awareness of his life span

Most of us, as we progress through life, have a sense of our age relative to those surrounding us. The child has a notion of who is 'bigger than me' or, for a 3-year-old 'she's just a baby', noticing a little girl still having a bottle. While the child is aware of his smallness, his aspiration is to be 'big'. The adolescents' scorn of the parents' wish to help and guide and the repudiation of dependency, marks his sense of 'who I am in relation to my child self and the adult I am striving to become'.

The established adult of the late twenties and thirties is a contributor to society, in work, in relationship and in the formation through partnership and marriage of the nuclear family. The adults, if they make this choice, take their place – man and woman – and assume the responsibility of founding a family and facing the task of rearing that family to adulthood. The overall attitude during these years is aspiration, looking forward, to the achievement of stability and advance for the family unit, for the individual in work and profession, for the safe, healthy development of children to be set on their way in life.

With the advent of mid-life, there arrives, however, a different mode. Perhaps one or two friends and colleagues succumb to an early death. Suddenly there is a jolt that brings into focus the fact of mortality. There are also the signs of physical ageing, perhaps accompanied by feelings of shame exacerbated by the preoccupation of our current culture with the idealization, even idolization of youthfulness. This awareness of physical ageing brings with it, however much the individual might wish to deny it, an awareness of death. Whatever else remains to be achieved, and there is much that can be accomplished in the mid-life to old age phase, what is incontrovertible is that the awareness of each puts in place an end point, and it is necessary for the individual to recognize this as it impinges on his/her sense of individual identity.

Development of the idea of mortality

A child's sense of mortality comes about as early as 3 or 4. 'Mummy's flowers have died' observes a 3-year-old, noticing the vase of wilting daffodils. When a family pet dies there is anxiety, puzzlement and at first an assumption that 'the hamster will wake up soon, won't he?' Children may announce that 'someone is dead' without really comprehending what this means. The sorting out of absence (with the possibility of a returning presence) from the permanent absence of death is a much later development. But the child is constantly trying to make sense of experience, that of external loss perceived when the flowers die, or the hamster dies, and to relate this to his inner experience of 'gone' and 'not coming back' and the ultimate incomprehension of this. What is most likely to go along with this is the experience of sadness, and further the depressive feelings that accompany a permanent loss. While these losses are part of the ongoing process of living, it is important that such losses and their accompanying affects are given their due, painful but deepening, of a child's experience of the world he inhabits. The child's first experience of loss of known persons in his world may be the death of a grandparent. Although this is a close figure in the child's life, grandparents are not generally the primary figures on whom the child depends. But a child will feel the loss directly and then secondarily as he sees his parents facing the loss of their parent, and can make an identification with their loss and sadness, and begin to experience what happens in old age, with its illness and infirmity moving towards death.

As one 9-year-old enquired on the death of her remaining paternal grandfather, 'Daddy, does that mean you are an orphan now?' Clearly she could envisage the predicament of a person left in the world without parents. While her father was perceived as the adult, a partner in a marriage, a man with a job in society, supporting his family, the person she most depended on alongside her mother, she could also see him as the bereaved child now without parents in *his* life. This suggests that, in our minds, our parents stand between us and death. When they are gone we feel the lack of that protection, even if it is in a real sense an illusion. But for adults established in their lives, there remain powerful vestiges of feelings of dependency that derive from childhood's essential dependency. For a child, the idea of the death of a parent evokes strong anxieties about who will be there to take care of the nurture the child needs until he is a viable adult. Such anxieties lie behind the 9-year-old girl's question to her father. The idea of being orphaned at her age was hard to think about, but she could bring the idea to bear on her father's position, to examine how he, as an adult, could face the predicament of being without parents in the world.

The teenager is usually more aware of his or her own mortality. The shock of this knowledge may come with the accidental death of one of the teenager's peer group. One thinks of the risk-taking that so often seems to be part of the psychological rites of passage that the mid- to late teens put themselves through, powered in most cases by the pressure exerted by a peer group. Whether it be street drugs, motor-bikes driven at high speed, excessive weight control to the point of anorexia, there is a sense of pushing life to the limit, as if it is vital to approach that limit and defy it. The expression 'death-defying' characterizes something of the drive to test oneself, the parental generation and society itself to the limit. This sort of behaviour, and the state of mind that engenders it, although largely unconscious, seems to represent the teenagers' attempt to experience the extremes of their destructiveness and their capacity to contain it, as some expression of establishing an identity separate from their parents. As D.W. Winnicott has observed, the parents' task is to survive this, adding ruefully 'there is only one cure for adolescence and this is the passage of time . . .'. He also observes that sometimes within a group who are dealing with these turbulent desires, there may be an actual death, as though there is something that has to be known, that death is a reality. One has only to think of Shakespeare's *Romeo and Juliet* and the intense rivalries of the Montague and Capulet families, with the teenagers acting out in their generation the feuding already established between the parental generation. As Friar Lawrence observes of the relationship between the two young lovers from the rival families caught up in the multiple struggles to which they add the power of their own passions: 'These violent delights will have violent ends.'

Domestic death of the elderly members of a family usually is not at home, and so the younger generation may not be aware of its coming, and it seems that to some extent it is felt appropriate to protect the young from direct experience of a dying person. It is questionable whether this is a wise move. It may be that we tend to reinforce the wish to deny the reality of death, and to foreclose on the opportunity to become acquainted with the processes of dying.

And also we may deprive the young of the chance to say and do the things to and for, for instance, a dying grandparent, to acknowledge that they have something to contribute to the process of leave-taking that the dying person is involved in.

The developmental tasks of adulthood represent the summation of what has been achieved in previous phases. By the thirties and forties the upward, aspirational movement of development continues and it is after this that the phase of mid-life appears. But sometimes, usually in the forties when an individual's children have reached late adolescence and are beginning to leave home, the sense of approaching middle age is borne in upon the apparently soon-to-be redundant parent. There may be a renewed concentration on the aims in life, a tighter focus on what the person wishes to achieve, perhaps especially those developmental tasks which have had to be put aside while the adult undertook the responsibilities of parenthood and the demands of work and wider social contributions.

The sense of the finite nature of the future life ahead enforces a radical reappraisal of what life is about and how it is now to be lived. It is no longer possible to deny anxiety about the future; it is time for both man and woman to search for a further interior rearrangement of priorities in their lives.

Middle age in men

Some of the factors described here also apply to women, particularly in relation to areas of work that are principally centred on physical expertise and skill. There is often a change to be faced when those who work essentially in a physical capacity, dancers, sportsmen and women, for example, whose talent and its honing to high levels of achievement depend on youthfulness and/or strength. While these are in the ascendant in early adult life, by mid-life a plateau will have been reached and a decline will be setting in. The narcissistic blows that this entails, and how these are dealt with by the individual personality, will to a great extent determine the degree of stable adjustment that can be made in later life. If too much of a person's self worth has been invested in the physical attributes and achievements, such that he is overly dependent on them for a stable sense of his identity, then the threat of decline and loss of these attributes may bring on debilitating depression or a sense that all is lost. If, on the other hand, there has been a realistic appreciation of the arc of aspiration, achievement and decline, and proper planning, the transition to the next stage, while inevitably marked by some sadness and regret, will hold the promise of future creativity in an allied field.

Athletes, sportsmen and sportswomen can make the move to coach, manager, writer or media person, writing or broadcasting about the sport they formerly competed in. Such a transition is also available to musicians, who have probably developed a coaching career alongside one of performance. Practitioners in many fields find themselves moving towards management as their careers develop, with mixed pleasures and regrets. There has to be scope for the mourning of the passing of the skills in younger life, while at the same time assuming the new roles that are opening up. To some extent, the roles that are on offer have a very different character to them. They are concerned with how things work – roles covered by the terms, 'management', 'administration' – the way the infrastructures of society, business, education, the health and social services, and commerce operate. These roles, like the parental roles in the family, are marked by the overall taking of full *responsibility* for getting things done, keeping the show on the road. One hugely important characteristic of this is its contribution to continuity – of the family, of the firm, of the clinic, the hospital, the school, whatever it may be. This is not about rigidifying or preserving tradition unchanged but assuming the work of making the institution, whatever its nature, viable for the future, just as parents strive to do similarly in the upbringing of their children. This is both for the satisfaction of the work itself, but is further to contribute to the future – so that society is viable for one's descendants to live and flourish in. It would be rash to assume that every harassed, middle-aged teacher, GP, or businessman or woman is consciously aware of such apparently altruistic motives as they labour through another difficult day of meetings, clinics, or bureaucratic battles. Yet perhaps the unconscious drive to do well, to contribute, to leave one's mark in these less than glamorous activities testifies to an ability to engage with commitments that are not entirely to do with individual satisfaction and gratification. These roles usually include the assumption of authority, and we are well aware of the ambivalence that can be met with when authority strives to make itself felt. One of the achievements of later years is the accumulation of experience, and traditionally this was recognized as grounds for respecting the authority this placed upon the person. The rapidity of technological change and its consequences for the work force has left many at mid-life facing redundancy – if not actually in the workplace then in the wider society where the expertise of the young, adapted to rapid change and often eager for it, can leave the older person bewildered and at a loss. 'Ageism', when there is a tendency to deny and undervalue the gains of experience built up through life, is the fate of many who feel they still have much to contribute to society.

But the opportunity to learn something new, not necessarily by way of work but to extend into new fields, offers something rejuvenating to many at mid-life. This is particularly so when there is an opportunity to take up something that, for whatever reason, was not able to be studied in earlier life. A long-cherished wish to paint watercolours, which a busy family and working life precluded, may open up a fertile world of the imagination not previously envisaged, giving chances for self-discovery and contentment. This may give scope to aspects of the personality that have never before found expression, while movement between the surface and the depth of the psyche may become more flexible, and a greater, and surprising, knowledge of the self become available.

Middle age in women

Of immediate significance here are two factors – the arrival of the menopause, and the gradual relinquishing of the maternal role in its immediate day-by-day manifestation as children grow up and leave home. These two challenges in the developmental process face women with tasks which have long-term consequences in their working out. For many women, the menopause brings with it the knowledge of the end of their fertile child bearing years, accompanied by difficult symptoms: night sweating, hot flushes, dizziness, weight gain, irregular and sometimes difficult periods. The availability of hormone replacement therapy is a boon to many women in tackling the worst of the physical symptoms, but few women escape the erratic mood changes which frequently mark the menopausal years, perhaps especially the particular depressive anxiety that seems to inflict many women and which is often overlooked as 'just part of the change' by those caring for her. It is not unusual for women to feel 'younger' in themselves when the distressingly turbulent years of the menopause are behind them.

Sexually, they may feel less attractive and although it is now very clear that sexual activity is in no way ended by the menopause, there may be psychological as well as physical factors that lead to disturbance and inhibition in sexual functioning. Here the previous sexual history of a couple can be of significance in determining how both partners negotiate these changes in their sexual relationship. The position of the woman who has not had children can be especially poignant at this time, suffused with regret and disappointment unless she has found satisfaction and fulfilment in sublimated forms of living, choosing to extend a form of maternal functioning perhaps in a career or in the wider family.

Children leaving home faces both parents with a range of new and unfamiliar situations. It will have been many years since the couple has been on their own, and they are certainly not the people they were 20 or more years ago. Again, radical adjustments call upon each person's capacity for adaptability and their mutual capacity to recognize the changes in themselves and in each other and to be able to encounter them with a creative response. It is not surprising that some couples find this too difficult a task and this is a prime contributory factor in marital breakdown at this phase of life. The explanations may be many and complex, ranging from a version of 'growing apart' to the causes and reasons for an extra-marital affair by one or other of the partners, that may be able to be weathered as a storm in the ongoing and continuing marriage, or may destroy a perhaps already shaky marital situation. While such a marital breakdown can be tumultuous and is often particularly painful for the 'betrayed' party, there is some sense that a new solution to the predicaments of the mid-life is being sought and sometimes achieved.

Mid-life crisis

This is generally recognized, as Jaques has described, as a stage in normal development, marked particularly by the acknowledgement that at least half of life is behind us. The ageing of the body and the fact of death cannot be denied any longer. When, in this normal development, anxiety and depression are present they are not usually pathological; this tends to occur only when there is a tendency for a person to attempt to cleave to patterns of thought, feelings, ways of life and images of the self that belong to previous, now age-inappropriate, stages of development. We would all recognize the woman who dresses as her teenage self, or indeed as her daughter does now, or the man who insists on attempting physical feats now beyond his scope. In both instances there is a failure to face the inevitable renunciation of one's past younger self, while simultaneously being contemptuous of the older self whose frame awaits to be occupied. There is a search for a new identity in some ways that have been mentioned, this representing a challenge and the route to the resolution of some of the conflicts which have been encountered.

But resolution, renunciation, acknowledgement of loss, sadness, depression and anxiety are not the whole story. Jaques (1970) has pointed out that in creative people, not just artists and writers, but men and women engaged in endeavours in the world, periods of intense, prolonged and sustained activity occur in mid-life and beyond. For men, one could instance the later works of Sibelius, Vaughan Williams, the writer Arthur Miller. For women, the striking recent example is of Britain's first woman prime minister, Margaret Thatcher. For people in public life it is often in the later years of mid-life that long-cherished ambitions to attain roles where power and authority can be exercised, and where the opportunity to make a significant contribution, presents itself.

The psychoanalyst D.W. Winnicott, talking on the day following the death of Sir Winston Churchill mused, 'Poor Winston Churchill, he had to wait until he was 64 so that he could achieve the expression of his true self in waging the Second World War!'

Further reading

Jaques, E. (1965) *Death and the mid-life crisis. International Journal of Psychoanalysis*, 46 no. 4: 502–514.

Levine, S.B. (1998) *Sexuality in Midlife*. New York: Plenum Press.

Sheehy, G. (1976) *Passages*. New York: Bantam Books.

Winnicott, D.W. (1976) Psychotherapy in adolescence. In: *The Maturational Processes and the Facilitating Environment*. London: Hogarth Press.

Chapter 15

Old age

Eric Rayner

Respect for the old

In a static or slow-changing culture we might expect the old to be respected more steadily than in a quickly moving one. Having lived longest, the old can act as the most assured carriers of techniques and beliefs that need to be passed on virtually unchanged from generation to generation. Reverence for the old occurs in many societies, especially if they have tight family organizations that need an old person's knowledge of traditions, and their authority, and with food supplies enough to cater for those who are too old to be producers themselves. Where food is scarce and living conditions hard, as, for instance, with the Eskimo in times past, the old become a burden and are often expected to discard themselves.

Our society seems to bear some resemblance to both these forms, with a prolonged expectation of life, a highly developed, fast-changing economy, and a large proportion of its population retired and unproductive, yet economically able to be be supported. At the same time, in Western Europe, old people are not often seen as essential carriers of culture. At work, they can be felt as useless and standing in the way of younger people. Many of the old can be thought of fondly, but not needed.

Ageing people thus have to live with quiet threats from two directions. First, there is the deterioration of bodily functions, especially of the brain and its memory. Second, there are the social expectations that they are useless because they are aged, irrespective of real capacities. Many people are compulsorily retired at an early, fixed age for the simple reason that middle-aged people can more surely be promoted; this of course happens particularly in times of high unemployment. There are more vague but influential attitudes that match the practice of compulsory retirement. For instance, an old person's ideas can be dismissed as outdated simply because of who they come from. The old may be cared for, but often not respected (Aitken, 2001; Burstock & Shana, 1976; Neugarten, 1968).

The crisis of retirement

Just as middle age has been epitomized by withdrawal from intimate parenthood, so, for many people, old age is usually marked by retirement from money-earning work. Many people welcome the chance of relaxation, but it is still a definite life crisis. New mental integrations must develop for life to continue in fruitful contentment. Retirement from paid work is only one facet of ageing, but it is clear-cut and easily recognized. Similar, smaller retirements and withdrawals occur throughout old age; they also call for *creative reorganizations*, and thus internal developments. We will emphasize retirement from paid work here simply because it epitomizes much about this time of life. For instance, retirement can be seen as a pleasant eternal holiday; but in reality it often leads to days of hanging around the house with men feeling unwanted and in the way. So new stresses can enter a marriage, along with any hoped for relaxation (Bromley, 1974; Brubaker, 1983; Nolan, 2001; Nusbaum, 1997).

A wage-earning man or woman's identity or sense of self will often have been largely oriented around work. He or she may or may not have invested much of themselves in it, but they will know themselves, and be known, by the work they do. With retirement this identity is largely taken away. 'I am a . . .' is replaced by 'I was a . . .'. At the same time, a lot of income disappears drastically. Here are a couple of examples of how this crisis may be experienced and managed:

Mr H. said he had mixed feelings when retirement was approaching. He looked forward to not having to work, but wondered what he was going to do with himself. His wife said she did not want him hanging around the house all the time. On the actual day, he went to work as usual and wished his friends good-bye at the end of it. They settled down to being pensioners. The greatest readjustment was living on a reduced income but they were both healthy. Mr H. took an allotment, so they never had to buy vegetables, and they lived close to their children and helped to look after the grandchildren. In the summer, Mr H. returned to work part-time, but in the winter they could relax with their friends and social activities.

Mr I. said he enjoyed every minute of his life as a mechanic. But he looked forward to retirement and, although offered a number of part-time jobs, turned them all down because he felt he needed a complete break. During the first months Mr and Mrs I. had a series of holidays, visiting children and grandchildren, and 2 weeks away on their own.

After this Mr I. turned into a jack-of-all-trades. He went around on a bicycle doing gardening, decorating and small repair jobs. His evenings were taken up with committee work. His health was good but he noticed that there was not so much 'spring' in his legs, and he now needed a rest after 2 or 3 hours work. His memory was also not so good and it took longer to think things out. He might not do as much as he used to but the quality of his work remained satisfyingly high. He also had a freedom that was denied him when in employment.

By contrast, here are two people who did not develop new patterns of life, and for whom despair set in:

Mrs F. went on working in a pub until she was over 70. Then one day she slipped and badly bruised herself. She lost her job through being off sick. She recovered quite quickly but never went back to work. Her husband remained lively and full of fun but she slowly became quiet and apathetic. She complained of aches and pains, but managed the housework and cooking. Then she began to lose weight and looked drawn, she gave up doing her hair and using make-up. She usually just shuffled about the house in boots and several layers of clothing.

Mr G. had been a pig farmer. He never gave a thought to retirement. By the time he was over 70 there was a noticeable deterioration in the farm. Roofs were leaking and fences broken. Mrs G. realized her husband could no longer keep up and suggested he employ a farm-hand. But he was too stubborn to admit his declining abilities and would not listen to his wife. Finally, he became acutely ill and was taken to hospital, where he was overcome with despair as he lay in bed. For many years he had dreamt of his family buying up the land around and continuing in his tradition of farming. But he had no sons, and his daughters had all married townsmen. When he dies he will be the last of a long line of farmers.

What functions come into play in these life crises? We have already noted the physical deterioration and its attendant depressive feelings. As with any loss, this usually sets in train a process of *mourning*. Here fear, rage, paranoid ideas and bitterness may or may not be followed by finding substitute satisfactions, which might lead to a peaceful sadness about the change.

On the positive side, the retirement crisis can involve finding new investments, as with Mr H. and Mr I. One particular psychological quality seems to be important here. You will remember that we saw how children can approach new activities with awe and enthusiastic romanticism. If a person has kept this childlike quality in his adult way of doing things, he is likely to be able to use it even late in life to discover and develop new investments. However, this can only happen when there are opportunities for new investment. For instance, Mr I. the mechanic lived in a fairly built-up area, so that his general skill with his hands met a local need. But Mr G. the pig farmer could not have turned to a job like this because there were few houses in his rural neighbourhood (Erikson et al., 1995).

The enjoyment of old age seems to rest, as it does throughout life, upon fusing the satisfaction of urges centred upon the self together with contributions to others. Naturally, the environment delimits both of these as much as does an individual's character.

One advantage of old age is that few responsibilities are now expected, and self-centred pursuits can be enjoyed without much recrimination. This, at least partial, absolution from guilt must often lie at the heart of many old people's enjoyments of life, which can often seem sparse to younger people. Perhaps the most common handicaps to feeling carefree in this way are bad health and lack of money, or fear of them. Anyone well acquainted with old people will have encountered real poverty as well as ill health.

Vital to many elderly people is the desire to continue *contributing to others* in a friendly way. This can give real happiness, and also keeps the rigidity of old age at bay. Keeping in touch with people and events probably helps prevent senility. Although people tend to lead longer lives today, they are still likely to have single careers, usually based on decisions made when youthful. The last quarter-century of a working life can then often be intellectually, emotionally and economically infertile. This is perhaps slowly being recognized, and some agencies for employment in part-time work by older people are being set up. It is tempting to think that, in the future, a life of several careers, each attuned to age, will become a more normal part of our society. But perhaps it is best to be sceptical about such pipe dreams, because younger people really do need to have freedom to advance without the old getting in their way.

The break-up of extended families living close to each other has lessened the opportunity for old people to help in child-rearing (Townsend, 1963). This does not mean that the need for such help has disappeared – as we have seen, things can be a great strain for a mother when bringing up children alone all day without help. What is more, a mother who has no-one to fall back on naturally tends to be chronically worried about exhaustion or illness. One or two of the illustrations given earlier in this chapter show how both old men and women often become invaluable auxiliaries to young parents. Very affectionate bonds can grow up between children and their grandparents, who are often not so burdened with responsibility as the parents. They can be more patient than parents and have time to relax and play. A sense of equality often grows between old and young, which makes them especially fond of each other.

The old can contribute to younger people in many other ways – volunteer work for good causes, part-time odd jobs, being on committees, and so on. There are also quieter things to do. For instance, old people are often the living *historians* of a society. By personal reminiscence they tell younger people how things were in the past, both in their own lives and in those of their parents and grandparents. For instance, an old person in the early twenty-first century can usually look back to his own childhood and remember people who were old then; and these people will have had memories going back at least to the mid-nineteenth century – 150 years ago. A young person in Europe is not likely to be called upon to copy the ways of their elders as happens in a traditional static society; but personal information about one's real roots is usually deeply moving and has a strange beauty about it.

More generally, old people, having been through many things, and feeling close to death, can often express themselves with a cool, dispassionate clarity, devoid of the grandiosity to which younger people can be prone. This kind of wisdom can broaden minds and make us humble. It tells young people, 'This sort of thing will happen to you one day.'

Depression and ageing

A common feature of ageing is the shrinkage of body functions. Cell tissue is not replaced as in youth, so that hair thins, skin, muscles and joints lose their vibrancy, blood circulation malfunctions. Brain cells die and memory quietly blurs. With ageing, 'small deaths' become widespread, and moods of both acute and chronic anxiety and depression can arise. This can happen at any time of life, whenever there is a loss of enjoyment. However, with old age there is less opportunity to hope for the future, so a valuable defence against depression is no longer effective. Coupled with physical deterioration is the loss of friends and loved ones, who will also be ageing and dying, and this is also depressing.

Many people accept the shrinkage of their lives with resigned equanimity. Perhaps one factor here is that loss of vitality can act as a release from guilt. The inner commands of 'ought, must and should' may lose their grip somewhat when it is no longer physically possible to obey them. The old person is in a good position to relax into unambitious contentment. Perhaps those people who have got used to being repeatedly forced to accept their fate find contentment in old age most easily. On the other hand, those who have characteristically been self-assertive may feel the losses more acutely. Those who feel they have been intensely hard working and useful in life, can often be old contentedly.

Nevertheless, no matter how it is received, ageing seems always attended by at least some painful depression. This can vary from utter misery to a quiet, peaceful resignation. It may sound strange to refer to depression as peaceful. However, after the first pain of a loss, acceptance can bring a dignified sense of peace, with a complexity of happy and utterly miserable feelings alternating with each other. Old people can be deeply happy – but depression may still be around the corner.

Persecutory, paranoid feelings in old age

Physical deterioration, with its ill-coordination, stooping, stiffness and shrinkage of body and brain, means that, mentally, there is depletion in ego-functioning and sense of self. The individual feels smaller and more helpless, so that the outside world becomes larger and less controllable. Events tend to be experienced passively, and thus can be more persecutory and threatening. This shows in more fear of roads, trains, flying and of whirl and bustle generally.

Psychologically, when ego-functioning and the sense of self shrink, so we would expect primitive, less integrated patterns of thought and feeling to emerge. This *regression* is manifest not only in generalized fearfulness but also in the use of *projective mechanisms*. In the prime of life, these defences are usually held in check or elaborately covered by rationalizations. With ageing, the more sophisticated defences tend to fall away and primitive disintegrated splitting, projection and denials emerge more obviously. This happens most catastrophically when *senile dementia* has taken hold.

Even people in full command of their intellectual faculties can subside into paranoid cantankerousness. For instance:

A woman had a very long, active life. She reared a large family and was much liked and respected throughout her town for being generally interested in people, kind and generously helpful. Her husband died, but she carried on alone in her kind, bustling way for a decade or so. Then, as her body slowed up, so she slipped into being chronically bitter and suspicious. The first sign was an argument with neighbours over a dilapidated garden fence. This spread to resentment about everyone, especially those she had helped in the past and who now seemed callously ungrateful. She would let no-one help her for she was convinced that they would make matters worse by taking advantage of her. Perhaps when young this woman had overcome a dread of being helpless (she came from a large family and had to leave school to work in a factory at a very early age) by developing a very active and rather bossy but deeply helpful character. When this was no longer possible, her bitter sense of threat and helplessness re-emerged and consumed her last years.

Another instance of projection is commonly seen with sensitivity to any physical deterioration. Here the sense of bodily malfunction, the 'little deaths' of old age, can be projected out onto the external world, so that dreadful things are dimly felt to be happening to outside things rather than inside the individual. For instance:

An intelligent old countryman was looking at the roof of a nearby cottage and said, 'That thatch is good for another 10 years yet. I'm 80 and never had a day of illness in my life, but the thatch will outlive me, no doubt.' He then lapsed into a generalized projection and said, 'But then such terrible things are happening in the world now that it will all be over for everyone on this earth before then, that's for sure.'

Such collapses into paranoid gloom are common but not universal. They seem most marked when physical functions are deteriorating and muscular activity is becoming limited. There is more to old age than this, but it is important to understand these background experiences of deterioration, depression and persecutory anxiety. *Gloom* probably has to be dealt with by everybody when growing old, however fit and active they may be. It is possible to get some fun out of cherishing this sad mood in order to make gloomy jokes, which anyone can enjoy.

Dependency on others

We have so far been considering the position of old people who still retain much of their vigour. So long as people can think and move, and can maintain their independence of judgement, they can still enjoy their individuality. But the progress of shrinkage is inevitable, so that the old person loses many freedoms of choice and has to sink into dependence upon others. This must be painful and is often bitterly resisted.

Dependence provides the ground for neurotic, and often nasty, satisfactions for both old and young. This is often seen between parents and their adult children. For instance, an old person losing their independence of action can gain malicious pleasure in behaving like a ruthless baby towards their own grown-up children. And the grown-up children can clothe their gloating upon how the tables have turned by being piously solicitous.

There are many ruthless games that can be played between old and young. No doubt such fantasies play through the minds of everyone at some time, and they become malign and ruthless only when they succeed in wiping out sympathy for the other's individuality. Note too that such games are not confined to parent–child relationships. Condescension mixed with cruel teasing can sometimes be seen being indulged in by staff working in old people's homes.

Even when sympathetic recognition of each other's dignity is maintained, underlying malicious fantasies are still likely to be active. But they will be held in check and likely to be used in conjunction with other feelings as a spur to helpful activity, rather than being a cruel, dominating force. When this occurs, care of the aged may still be stressful and sad but also deeply rewarding. Both old and young can feel together in being close to the elements and ultimates of life and death.

Senility and Alzheimer's disease

Progression into muscular incapacity is depressing enough, but deterioration of brain functioning is usually worse, because both communication and curiosity become more transient and difficult. The usual modes of conversation can disappear, so that helpers are embarrassed and confused. Then, with the lapse of integrated thought processes, which involve very complex neural coordination, more primitive mental functions emerge unfettered. In particular, paranoid projective mechanisms can dominate a senile person's thoughts. Speech can be angry and even cruelly directed at helpers, who can be made to feel hurt, confused and inadequate, thence prone to retaliate with little mercy.

Such bitter paranoia does not occur with every old person losing their faculties; but senility and Alzheimer's disease, or pre-senile dementia, always revert to primitive modes of symbolic thought and communication. Speech takes on 'unconscious' qualities only known otherwise in psychosis. It is like a person in a waking dream, sometimes like a nightmare, at other times like a sweet holiday – but both are delusory. This can be disturbing to inexperienced helpers, who naturally expect objective speech. The primitive symbolism of such dementia can, however, often be deciphered by an experienced listener. When this is achieved, the contact between helper and old person can be very moving and even enjoyable for both.

The code of this primitive symbolism, being like that of dreaming, can be roughly described as one where *abstract ideas are expressed in terms of specific body functions* and, conversely, *body functions are expressed in terms of, often grand, external events.*

This is the 'language of the unconscious'. We discussed it, all too briefly, in the early chapters of this book. We saw there a strange phenomenon occurring in primitive imagination. It happens particularly in dreams, neurotic symptoms, and psychosis – but also in the background of little children's thoughts. Here an intellectual concept about something *external* can be experienced as *identical* to an *internal* bodily function if they have a *similarity of form* in common. Now, in senility, such ideas can be heard naked.

Hearing such equations of mind and body can be very disturbing, but when a listener has mastered the code, and knows the old person well, he can often carry out the necessary translation, so that he understands what is being said – to the benefit of old and young. Incidentally, Ignacio Matte-Blanco (1975) has developed a difficult but vital theory about the *logical form* of such unconscious ideas. This was achieved by using a combination of psychoanalysis and mathematical logic (Rayner, 1995).

Here is an example of an abstract idea being expressed in terms of body functions:

> An old man was clouded and wandering in his mind. His son came to ask for his signature for a 'power of attorney' to manage affairs and was worried whether his father would understand and comply. The old man seemed to wander off to another subject when he said, 'I must climb up onto your shoulders. I hope I won't be too heavy for you.' The son realized what he meant and said, 'Oh no, everything in the accounts is in order and I think we'll be able to manage things quite well.' He then handed him the pen and paper. The father readily signed it and with a sigh said, 'That's much more comfortable now, you always were a broad-shouldered boy.'

Here is an example of a body function being expressed in terms of an external event:

> An old woman was found crawling in the corridor whimpering, 'There has been an earthquake, the dam has burst.' The nurse knew what this meant, looked, and found that she had soiled herself.

We can see that external and internal reality have become confused, as may happen to all of us when waking up from a dream, or like a person in psychosis. A young baby has also probably not yet discovered the difference between inside the self and external reality. This differentiation is one of the great tasks of early childhood. In adult life we use our inner fantastical symbolization to feed our creative imagination in relation to the outside world. This can be great fun and richly rewarding so long as external reality is still also safely present. With dementia, awareness of the differentiation between outer and inner breaks down, and we can communicate only through concrete symbolic language. Perhaps, as people become more sensitive to this, the loneliness of old and senile people will be somewhat alleviated.

Further reading

Aitken, L.R. (2001) Aging and Later Life: Growing Old in Modern Society. Springfield, IL: Thomas.

Nolan, M. (2001) *Working with Older People and their Families.* Maidenhead, UK: Open University Press.

Nusbaum, P.D. (1997) *Handbook of Neuropsychology of Aging.* London: Plenum Press.

Chapter 16

Dying, grief and mourning

Eric Rayner

We all need to be brought to awareness of death – among other things it gets us to appreciate living. From childhood onwards death is frightening, and taboos often grow to keep the fear away. Particularly in the suburbs, and in high-rise flats, death can be private and lonely for old people. Perhaps this helps the living to ignore its inevitability.

Younger people then have little practice in experience of actual deaths – or the certainty that it will happen to them. But experience of death can foster a humble feeling of just being ordinary, and can help negate grandiosity and egocentrism. The isolation of much modern society also means that the old and dying can be left lonely, for family and old friends may live a long way off. What is more, many people die in hospital, often alone except for the staff. Then, within a hospital, staff need to develop their own ways of coping with deaths day in and day out – they need to keep detached, and this can continue the isolation of the dying person. On the other hand, thanks largely to campaigning authors who have brought death to our attention, perhaps the taboos are beginning to melt away (Hinton, 1967; Kavanagh, 1972; Kubler-Ross, 1975; Parkes, 1972; Stott, 1973).

In contrast to suburbs, close-knit rural communities have often had traditions for a dying person to be surrounded by people who know them well. Death may then be almost a public, shared event of friendly living. In some rural areas of the British Isles, particularly Wales, Ireland and the West of England, this has been common for centuries – local people have naturally helped in nursing their neighbours. Then, after death, it has usually been assumed that any acquaintance, old or young – even children – could pay their last respects to the body laid out in the bedroom or the parlour (Gorer, 1965).

Terminal illness

Here is a description of the last weeks of an old man. He was very much of an individual, so his way of growing old and dying was his own, but many of the features are common to others' experiences. (I am indebted to Barry Palmer for this description):

For 4 years, Mr J. had been partially paralysed and unable to move outside his home except in a wheelchair. Even so, although 87 years old, he was very alert and able to converse on many subjects through daily reading. His favourite topic of conversation was, nevertheless, his past career as an army officer. He was very proud of being an active man.

He had steadily deteriorated in physical health, and on many occasions it was thought that he might die. But he was never willing to admit that his health was declining and, when asked how he was, he would say that he was better, and even demonstrate this by getting out of his chair and walking across the room. Each step might take upwards of 10 seconds, but it would satisfy him that he had convinced the onlookers that he was not dead yet. His will to live was extraordinarily great. Mr J. was afraid of being forcibly admitted to hospital. On many occasions it was advisable for the sake of his wife's health that he should leave home for a couple of weeks. He refused on every occasion, and one felt that this was because he had the fear that entry to hospital would be the end of him. On one occasion his wife had to go into hospital and, in spite of the fact that he was most uncomfortable and not properly cared for, he would not leave the house.

Mr J. was always conscious of death. He was very fond of his children, but if they called without warning he would get very heated and suggest that they had been sent for. I do not know whether it was death he was afraid of, or losing command of his life situation. It was always clear that he wished to be the boss of the house and in command of every aspect of his life. The thought of losing his independence, which he had largely done but would not admit, was very apparent.

Three weeks before he died, Mr J. was walking to the toilet when he began to slip, and eventually sat helplessly on the floor. Normally he would claim that he was alright, although someone would have to help him to his feet. On this occasion he said, 'Joan, I'm going.' He did not say much more, except that he wanted to see his children. From this point on he was no longer the man who wished to appear in command, but allowed himself to be cared for. A few days later, having seen his children, he became unconscious much of the time. The one thing that differed from his former collapse was that, although it appeared much the same to the onlookers, he knew that this time he was going to die.

This was one man's way of dying. Although there have been countless millions of deaths in human history, many of us in urban and suburban Britain often know very little about it. This is not surprising because, apart from the dread that makes the living shy away, it is, perhaps, essentially a private, silent and solitary time. Dying people are not much given to talk. It is perhaps mostly nurses, even more than doctors, who have a wide personal experience of the emotions of the last weeks of life.

There has been some disagreement about when an organism can be said to be dead. Some argue that absence of cerebral activity is decisive, others that it is absence of heartbeat, but for ordinary purposes this is a specialist's question. What happens before death and after does concern us. Traumatic deaths, of course, may be instantaneous. But in other cases a terminal phase can usually be recognized. It may last only a few hours, in say a coronary thrombosis, or be drawn out over weeks and months in slow-working diseases like cancer.

The terminal phase has begun when a disease or deterioration of tissue has an irreversible hold. Those around may not be aware of it but there is some evidence that the grip of the lethal process is signalled to the mind of the dying person. For instance, it has been noted that the quality of dream imagery changes. Thus dying people are probably fundamentally aware of their dying, even though it may be dim and often ignored or denied.

The months after the diagnosis of a fatal illness are usually awful; brightened often for those around only by the sheer courage of the dying person, and by guilty day-dreams about when it will all be over. Thanks to recent writers, the thoughts and ideas of people who have only a short time to live are much more common knowledge than a few years ago. There is much to be done in a short time to prepare to complete one's life. Elisabeth Kubler-Ross (1975) called it the *final stage of growth*.

It has been pointed out that a clear emotional sequence can show itself in the period following diagnosis of terminal illness. First, there is shock and denial of the illness, followed by loneliness, dread, internal conflict, guilt about one's life and a sense of its meaninglessness. This can turn to anger at one's fate, followed perhaps by bargaining with fate or one's God. Then comes a gradual realization of the consequences of dying, which leads to deep-down fear and depression. After this trough there is a movement of increased self-awareness and enjoyment of contact with others, often leading to a self-reliant acceptance of dying. Such a sequence cannot be clear-cut, and probably not many people work through, or 'pain' through, to equanimity – but it is not so very rare.

One of the worst experiences in this time seems to be uncertainty: 'How long have I to live?' 'How long will my mind be clear?' With such indefiniteness, preparation is difficult. It is not uncommon to hear things like, 'I'm ready now; the pain isn't worth it any more. I wish they'd let me die? What are they keeping me alive for? Not for my benefit, I'm sure.'

Physical pain is often the greatest dread. Many dying people do experience chronic pain; and with it comes exhaustion, and often deep depression. Pain is usually made worse by anxiety. Perhaps because of this, old people tend to feel less pain than younger ones, who are usually not so prepared for death. They have more to lose and are often distraught about dependants left behind and life-work uncompleted. Nurses frequently say that the most harrowing experiences they have are caring for dying young children – and also dying mothers of young children.

Almost as bad as pain is chronic discomfort and immobility: both are terribly depressing; so also is the guilt and shame of being an *incontinent nuisance* to others. These feelings are probably all at their worst in the earlier stages of terminal illness. A person is, at that time, still acutely aware of other people, attached to them and worried about what they think. There are often many memories to be relived, and settled in the mind. There are also bonds of affection to things and people to say goodbye to. This is rarely done explicitly in an orderly way, but it is usually vital.

Then, perhaps a day or so before the end, a person usually seems to release their interest in life. They withdraw into themselves – perhaps talk a bit to those around them; but apart from this they just seem to be dreamily waiting for death. He or she may become unconscious, but, even if this does not happen, a quiet change takes place and it is usually possible to see that death is close. However, the dying person may still have work to do, mostly in bidding farewell. The relatives and nurses can actively help in this. In other aspects the dying person needs to be quiet, alone perhaps, or with another person in the room. This helps the natural process which dying is.

Many people around may be more frightened and frantic than is the dying person. With their anxious jumps of mind, they can often make dying more confusing, painful and lonely than it need be. People quite often say to an attendant, 'I know I'm dying, but don't tell my relatives – they'd be too upset.' This will be the fruit of the taboo of death – probably still too common in our own culture.

Awareness of death and its recognition by those around can mean that a person ends with dignity and peace, which can be remembered with gratitude by those remaining. Here are four instances:

An old man in considerable pain said to his son, 'When this non-sense is over, you will find the will in the desk downstairs'. He then proceeded to give instructions about his affairs.

An old man said to his niece, 'I think I shall be gone by the time you visit me again next week – so I think we'd better say goodbye now'.

An old woman was near the end, and her son-in-law rather import-antly turned to a phone that was in the room to let the relatives know. She muttered, 'John, don't get making arrangements, I'm not dead yet'. She died a week later. John had learnt a lesson.

An old woman in Nigeria was nearly 90 when she fell ill. How-ever, she said to her children, 'Don't waste your money preparing for a funeral now, because I am not going to die yet'. She did not die, but one day some months later she got up and began to make her preparations by walking round to all her friends saying goodbye. The next morning her daughter was due to go to market and the old lady said, 'I think we had better say goodbye now before you go'. A few hours later she died.

After this, the living person changes into inert, shrunken, grey remains. What is left alive of them on this earth now lies in the minds of other people. These will be their children if any, surviving relatives, friends and acquaintances – all those who have experienced and often enjoyed the dead person. They will probably have learnt from them, and have something from them inside themselves.

Let us now turn to the survivors. They have the task of transforming their experiences of the dead person, from someone really outside themselves into an internal, living and usable memory.

Grief and mourning

Here is a description by a woman of her encounters with death, remembered from many years ago:

When I was 13 my grandmother died. She was a much-loved, very elegant lady, with long, black skirts and button boots. I thought as a very young child that she must be a close friend of the Queen. One Saturday she decorated my bedroom, putting on wallpaper that I had been allowed to choose myself for the first time. She sat eating her tea with my new puppy trying to bite the buttons off her boots. She was laughing and happy. I slept in my newly-decorated bedroom that smelt of the new wallpaper. That night I was very conscious of how much my grandmother loved me. On Monday morning an aunt came round to our house, just as I was leaving for school. It was the day I was due to take an English examination. My mother and aunt tried to make me go to school, but something in their faces terrified me and I refused to go. Eventually they told me that my grandmother was dead. She had died very suddenly the previous night. I then went to school, sat the examination and did not think about my grandmother. I did not think about her again until the funeral, when I sat in the carriage with the hearse and the coffin covered in flowers, surrounded by relatives, dressed in black, and I had a black coat too. I did not think about my grandmother herself, because I was too busy trying not to laugh and laugh, and I knew that if I did nobody would understand why, and my mother would be ashamed. When the results of the examinations came out I was top of my class. It seemed as though this was the most shameful thing I had ever done.

A year later my school-friend died. She had pneumonia. I had seen her and she was getting better. The next day my mother told me when I came home from school that she was dead. I did not believe her. I went to see her mother, who told me that my friend died because the doctor would not wake her up to give her medicine. I was very afraid. I dared not go to sleep that night in case I should see my friend. I had loved her, but her death had turned into a terrifying horror.

When I was 15 my grandfather died. He was ill for a long time, and we knew for a week that he was going to die any day. Perhaps he wanted to die because my grandmother was dead. We had an end-of-term school dance on the Friday, and all I could think of was that I hoped he wouldn't die until that was over, or I should not be able to go. He died on Friday night whilst I was enjoying myself at the dance. I hated him for dying then, and became even more afraid of death.

My next experience was years later, when my own daughter was 15. Normally she came home from school with three friends, two boys and a girl. This particular day she was delayed at school and they left without her. A thunderstorm broke as they came across the common. They sheltered under a tree with their bicycles – lightning struck them and all were killed. I could not find words to console my daughter. I could only be thankful that she was alive.

A little later my father died, driving his car home from a football match. My mother did not ring me to tell me until 2 hours after his death, because she 'wanted me to have my tea first'. I was kept very busy looking after her during the next 2 weeks, and hardly thought about him.

When I was 44 my mother died. She had insisted on living alone. She was very independent and had enough money to do so comfortably. I was always afraid she would have an accident and be unable to get help. She had a minor stroke and lay unconscious for a whole day before I could get there. I did not say goodbye to her. My aunt said she didn't tell me that she was ill. She thought I might be upset and I 'couldn't do anything anyway'.

A few months later my dearly loved father-in-law died. He died of cancer and we knew that the end was near. We received a telephone call to go to the hospital. Our car was caught in a traffic jam and we arrived at the hospital 5 minutes after he died. We never talked of any of these people and their deaths.

The last one was my husband, and he died after 3 months of torture. He had cancer and refused an operation, which would have been useless anyway. I used to pray that he would hurry up and die, and was glad when he did.

After they had taken him away his dog ripped up his bed and his pillows and scattered the feathers all over the stairs. I changed all the furniture around the day he died, and then I carried on doing all the same things that I had done before. I used to pretend he was at work.

I couldn't stop buying the foods he liked from the grocers. I didn't know when to go to bed or when to get up. My son drove his father's car, and the dog nearly went mad every day when the car came down the drive. We sold the car.

Eventually we had to find a new home for the dog, who would have died of misery if we hadn't. My friends were all very kind. They kept me very busy with empty business. I was lonelier with people than without them. Nobody could talk about my husband. Christmas was hell. We always wound up our special clock on Christmas Day. I let it stop. My birthday, our wedding anniversary, his birthday and his children's birthdays were hell, but we never spoke about him. After a few months people started to say how brave I'd been, and what a wonderful new life I'd made. There was relief in their voices. They could look me in the eye again and didn't need to be embarrassed. I remember the relief that he was dead and couldn't suffer any more, or was it that I didn't have to watch him suffer? I never talked about him.

More recently I have thought about the cruelties of our culture, that demands a 'stiff upper lip' and no embarrassing show of emotion. I think I may have learnt how to say goodbye, and that, through sorrow and conscious weeping, the horror of pain and disease-riddled bodies can be allowed to sink into the background and mourning to become more joyful. When this happens, memories can be of the happiness known of a loving mother, warm and alive, of a husband walking in the sunshine across the paddock, his pipe in his mouth, his dog by his side, coming in to tea.

This is not only a report, it is also a plea for greater openness about death. Fortunately, the careful thought given to bereavement more recently makes many things less obscure and less lonely for the dying. This coherent knowledge can amplify traditional wisdom, and consistent and thoughtful ways of caring can be learnt by any ordinary intelligent person. Two classic works are by Lindemann (1979) and Parkes (1972): they are beautiful books. Others of value are Langer (1957); McNeil (1983); Parker & Weiss (1983); and Schneideman (1984).

Parkes summarized the evidence, making it plain that bereavement is a state of *acute stress*. Cerebral dysrhythmia, cardiovascular changes, hyperactivity, panic and fight-flight reactions all occur. Being in a state of distress means that *grief is a normal illness*, and should be seen as such. However, not only do mental disturbances arise from it very commonly indeed, but physical disease as well. This occurs to such an extent that it has been found that the death rate among certain groups of bereaved people is very significantly higher than that of similar non-bereaved people. After the death of a close loved one, a person is 'at risk'.

Following on from this, it is fairly clear that a sequence can be detected in the months after a death. From the storms of emotional pain that goes with mourning, Parkes suggested that the following movements can be seen as the essence of it. Acute grief in the few days after a death is when distress is at its height and is best epitomized by the term *alarm*. The whole organism is in a biological state of alarm, the person is not likely to be noisy, on the contrary, he or she is usually very quiet. But the signs of alarm are omnipresent: sleep is disturbed, there is often subdued hyperactivity and even hallucination in otherwise normal people. At this time, it is still difficult for a grieving person to fully believe that the loved one has gone; they can be automatically spoken to, or heard around the corner – their place even automatically laid at table. As the loss begins to sink home, a phase of *searching*, usually quite unconscious and automatically driven, sets in. Then this is felt as hopeless, with waves of weeping and despair. Somehow, arising out of these tears, periods of calm begin to emerge which come in mitigation of the loss. A person begins to warm again inside and becomes interested in the world around – sad at the loss but feeling glad to be alive.

All this is laid out neatly here, but it does not happen in so simple a way in life, for moods come and go. Past life together with the dead person is re-lived and re-sorted. Waves of guilt assail the bereaved, as does rage at being let down. Old recriminations can gnaw and more guilt wells up. Grief is not only a state of distress – it is an acute crisis (just as mid-life was a more chronic one). It is a crisis which strikes a person from the outside rather than from within. And, like any crisis, it entails the breaking of old patterns, regression to more primitive states and withdrawal – followed by the slow discovery of a slightly new identity and testing that out.

It is his or her disintegrated state and shattered distress that makes it important for a mourner to have the opportunity to talk things over with another understanding person. This can allow a person to continue, probably unconsciously, re-connecting with the primitive patterns of the earliest conversations of life. These are the early dialogues with one's mother, which perhaps are nakedly closest to our innate propensities. Sometimes it hardly matters what is actually talked about – the *tone* itself is enough.

Without sympathetic company, the 'falling to bits' caused by distress can be unforgettably lonely and terrifying; things can get so vivid they are near to hallucination. The frantic defensive manoeuvres that arise often become wild and even self-destructive.

Open destructiveness towards others is not much reported upon, but it does happen. For instance, an observer in South Africa more than a century ago reported that the grief of the great king Shaka Zulu led to his ordering the massacre of about 7000 people on the day after his mother's death! Vendettas and vengeance are practised in some cultures, even in Britain today, and if not openly practised can nonetheless be painfully present in hidden feelings. Relatives can become particularly vicious with each other, not usually at the time of the funeral but in the months after. The time of 'reading the will' is often quietly tense with, not always hidden, nasty, rivalrous ideas between relatives.

The soothing presence of a wise and firm but uncomplicated friend or relative can be wonderfully helpful. They can act as a check to the mourners' scatterbrained storms of ideas and perhaps more violent impulses. They can be a continuing reminder of enjoyable benevolence at a time when things feel empty. In addition, a regressed, grieving person often needs a vigilant helper to carry out essential tasks that the mourner cannot do – or forgets about.

However, most bereaved people are adults, and they usually have their own self-contained dignity. They need to be alone frequently and also to prove their own competence to themselves. Fussing, while particularly seductive at this time, is fundamentally choking and usually extremely irritating.

In the later phases, working out what to do next, together with finding a new integrity or identity, is mostly done alone. But people nearly always need to voice their ideas, to check them with another person. Remember, too, that the time a person takes to die can result in very different forms of mourning. When a death has not come as a surprise, much of the mourning can have been gone through *before death*, during the months of the terminal phase. Relatives can then often get to the point of feeling, 'Oh! I do wish they would hurry up and die now'. Charles II is reported as apologizing on his death-bed, with wry sarcasm, to his impatient brother and heir to the throne, James, for taking 'such an unconscionable time a-dying'.

With our greater awareness of the crisis of mourning, it is now not only psychiatrists and other specialists who are alerted to attendant dangers of long-standing disturbance and pathology, which can continue for years. The clergy have known about grief intimately for centuries and can speak about it with great beauty at funerals; they take special care of parishioners who are bereaved.

Other organizations, too, like Cruse and the Samaritans, have forged a wider new awareness about death, grief and mourning in our culture.

Grief in childhood

A young child's inner representations of the world and loved people are, of course, less articulated and stable than an adult's. He or she is rarely able to recognize, or voice, their sense of loss, and rarely weeps alone at a loved person's death. At that age, the mental organization is not sufficiently coherent to recognize the extent of a loss. This raises the question whether little children who have lost a parent should be told about it or not and, if so, how. Many people avoid the issue by saying children are too young to understand. So a young child, usually in a state of puzzlement and cataclysmic shock, rarely asks questions about death spontaneously. Their integrative capacity has not developed enough to put these ideas into words. A child's silence can then make not very sensitive adults assume that grief means nothing to them.

Some people will go to remarkable lengths to prevent a child knowing about a parent's death. For example:

The mother of three young children died after a long illness. Their father decided it was best to pretend that their mother was still in hospital and would be home again one day. He asked the children's head-teacher to keep the news from them. The teacher, trying to be considerate and helpful, asked all the other children in their classes and their parents not to talk about the death. However, the school was large and many children in other classes knew what had happened and naturally talked about it. Throughout the neighbourhood, children were baffled and ill at ease. Some had been told not to talk about it, but did not know why, while others felt guilty for talking quite freely, having had no instructions to the contrary. Eventually matters were sorted out. Someone mentioned the problem to the teacher, who got someone to talk things over with the father.

Here the father cannot really be condemned; he was distraught after the death of his wife, with three young children to look after. The teacher, too, was trying to help him. But a lie arose which caused far more trouble to his children than it was worth, for not only were they surrounded by grief at home but also by embarrassment, secretiveness, and confusion among their friends.

There seems to be a clear conclusion following on from this. It is that not telling a child about the death of their parent *withholds the truth* about a very important reality. Naturally, this may seem not to matter much if the child is too young to attach meaning to spoken words. It might, for instance, seem to be inappropriate to talk to a young baby of a parent's death. So the question arises, first as to how much children understand about what has happened when someone has died, and second, how much verbal explanation is helpful.

It is clear that children dimly realize at a very early age that something terrible has happened. They will usually have seen death, whether of birds in the garden, or pets, or from coming upon road accidents. More poignantly, even if children do not show much feeling at the time, the death of a parent, say, must soon be evident – for they are never seen again. A parent has simply disappeared, and never returns. Then, as earlier chapters here showed: loss and separation can have even life-long effects upon the child's capacity to feel and think.

The situation is made more complex by the fact that a young child cannot yet communicate grief coherently. He or she may act in a disturbed way, but not yet have organized their ideas enough to speak openly and coherently, or weep as older mourners do. A helping adult cannot wait until the child is ready to talk, because they may then never be able to verbalize their early grief coherently. It seems best for adults to actually *talk with feeling* about the death, even to an infant, who will probably feel better to be included in that realm of feeling, rather than be excluded from the family's emotion. This allows children to take part in the family's grief, such as going to the funeral.

It is usually also valuable to give quite detailed explanations to a child who can understand the words. It can then be largely left to him or her to find their way to asking questions as time goes by. Answers can then be simple and truthful, confined to what is understandable. As well as this, the adult needs to expect anxiety and disturbed behaviour from a little child who has been affected by puzzling and awesome ideas and feelings, which cannot yet be put into words but are there all the same. Sensitive people find their own intuitive ways about how to respond. Formally stated rules and procedures are obviously out of place. Without sympathetic understanding, the child is left alone with their grief in an alien, uncommunicative world. This aberration is likely to continue to haunt a child if the adults do not recognize it and openly feel for the anxiety and loss, however kind they may be in other ways (Berlinsky & Biller, 1982; Bowlby 1979; Furman, 1980; Harris, 1995; Worden, 1996).

Completion of mourning

The stage of acute distress may last for only a few weeks, but critical changes of feeling structures inside the individual probably go on less dramatically for many months, and more quietly, even for years.

Slowly, the grieving person finds a new distribution of feeling and awareness, and hopefully other people to love and hate. But if mourning is successful, awareness of the dead person is definitely not lost. The immediate experience, of the person as dead and gone for ever, loses force and gives way to living memories of them as they were when alive. In doing this, the mourner has not necessarily been 'taken over' by the dead person, although this can happen. Rather, an *internalization* has taken place. Then, firm memories from experiences of the lost person are present and ready to use in the future.

This is the natural end product of successful and 'decent' mourning. The mourner slowly comes alive again. The dead person is remembered with gratitude, if fondness was present before, and has gained some immortality in the memory of his or her loved ones. They themselves are then perhaps ready to carry on living, and are a little more prepared to die themselves one day – for other generations to carry them on also into the future.

Further reading

Bowlby, J. (1979) *The Making and Breaking of Affectional Bonds*. London: Tavistock.
Furman, E. (1980) *A Child's Parent Dies*. London: Yale University Press.

Harris, M. (1995) *The Loss is for Ever: The Lifelong Impact of the Early Death of a Mother or Father*. New York: Dutton.

Hinton, J. (1967) *Dying*. Harmondsworth: Penguin. A classic, short, must be read.

Kubler-Ross, E. (1975) *Death, the Final Stage of Growth*. London: Prentice-Hall. An easily readable book by one of the world's best known and respected authorities on dying.

Lindemann, E. (1979) *Grief: Studies in Crisis Intervention*. New York: Aronson.

Parkes, C.M. (1972) *Bereavement*. Harmondsworth: Penguin. A classic.

Pincus, L. (1997) *Death in the Family*. London: Faber. A much-read book over many years.

Stott, M. (1973) *Forgetting's No Excuse*. London: Faber. A brave and painful autobiography about confronting widowhood.

Worden, J.W. (1996) *Children and Grief: When a Parent Dies*. New York: Guildford.

Conclusion

Eric Rayner

We have come to the end of this excursion through life, with its way of thinking about emotions and intellect together, within a developmental framework. We hope you will find it useful, not just now, but as a book you will return to over the years, both when reflecting about people and introspecting about yourself.

When approached by friends with a problem, or by patients and clients, our natural instinct is surely always to listen carefully to what they have to say, and then to wonder about the setting of their life situation. We formulate and check over, to ourselves and them, such aspects as the network of their relatives and friends, the nature of their contributions to and fro, as well as their special abilities and weaknesses. With increased experience, we may then go on roughly listing immediate and more distant future problems that may have to be faced and solved. Using this developmental structure, we can then begin to estimate the nature and extent of their successes, competence, failures, disturbance and handicap. We can know them better, and thence perhaps be helpful as we suffer and enjoy their predicaments with them.

Developing this kind of understanding as you ponder upon the more distant as well as immediate problems that have to be faced any time in life can sometimes be frightening; however, as well as useful, it can also often be deeply satisfying. It is a way of thinking akin to the exercise of meditation, giving the reward of deep understanding as well as of finding new ideas. Most important, too, is that it serves to check absurdities.

If we continue to exercise this way of thinking and feeling about life, we can become aware of the way that some sides of the questions that preoccupy us arise from events and people outside us, while others are self-generated and come from within. We can also often sense our minds fleeing or switching off from some of the questions – usually the embarrassing, unpleasant or frightening ones. In order to go further, and make a general policy of exploring our feelings in relation to each new problem that faces us, we will find it necessary to move continuously to new points of view, and compare them with previous ideas, while being aware of the feelings that this process stirs. We are then beginning to *argue within ourselves* – trying to develop our understanding by using both old and new points of view together. I hope that, in reading this book, you have not felt yourself to be a passive audience but will have been stirred to argue some points fiercely in your mind, and will have enjoyed coming up with new ideas of your own.

Suggested films and videos

Below is a list of suitable films for use with all chapters of this book. Each entry gives: title of film (country of origin), short description, running time in minutes, film (F) or video (V).

Unless otherwise stated, all are obtainable from:

Concord Films Council Ltd., 201 Felixstowe Road, Ipswich, Suffolk IP3 9BJ. Tel: 01473 726012

Chapter 1 Introduction

Development (USA). Current research methods and   33 F
ideas in the study of development.
Sensory world (USA). An examination of the   33 F
mechanics of man's perception of his environment.

Chapter 2 Being pregnant

Bamet – the child (Sweden). Complete account of   48 F
conception, gestation and delivery of a child.
Family matters (UK). Part 1: Account of fetal growth, 20 F & V
a voice-over of mother's story in pregnancy.
    Part 2: The birth of a baby.   20 F & V
    Part 3: A home confinement.   20 F & V
Five women, five births (USA). Five births filmed   29 F & V
together with conversations with the women.
Having a baby (UK). A series of five short   7–11 F & V
films illustrating different aspects of pregnancy   each
and childbirth.

Chapter 3 The first six months

Amazing newborn (USA). A condensation from   25 F
hours of observation of babies from one to seven
days old.

Breast feeding: a special closeness (USA). Emotional   30 F
and practical issues of breast-feeding.

Family matters. Parts 3, 4, 5 and 6 (UK).   20 F & V each
Granada film about events of the first two years.

Growth through play (UK). A baby's awareness of   21 F
environment from two to sixteen weeks.

Sunday's child. The development of an individual (UK).   60 V
In eight parts. This is the most detailed film yet
made of one infant's development over two years.
Invaluable, especially for those who cannot observe
an infant for themselves.
Also a summary film of 45 minutes and excerpts
on special topics: play, role of father, language,
day-minding.

Hire orders to: Lynn Bamett, Iddesleigh House Clinic,
97 Heavitree Road, Exeter, Devon, EX1 2ND,
Tel. 01392 76348.

Chapter 4 The second six months

A baby is weaned. Parts 1 and 2 (UK). Two short   7–9 V
videos to stimulate discussion about weaning and
development.

The child watchers (USA). This illustrates some of   30 F
Piaget's observations about development.

From hand to mouth (UK). Beginning to explore.   20 F

Katie's first year (UK). Traces a first year of one   25 F & V
baby and her family.

Moving off (UK). Mastering locomotion.   20 F

Sunday's child. For details see entry under *The first*   60 V
six months above.   each part

A two-year-old goes to hospital (UK). The   30 F & V
Robertsons' classic about separation. Not about a
young infant but it illustrates the problem that
has been introduced in this chapter.

Young children in brief separation (UK). A series   33–43 F & V
of five complementary films by the Robertsons
on young children separated from their mothers.
They show the factors that affect the child's
ability to cope. Not about infancy but the film
is included here because separation is raised in
this chapter.

Chapter 5 One to two years old

Language and development (USA). Recent studies   20 F
of language acquisition.
Looking at children, series 3, part 1 (UK). A study   30 F
of one-year-olds and their movements.
Out of the mouths of babes (Canada). Investigates   27 F
research on the innate basis of language.
Sunday's child. For details see entry under *The first*   60 V
six months above.   each part

Chapter 6 Two to three years old

At least let me play (UK). Shows the importance   20 F
of play and the condition of children deprived of it.
Childhood, right of every child (UK). A group of   30 F
young children having early experiences of play.
Children and play series (UK). A series of short   5 F
films about play materials and places, clay, dough,
paint, sand, water, indoors, etc.
Looking at children, series 3, part 2 (UK). A continuation   30 F
of Part 1 of this series showing the children one
year later.

Chapter 7 Three to five years old

Looking at children, series 3, part 3 (UK). The same   20 F
children seen earlier in the series now three years old.
Playing (UK). This looks at a cross section of play   28 F
invented by children of four to eleven.

Chapter 8 Early school days

Buckets, spades and hand grenades (UK). TV film of   52 F
observation of children in playground from different
backgrounds.

Seven up (UK). Classic Granada study of seven-year-   30 F & V
old children from different backgrounds. Followed
by 'Seven Plus Seven', 'Twenty-One' and 'Twenty-
Eight', all at seven year intervals.

Chapter 9 Adolescence

Seven plus seven (UK). The first sequel to *Seven up*   30 F & V
(see above)

Chapters 10, 11, 12, 13, 14 and 15

For these years of adulthood there are a vast array of films about
specific topics and questions but few that are both general and
searching. For titles consult a catalogue such as that of Concord
Films.

Chapter 16 Dying, grief and mourning

Begin with goodbye (USA). Seven parts. A series of   28 F
films to make us think about changes in ordinary
life. Particularly concerned with the losses when
going through developmental crises. *Time to cry*
and *The Death of Ivan Ilych* deal with death
and grief specifically.

Facing death (UK). A series of films for TV   30 F & V each
about people dying and their bereaved relatives.

Hospice – St Christopher's (UK). An explanation   38 F & V
of the method of this world-renowned hospice.

References

Chapter 1 Introduction

Beckett, B.S. (1981) *Illustrated Human Biology*. Oxford: Oxford University Press.

Bowlby, J. (1969) *Attachment*. Harmondsworth: Penguin.

Bowlby, J. (1973) *Separation*. Harmondsworth: Penguin.

Bowlby, J. (1980) *Loss*. Harmondsworth: Penguin.

Dunbar, R. (1996) *Grooming, Gossip and the Evolution of Language*. London: Faber & Faber.

Erikson, E.H. (1963) *Childhood and Society*. London: Paladin.

Erikson, E.H. (1995) *A Way of Looking at Things*. New York: Norton.

Fonagy, P. (2001) *Attachment Theory and Psychoanalysis*. New York: The Other Press.

Hindle, D., & Smith, M. (eds) (1991) *Personality Development*. London: Routledge.

Karen, R. (1994) *Becoming Attached*. New York: Warner.

Klein, J. (1987) *Our Need for Others and its Roots in Infancy*. London: Methuen.

Marrone, M. (1998) *Attachment and Interaction*. London: Jessica Kingsley.

Pally, R. (2000) *The Mind–Brain Relationship*. London: Karnac.

Piaget, J. (1929) *The Child's Conception of the World*. London: Routledge.

Piaget, J. (1935) *The Moral Judgments of the Child*. London: Routledge.

Piaget, J. (1951) *Play, Dreams and Imitation in Childhood*. London: Routledge.

Piaget, J. (1953) *The Origins of Intelligence in the Child*. London: Routledge.

Piaget, J. (1999) *The Psychology of Intelligence*. London: Routledge.

Rutter, M. (1993) *Developing Minds Across the Life Span*. Harmondsworth: Penguin.

Sroufe, L.A., Cooper, R.G., & DeHart, G.B. (1996) *Child Development, Its Nature and Course*. New York: Basic Books.

Stern, D. (1985) *The Interpersonal World of the Infant.* New York: Basic Books.

Sugarman, L. (1986) *Life-Span Development.* London: Routledge.

Chapter 2 Being pregnant

Winnicott, D.W. (1956) Primary Maternal Preoccupation. In: *Through Paediatrics to Psychoanalysis.* London: Hogarth. p. 184.

Chapter 3 The first six months: the baby getting started

Ainsworth, M., Blehar, M., Waters, E., & Wall, S. (1978) *Patterns of Attachment: A Psychological Study of Strange Situations.* Hillsdale, NJ: Lawrence Erlbaum Associates Inc.

Argyle, M. (1988) *Bodily Communications.* London: Routledge.

Beebe, B., Lachmann, F., & Jaffe, J. (1997) Mother-infant structures and pre-symbolic self and object representations. *Psychoanalytic Dialogues,* 7.

Belsky, J. (1999) Quality of Non-maternal Care and Boys' Problem Behaviour/Adjustment at Ages 3 & 5. *Psychiatry,* 62.

Bion, W. (1967) *Second Thoughts.* London: Heinemann.

Blaffer Hrdy, S. (1999) *Mother Nature: Natural Selection and the Female of the Species.* London: Chatto and Windus.

Bowlby, J. (1958) The nature of the child's tie to his mother. *International Journal of Psychoanalysis,* 39: 350–373.

Bowlby, J. (1969) *Attachment and Loss,* Vol. 1. London: Hogarth Press and the Institute of Psychoanalysis.

Clarke, A.M., & Clarke, A.D. (1975) *Early Experience: Myth and Evidence.* London: Open Books.

Dunn, J. (1977) *Distress and Comfort.* London: Fontana Open Books.

Fonagy, P. (1999) Final remarks. In: Perelberg, R.J. (ed) *Psychoanalytic Understanding of Violence and Suicide.* London: New Library of Psychoanalysis.

Fonagy, P., Steele, H., Moran, G., Steele, M., & Higgitt, A. (1993) Measuring the ghost in the nursery: An empirical study of the relationships between parents' mental representations of childhood experiences and their infants' security of attachment. *Journal of the American Psychoanalytic Association,* 41: 957–989.

Fraiberg, S. et al. (1987) Ghosts in the Nursery: A psychoanalytic approach to the problems of impaired infant–mother relationships. In: Fraiberg, S. (ed) *Selected Writings of Selma Fraiberg.* Columbus: Ohio State University Press.

Freud, S. (1905) *Three Essays on Sexuality*. Standard Edition, Vol. 7. London: Hogarth Press.

Hoffer, W. (1947) *Mouth, Hand and Ego Integration*. London: Hogarth Press and the Institute of Psychoanalysis.

Isaacs, S. (1970) The nature and function of phantasy. In: Jones, E. (ed) *Developments in Psychoanalysis*. London: Hogarth Press and the Institute of Psychoanalysis.

Klaus, M., & Klaus, P. (1998) *Your Amazing Newborn*. New York: Perseus Books.

Klaus, M., Kennel, J., & Klaus, P. (1995) *Bonding*. New York: Addison-Wesley.

Mahler, M., Pine, F., & Bergmann, A. (1975) *The Psychological Birth of the Human Infant*. London: Hutchinson.

Meltzoff, A., & Moore, M. (1977) Imitation of facial and manual gestures by human neonates. *Science*, 198.

Murray, L., & Andrews, E. (2000) *The Social Baby*. Richmond, UK: CP Publishers.

Murray, L., & Trevarthan, C. (1986) The infant's role in mother–infant communications. *Journal of Child Language*, 13, no. 1: 15–29.

Perry, B.D., Pollard, R., Blakely, T., Baker, W., & Vigilante, D. (1995) Childhood trauma. The neurobiology of adaptation and 'use-dependent' development of the brain: how 'states' become 'traits'. *Infant Mental Health Journal*, 16, no. 4.

Pine, F. (1981) In the beginning: Contributions to the Psychoanalytic Developmental Psychology. *International Review of Psychoanalysis*, 8: 15–33.

Rutter, M. (1972) *Maternal Deprivation Reassessed*. Harmondsworth, Penguin.

Schore, A. (1994) *Affect Regulation and the Origins of the Self: The Neurobiology of Emotional Development*. Hillsdale, NJ: Lawrence Erlbaum Associates Inc.

Schore, A. (2001) Effects of secure attachment relationships on right brain development, affect regulation, and infant mental health. *Infant Mental Health Journal*, 22.

Segal, J. (1995) *Phantasy in Everyday Life: A Psychoanalytical Approach to Understanding Ourselves*. Lanham, MD: Jason Aronson.

Spitz, R. (1965) *The First Year of Life*. New York: International Universities Press.

Stern, D. (1985) *The Interpersonal World of the Human Infant*. New York: Basic Books.

Trevarthan, C., & Aitken, K. (2001) Infant intersubjectivity: research, theory and clinical applications. *Journal of Child Psychology and Psychiatry Annual Research Review*, 42.

Tronick, E. et al. (1989) *The Structure of Early Face-to-face Communicative*

Interactions. Before Speech: The Beginning of Interpersonal Communication. New York: Cambridge University Press.

Von Klitzing, K. et al. (1999) Child Development and Early Triadic Relationships. *International Journal of Psychoanalysis,* 80.

Winnicott, D.W. (1956) *Through Paediatrics to Psychoanalysis.* London: Hogarth Press and the Institute of Psychoanalysis.

Winnicott, D.W. (1960) Ego distortions in terms of the true and false self. In: *The Maturational Processes and the Facilitating Environment.* London: Hogarth Press and the Institute of Psychoanalysis.

Winnicott, D.W. (1965) *The Maturational Processes and the Facilitating Environment.* London: Hogarth Press and the Institute of Psychoanalysis.

Winnicott, D.W. (1988) *Human Nature.* London: Free Association.

Wolff, P. (1959) Observations on Newborn Infants. *Psychosomatic Medicine,* 21.

Chapter 4 The second six months: the baby getting organized

Bowlby, J. (1969) *Attachment and Loss,* vol. 1. London: Hogarth Press and the Institute of Psychoanalysis.

Bowlby, J. (1973) *Attachment and Loss,* vol. 2. London: Hogarth Press and the Institute of Psychoanalysis.

Bowlby, J. (1980) *Attachment and Loss,* vol. 3. London: Hogarth Press and the Institute of Psychoanalysis.

Bretherton, I. (1992) Social referencing, intentional communication and the interfacing of minds in infancy. In: Feinman (ed) *Social Referencing and the Social Construction of Reality in Infancy.* New York: Plenum Press.

Edgcumbe, R. (2000) *Anna Freud.* London: Routledge.

Emde, R., Klingman, D.H., Reich, J.H., & Wade, J.D. (1978) Emotional expression in infancy. In: Lewis, M., & Rosenbaum, M. (eds) *The Development of Affect.* New York: Plenum Press.

Fraiberg, S. (1987) Pathological Defences in Infancy. In: Fraiberg, L. (ed) *Selected Writings of Selma Fraiberg.* Columbus: Ohio State University Press.

Freud, A. (1936) *The Ego and Mechanisms of Defence.* London: Hogarth Press.

Freud, A. (1965) *Normality and Pathology in Childhood.* London: Hogarth Press.

Freud, S. (1915) *Introductory Lectures in Psycho-Analysis.* S.E. Vol.

Freud, S. (1921) *Beyond the Pleasure Principle.* S.E. Vol.

Freud, S. (1923) *The Ego and the Id.* S.E. Vol.

Hopkins, J. (1996) The dangers and deprivations of too good mothering. *Journal of Child Psychotherapy*, 22, no. 3.

Klein, M. (1948) *Contributions to Psycho-Analysis*. London: Hogarth Press.

Lebovici, S. (1985) Clinical studies in infant mental health. The first year of life. *Journal of the American Psychoanalytic Association*, 33: 687–691.

Mahler, M., Pine, F., & Bergmann, A. (1975) *The Psychological Birth of the Human Infant*. London: Hutchinson.

Piaget, J. (1953) *The Origins of Intelligence in the Child*. London: Routledge and Kegan Paul.

Pine, F. (1981) In the beginning: contributions to a psychoanalytic developmental psychology. *International Review of Psycho-Analysis*, 8: 15–33.

Rovee-Collier (1987) *Handbook of Infant Development*. J. Osofsky, 2nd edn.

Sandler, J., & Rosenblatt, B. (1962) The representational world. In: *From Safety to Superego*. London: Karnac.

Schore, A. (1994) *Affect Regulation and the Origins of Self*. Mahwah, NJ: Lawrence Erlbaum.

Spitz, R. (1965) *The First Year of Life*. New York: International Universities Press.

Steele, M. et al. (1991) Measuring the ghost in the nursery. *The Bulletin of the Anna Freud Centre*, 14: 115–131.

Stern, D. (1985) *The Interpersonal World of the Human Infant*. New York: Basic Books.

Stern, D. (1995) *The Motherhood Constellation*. New York: Basic Books.

Trevarthan, C. (1979) Communication and co-operation in early infancy: a description of primary inter-subjectivity. In: Budlowa, M. (ed) *Before Speech*. Cambridge: Cambridge University Press.

Trevarthan, C., & Aitken, K. (2001) Infant intersubjectivity: research, theory and clinical applications. *Journal of Child Psychology and Psychiatry Annual Research Review*, 42.

Waddell, M. (1998) *Inside Lives*. London: Duckworth.

Winnicott, D.W. (1971) *Playing and Reality*. London: Penguin.

Winnicott, D.W. (1982a) The observation of infants in a set situation 1941. In: *Through Paediatrics to Psycho-analysis*. London: Hogarth Press.

Winnicott, D.W. (1982b) Transitional objects and transitional phenomena 1951. In: *Through Paediatrics to Psycho-analysis*. London: Hogarth Press.

Winnicott, D.W. (1982c) Primary maternal pre-occupation 1956. In: *Through Paediatrics to Psycho-analysis*. London: Hogarth Press.

Winnicott, D.W. (1984a) Psycho-analysis and a sense of guilt (1958). In: *The Maturational Processes and the Facilitating Environment*. London: Karnac.

Winnicott, D.W. (1984b) Communicating and not communicating leading to a study of certain opposites (1963). In: *Maturational Processes and the Facilitating Environment*. London: Karnac.

Chapter 5 One to two years old: junior toddlers

Bower, T. (1977) *A Primer of Infant Development*. Reading, UK: W.H. Freeman.

Britton, J. (1985) *Language and Learning*. Harmondsworth: Penguin.

Dorr, D., Zax, M., & Danner, T. (eds) (1978) *The Psychology of Discipline*. New York: International Universities Press.

Dunbar, R. (1996) *Grooming, Gossip and the Evolution of Language*. London: Faber and Faber.

Edgcumbe, R. (1981) Toward a developmental line for the acquisition of language. *Psychoanalytic Study of the Child*, 36: 71–104.

Freud, A. (1936) *The Ego and the Mechanisms of Defence*. London: Hogarth Press.

Freud, A. (1965) *Normality and Pathology in Childhood*. London: Hogarth Press.

Freud, S. (1915) *Introductory Lectures on Psychoanalysis*. Standard edition, vol. XV. London: Hogarth Press.

Freud, S. (1917) *Mourning and Melancholia*. Standard edition, vol. XIV. London: Hogarth Press.

Freud, S. (1921) *Beyond the Pleasure Principle*. Standard edition, vol XXX. London: Hogarth Press.

Klein, M. (1932) *The Psychoanalysis of Children*. London: Hogarth Press.

Kohlberg, L. (1969) State and sequence. In: *Handbook of Socialisation Theory*. Chicago: Rand McNally.

Leach, P. (1974) *Babyhood*. Harmondsworth: Penguin.

Lewin, R. (ed.) (1975) *Child Alive*. London: Temple Smith.

Lieberman, A. (1993) *The Emotional Life of Toddlers*. New York: The Free Press.

Mahler, M., Pine, F., & Bergmann, A. (1975) *The Psychological Birth of the Human Infant*. London: Hutchinson.

Mead, G.H. (1932) *Mind, Self and Society*. Chicago: University of Chicago Press.

Palombo, S.R. (1978) *Dreaming and Memory*. New York: Basic Books.

Phillips, J.L. (1975) *The Origins of Intellect*. Reading, UK: W.H. Freeman.

Piaget, J. (1935) *Moral Judgements of Children*. London: Routledge and Kegan Paul.

Piaget, J. (1951) *Plays, Dreams and Imitation in Childhood*. London: Routledge and Kegan Paul.

Pincus, L. (ed.) (1955) *Marriage: Studies in Emotional Conflict and Growth*. London: Methuen.

Pinker, S. (1994) *The Language Instinct*. New York: Morrow.

Rycroft, C. (1979) *The Innocence of Dreams*. Oxford: Oxford University Press.

Schore, A. (1994) *Affect Regulation and the Origins of the Self: The*

Neurobiology of Emotional Development. Hillsdale, NJ: Lawrence Erlbaum Associates Inc.

Segal, H. (1973) *An Introduction to the Work of Melanie Klein*. London: Penguin.

Skinner, B.F. (1953) *Science and Human Behaviour*. New York: Macmillan.

Smith, A.J.W., & Danielson, J. (1982) *Anxiety and Defensive Strategies in Childhood and Adolescence*. New York: International Universities Press.

Tyson, P., & Tyson, R. (1990) *Psychoanalytic Theories of Development*. Princeton: Yale University Press.

Winnicott, D.W. (1965a) The capacity for concern (1963). In: *The Maturational Processes and the Facilitating Environment*. London: Hogarth Press.

Winnicott, D.W. (1965b) Communicating and not communicating leading to a study of certain opposites (1963). In: *The Maturational Processes and the Facilitating Environment*. London: Hogarth Press.

Wolman, B.B. (ed.) (1979) *Handbook of Dreams*. New York: Van Nostrand Rheinhold.

Chapter 6 Two to three years old: senior toddlers

Abraham, K. (1927) *Selected Papers on Psychoanalysis*. London: Hogarth Press.

Archer, I., & Lloyd, B. (1982) *Sex and Gender*. Harmondsworth: Penguin.

Backett, K.C. (1982) *Mothers and Fathers*. London: Macmillan.

Bowlby, J. (1969) *Attachment*. Harmondsworth: Penguin.

Bowlby, J. (1973) *Separation*. Harmondsworth: Penguin.

Bruner, J. (1976) *Play and Its Role in Development and Evolution*. Harmondsworth: Penguin.

Coates, S. (1997) Is it time to jettison the concept of developmental lines? *Gender and Psychoanalysis*, 2: 35–53.

Fraiberg, S.H. (1959) *The Magic Years*. London: Methuen.

Freud, S. (1900) *The Interpretation of Dreams*. Standard edition, vol. IV. London: Hogarth Press.

Freud, S. (1905) *The Three Essays on Sexuality*. Standard edition, vol. XII. London: Hogarth Press.

Freud, S. (1915) *Instincts and their Vicissitudes*. Standard edition, vol. XIV. London: Hogarth Press.

Fromm, E. (1973) *The Anatomy of Human Destructiveness*. Harmondsworth: Penguin.

Hayman, A. (1974) Some unusual anal phantasies in a young child. *Psychoanalytic Study of the Child*, 29: 265.

Isaacs, S. (1930) *Intellectual Growth in Children*. London: Routledge and Kegan Paul.

Isaacs, S. (1933) *Social Development in Young Children*. London: Routledge and Kegan Paul.

Kline, P (1972) *Fact and Fantasy in Freudian Theory*. London: Methuen.

Kuhn, D., Nash, S.C., & Brucken, L. (1978) Sex role concepts of 2 and 3 year olds. *Child Development*, 49: 445–451.

Lamb, M.E. (ed.) (1981) *The Role of the Father in Child Development*. New York: Wiley.

de Marneffe, D. (1997) Bodies and words: a study of young children's genital and gender knowledge. *Gender and Psychoanalysis*, 2.

Matte-Blanco, I. (1975) *The Unconscious as Infinite Sets*. London: Duckworth.

Millar, S. (1968) *The Psychology of Play*. Harmondsworth: Penguin.

Overton, W.F., & Gallagher, J.M. (1977) *Knowledge and Development*. London: Plenum.

Parke, R.D. (1981) *Fathering*. London: Fontana.

Piaget, J. (1950) *The Psychology of Intelligence*. London: Routledge and Kegan Paul.

Piaget, J. (1951) *Play, Dreams and Imitation in Childhood*. London: Routledge and Kegan Paul.

Segal, L. (1985) *Fantasy in Everyday Life*. Harmondsworth: Penguin.

Van Heeswyk, P. (1997) *Analysing Adolescence*. London: Sheldon Press.

Winnicott, D.W. (1982) The mind and its relation to the psyche soma (1949). In: *Through Paediatric to Psychoanalysis*. London: Hogarth Press.

Chapter 7 Three to five years old

Edgcumbe, R. (2000) *Anna Freud*. London: Routledge.

Emanuel, L. (2005) Understanding Your 3 Year Old. London: Tavistock Clinic & Jessica Kingsley.

Erikson, E. (1963) *Childhood and Society*. London: Paladin.

Freud, S. (1905) *Three Essays on Sexuality*. Standard edition, vol. 7. London: Hogarth.

Freud, S. (1915) *Introductory Lectures on Psychoanalysis*. Standard edition. London: Hogarth.

Hamilton, V. (1982) *Narcissus and Oedipus*. London: Karnac.

Holditch, L. (1992) *Understanding Your 5 Year Old*. London: Tavistock Clinic & Rosendale Press.

Miller, L. (1992) *Understanding Your 4 Year Old*. London: Tavistock Clinic & Rosendale Press.

Piaget, J. (1953) *The Origins of Intelligence*. London: Routledge.

Piaget, J. (1955) *The Child's Construction of Reality*. London: Routledge.

Segal, H. (1973) *Introduction to the Work of Melanie Klein*. London: Hogarth Press.

Snow, E. (1968) *Red Star Over China*. Harmondsworth: Penguin.

Sroufe, L. et al. (1996) *Child Development, International Edition*. New York: McGraw-Hill.
Sugarman, L. (1986) *Life Span Development*. London: Routledge.
Winnicott, D.W. (1964) *The Child, the Family and the Outside World*. Harmondsworth: Penguin.
Winnicott, D.W. (1971) *Playing and Reality*. London: Tavistock.
Winnicott, D.W. (1986) *Home is Where We Start From*. Harmondsworth: Penguin.

Chapter 8 Early school days

Barrett, M., & Trevatt, C. (1991) *Attachment Behaviour and the School Child*. London: Routledge.
Erikson, E.H. (1993) *A Way of Looking at Things*. New York: Norton.
Floyd, A. (ed.) (1979) *Cognitive Development in the School Years*. London: Croom Helm.
Green, L. (1968) *Parents and Teachers, Partners or Rivals*. London: Allen & Unwin.
Hale, G. (1979) *Attention and Cognitive Development*. London: Plenum Press.
Holt, J. (1982) *How Children Fail*. Harmondsworth: Penguin.
Holt, J. (1983) *How Children Learn*. Harmondsworth: Penguin.
Kohlberg, L. (1976) Moral stages. In: Lickona, R. (ed) *Moral Development*. Chicago: Rand McNally.
Piaget, J. (1972) *The Child and Reality*. Harmondsworth: Penguin.
Salzberger-Wittenberg, I., Osborne, E., & Henry, G. (1983) *The Emotional Basis of Learning and Teaching*. London: Karnac.
Segal, H. (1973) *An Introduction to the Work of Melanie Klein*. London: Hogarth Press.
Sroufe, L. (1996) *Child Development*. New York: McGraw-Hill.

Chapter 9 Adolescence

Brooks-Gunn, J. (1987) Pubertal processes and girls' psychological adaptation. In: Lerner, R., & Foch, T.T. (eds) *Biological-Psychosocial Interactions in Early Adolescence* (pp. 123–153). Hillsdale, NJ: Lawrence Erlbaum Associates Inc.
Chumlea, W.C. (1982) Physical growth in adolescence. In: Wolman, B.B. et al. (eds) *Handbook of Developmental Psychology* (pp. 471–485). Englewood Cliffs, NJ: Prentice Hall.
Coleman, J., & Hendry, L. (1990) *The Nature of Adolescence*, 2nd edn. London: Routledge.
Dorn, L.D., Crockett, L.J., & Petersen, A.C. (1988) The relations of

pubertal status to intrapersonal changes in young adolescents. *Journal of Early Adolescence*, 8: 405–419.

Egeland, J.A., & Hostetter, A.M. (1983) Amish study. I. Affective disorders among the Amish 1976–1980. *American Journal of Psychiatry*, 140: 56–61.

Farrell, C. (1978) *My Mother Said . . . The Way Young People Learn about Sex and Birth Control*. London: Routledge and Kegan Paul.

Fonagy, P., & Moran, G. (1991) Understanding psychic change in child psychoanalysis. *International Journal of Psycho-analysis*, 72: 639.

Freud, A. (1949) On certain difficulties in the pre-adolescent's relation to his parents. In: *The Writings of Anna Freud*, vol. 4, pp. 95–106. New York: International Universities Press.

Freud, A. (1958) Adolescence. *Psychoanalytic Study of the Child*, 13: 255–278.

Freud, S. (1905) Three essays on the theory of sexuality. Standard edition, vol. 7 (pp. 125–243). London: Hogarth Press.

Freud, S. (1923) The infantile genital organization of the libido. Standard edition, vol. 19 (pp. 155–170). London: Hogarth Press.

Frisch, R.E. (1990) The right weight: body fat, menarche and ovulation. *Balliere's Clinical Obstetrics and Gynaecology*, 4: 419–439.

Graham, P., & Rutter, M. (1985) Adolescent disorders. In: Rutter, M., & Hersov, L. (eds) *Child and Adolescent Psychiatry: Modern Approaches* (pp. 351–367). Oxford: Blackwell.

Gutton, P. (1998) The pubertal, its sources and fate. In: Perret-Catipovic, M., & Ladame, F. (eds) *Adolescence and Psycho-analysis*. London: Karnac.

Laufer, M. (1965) Assessment of adolescent disturbances – the application of Anna Freud's diagnostic profile. *Psychoanalytic Study of the Child*, 20: 99–123.

Laufer, M. (1968) The body image, the function of masturbation, and adolescence. *Psychoanalytic Study of the Child*, 23: 114–137.

Laufer, M. (1998) The central masturbation fantasy, the final sexual organization and adolescence. In: Perret-Catipovic, M., & Ladame, F. (eds) *Adolescence and Psycho-analysis*. London: Karnac.

Laufer, M., & Laufer, M.E. (1984) *Adolescence and Developmental Breakdown*. New Haven: Yale University Press.

Leffert, N., & Petersen, A.C. (1995) Patterns of development during adolescence. In: Rutter, M., & Smith, D.J. (eds) *Psychosocial disorders in young people*. Chichester, UK: Wiley.

Perret-Catipovic, M., & Ladame, F. (1998) Normality and pathology in adolescence. In: Perret-Catipovic, M., & Ladame, F. (eds) *Adolescence and Psycho-analysis*. London: Karnac.

Piaget, J. (1935) *Moral Judgements in the Child*. London: Routledge and Kegan Paul.

Piaget, J. (1950) *The Psychology of Intelligence*. London: Routledge and Kegan Paul.

Robins, L.N., & Hill, S.Y. (1966) Assessing the contributions of family structure, class and peer groups to juvenile delinquency. *Journal of Criminal Law, Criminology and Police Science*, 57: 325–334.

Rutter, M., Graham, P., Chadwick, O., & Yule, W. (1976) Adolescent turmoil; fact or fiction? *Journal of Child Psychology and Psychiatry*, 17: 35–36.

Rutter, M., & Hersov, L. (1985) *Child and Adolescent Psychiatry: Modern Approaches*. Oxford: Blackwell Scientific Publications.

Schofield, M. (1965) *The Sexual Behaviour of Young People*. Harmondsworth: Penguin.

Shapland, J.M. (1978) Self-reported delinquency in boys aged 11–14. *British Journal of Criminology*, 18: 255–266.

Simmons, R.G., & Blythe, D.A. (1987) *Moving Into Adolescence: The Impact of Pubertal Change & School Context*. New York: Aldine de Gruyter.

Simmons, R., Blythe, D., & McKinney, K. (1983) The social and psychological effects of puberty on white females. In: Brookes-Gunn, J., & Petersen, A.C. (eds) *Girls at Puberty; Biological and Psychosocial Perspectives* (pp. 229–272). New York: Plenum Press.

Tanner, J.M. (1989) *Foetus into Man: Physical Growth from Conception to Maturity*, 2nd edn. Ware, UK: Castlemead Publications.

Van Heeswyk, P. (1997) *Analysing adolescence*. London: Sheldon Press.

Wellings, K. et al. (1994) *Sexual Behaviour in Britain: The National Survey of Sexual Attitudes and Life Styles*. London: Penguin.

Wellings, K. et al. (2001) Sexual behaviour in Britain: early heterosexual experience. *The Lancet*, 358: 1835–1842.

Westin-Lindgren, G. (1982) Achievement and mental ability of physically late- and early-maturing schoolchildren related to their social background. *Journal of Child Psychology and Psychiatry*, 23: 407–420.

Winnicott, D.W. (1971) Contemporary concepts of adolescent development and their implications for higher education. In: Winnicott, D.W. (ed) *Playing and Reality*. London: Tavistock.

Chapter 10   Work, identity and love

Adorno, T., Fenkel-Brunswik, E., Lewinson, D.J., & Sanford, R.N. (1982). *The Authoritarian Personality*. New York: Norton.

Bazelgette, J. (1978) *School Life and Work Life: A Study of Transition in the Inner City*. London: Hutchinson.

Cahn, R. (1998) On becoming a subject. In: Perret-Catipovic, M., & Ladame, F. (eds) *Adolescence and Psycho-analysis*. London: Karnac.

Cameron, N. (1963) *Personality Development and Psychopathology*. Boston: Houghton Mifflin.

Carter, M. (1966) *Into Work*. London: Penguin.

Chasseguet-Smirgel, J. (1980) *Female Sexuality*. Ann Arbor, MI: University of Michigan Press.

Erikson, E.H. (1964) *Insight and Responsibility*. New York: Norton.

Erikson, E.H. (1968) *Identity, Youth and Crisis*. London: Faber.

Foucault, M. (1987) *The Uses of Pleasure; The History of Sexuality*, vol. 2. London: Penguin.

Freud, S. (1905) *Three Essays on Sexuality*. Standard edition, vol. XII. London: Hogarth Press.

Friedman, R., & Downey, J. (1993) Psychoanalysis, psychobiology, and homosexuality. *Journal of the American Psychoanalytical Association*, 41: 1159–1198.

Geer, J., Heinman, J., & Lentenberg, H. (1984) *Human Sexuality*. Englewood Cliffs, NJ: Prentice-Hall.

Holleran, A. (1983) *Dancer from the Dance*. New York: Bantam.

Laufer, M., & Laufer, M.E. (1984) *Adolescence and Developmental Breakdown*. Princeton, NJ: Yale University Press.

Lichenstein, H. (1977) *The Dilemma of Human Identity*. New York: Aronson.

Lynd, H.M. (1958) *Shame and the Search for Identity*. London: Routledge and Kegan Paul.

Masters, W.M., & Johnson, V.F. (1966) *The Human Sexual Response*. New York: Bantam.

Milner, M. (1957) *On Not Being Able to Paint*. London: Heinemann.

Robinson, P. (1989) *The Modernization of Sex*. Ithaca, NY: Cornell University Press.

Rosen, I. (1979) *Sexual Deviation*. Oxford: Oxford University Press.

Ruitenbeck, H.M. (1973) *Homosexuality*. London: Souvenir.

Scharff, D.E. (1982) *The Sexual Relationship*. London: Routledge and Kegan Paul.

Schofield, M. (1973) *Sexual Behaviour of Young Adults*. Harmondsworth: Penguin.

Shor, J., & Sanville, J. (1978) *Illusions in Loving*. Harmondsworth: Penguin.

Smelser, N., & Erikson, F. (1980) *Theories of Work and Love*. London: Grant McIntyre.

Stevens, T. (1979) *Adult Life Processes*. Palo Alto, CA: Mayfield.

Terkel, S. (1985) *Working*. Harmondsworth: Penguin.

Tiefer, L. (1983) *Human Sexuality*. London: Harper Row.

Tunnadine, I. (1983) *The Making of Love*. London: Jonathan Cape.

West, D.J. (1960) *Homosexuality*. Harmondsworth: Penguin.

White, R.W. (1975) *Lives in Progress*. New York: Holt Rinehart.

Winnicott, D.W. (1963) On Communication. In: *The Maturational Processes and the Facilitating Environment*. London: Institute of Psychoanalysis and Karnac Books.

Winnicott, D.W. (1971) Contemporary concepts of adolescent development and their implications for higher education. In: Winnicott, D.W. (ed) *Playing and Reality*. London: Tavistock.

Chapter 11 Partnership and marriage

Austen, J. (1813/1985) *Pride and Prejudice* (pp. 236–237). Harmondsworth: Penguin.

Boswell, J. (1791/1990) Life of Samuel Johnson. Cited in: Rubinstein, H. (ed) *The Oxford Book of Marriage*. Oxford: Oxford University Press.

Britton, R. (2000) On sharing psychic space. *Bulletin of the Society of Psychoanalytical Marital Psychotherapists*, 7: 10–16.

Clulow, C. (2001) Attachment, narcissism and the violent couple. In: Clulow, C. (ed) *Adult Attachment and Couple Psychotherapy. The 'Secure Base' in Practice and Research*. London: Brunner-Routledge.

Colman, W. (1993) Fidelity as a moral achievement. In: Clulow, C. (ed) *Rethinking Marriage: Public and Private Perspectives*. London: Karnac.

Gibran, K. (1926) *The Prophet*. London: Heinemann.

Giddens, A. (1992) *The Transformation of Intimacy. Sexuality, Love and Eroticism in Modern Societies*. Cambridge: Polity Press.

Haley, J. (ed.) (1985) Conversations with Milton H. Erickson. In: *Changing Couples*, vol. 2. New York: Triangle Press.

Hudson, J., & Jacob, B. (1991) *The Way Men Think: Intellect, Intimacy and the Erotic Imagination*. New Haven, CT: Yale University Press.

Mill, J.S. (1873/1989) *Autobiography*. Cited in: Mooney, B. (ed) *From This Day Forward. An Anthology of Marriage*. London: Murray.

Orbach, S. (1993) Women, men and intimacy. In: Clulow, C. (ed) *Rethinking Marriage: Public and Private Perspectives*. London: Karnac.

Powell, A. (1972) *Books Do Furnish a Room*. London: Heinemann.

The Stationery Office (2003) *National Statistics (2003). Social Trends, 33*. London: The Stationery Office.

Chapter 12 Parenthood

Anthony, E.J., & Benedek, T. (1970) *Parenthood*. Boston: Little Brown.

Borstein, M.H. (1995) *Handbook of Parenting*. Hove, UK: Lawrence Erlbaum Limited.

Brazelton, T.B. (1988) Stress for families today. *Infant Mental Health Journal*, 9: 65–71.

Brazelton, T.B., & Cramer, B. (1991) *The Earliest Relationship*. London: Karnac.

Byng-Hall, J. (1995) *Re-writing Family Scripts*. London: Guilford.

Carter, E.A., & McGoldrick, M. (1980) *The Family Life Cycle*. New York: Gardiner Press.

Clulow, C. (1982) *To Have and to Hold, Managing the First Baby*. London: Karnac.

Daws, D. (1993) *Through the Night: Helping Parents and Sleepless Infants*. London: Free Association.

Dunn, J. (1984) *Sisters and Brothers*. London: Fontana.

Fraiberg, S.H. (1977) *Every Child's Birthright*. New York: Basic Books.

Gorrell-Barnes, G., & Dowling, A. (1999) *Working with Children and Parents through Separation and Divorce: The Changing Lives of Children*. London: Macmillan.

Hollway, W., & Featherstone, B. (1997) *Mothering and Ambivalence*. New York: Guilford.

Murray, L., & Cooper, P. (1997) *Post-Partum Depression*. London: Guilford.

Oakley, A. (1974) *Housewife*. Harmondsworth: Penguin.

Oakley, A. (1979) *Becoming a Mother*. Oxford: Martin Robertson.

Parke, R.D. (1981) *Fathering*. London: Fontana.

Parker, G. (1983) *Parental Overprotection*. New York: Grune & Stratton.

Parker, R. (1995) *Torn in Two: Motherhood and Ambivalence*. London: Virago.

Ruszczynski, S., & Fisher, J. (eds) (1995) *Intrusiveness in the Couple*. London: Karnac.

Stern, D. (1995) *The Motherhood Constellation*. New York: Basic Books.

Trowell, J., & Bower, M. (1995) *The Emotional Needs of Young Children and Their Families*. London: Routledge.

Trowell, J., & Etchegoyen, A. (2002) *The Importance of Fathers*. London: Routledge.

Winnicott, D.W. (1964) *The Child, the Family and the Outside World*. Harmondsworth: Penguin.

Chapter 13 Being alone

Storr, A. (1988) *The School of Genius*. London: Andre Deutsch.

Winnicott, D.W. (1969) The capacity to be alone. In: *The Maturational Processes and the Facilitating Environment*. London: Hogarth Press.

Chapter 14 Mid-life

Erikson, E. (1968) *Childhood and Society*. London: Penguin Books.

Hildebrand, P. (1995) *Beyond Mid-life Crisis*. London: Sheldon Press.

Jaques, E. (1970) *Work, Creativity and Social Justice*. New York: International Universities Press.

Nemiroff, R., & Colarusso, C. (1985) *The Race Against Time: Psychotherapy and Psychoanalysis in the Second Half of Life*. New York: Plenum Press.

Neugaten, B., & Hagestad, G. (1976) Age and the life-course. In: Binstock, R., & Shanas, E. (eds) *Handbook of Ageing and the Social Sciences*. New York: Van Nostrand.

Chapter 15 Old age

Aitken, L.R. (2001) *Aging and Later Life: Growing Old in Modern Society*. Springfield, IL: Thomas.

Bromley, D.B. (1974) *The Psychology of Human Ageing*. Harmondsworth: Penguin.

Brubaker, T.H. (1983) *Family Relationships: Later Life*. Beverley Hills: Saga Press.

Burstock, R., & Shana, C. (1976) *Handbook of Ageing and the Social Sciences*. New York: Van Nostrand.

Erikson, E.H., Erikson, J.H., & Kivnik, H.Q. (1995) *Vital Involvement in Old Age*. New York: Norton.

Matte-Blanco, I. (1975) *The Unconscious as Infinite Sets: An Essay in Bi-logic*. London: Duckworth.

Neugarten, B.C. (1968) *Middle Age and Aging*. Chicago: University of Chicago Press.

Nolan, M. (2001) *Working Older People and their Families*. Maidenhead, UK: Open University Press.

Nusbaum, P.D. (1997) *Handbook of Neuropsychology of Aging*. London: Plenum Press.

Rayner, E. (1995) *Unconscious Logic*. London: Routledge.

Townsend, P. (1963) *The Family Life of Old People*. Harmondsworth: Penguin.

Chapter 16 Dying, grief and mourning

Berlinsky, E., & Biller, H. (1982) *Parental Death and Psychological Development*. Lexington: Lexington Books.

Bowlby, J. (1979) *The Making and Breaking of Affectional Bonds*. London: Tavistock Clinic.

Furman, E. (1980) *A Child's Parent Dies*. London: Yale University Press.

Gorer, G. (1965) *Death, Grief and Mourning in Contemporary Britain*. London: Cresset.

Harris, M. (1995) *The Loss is for Ever: The Lifelong Impact of the Early Death of a Mother or Father*. New York: Dutton.

Hinton, J. (1967) *Dying*. Harmondsworth: Penguin.

Kavanagh, R.E. (1972) *Facing Death*. Harmondsworth: Penguin.

Kubler-Ross, E. (1975) *Death, the Final Stage of Growth*. London: Prentice-Hall.

Langer, M. (1957) *Learning to Live as a Widow*. New York: Gilbert Press.

McNeill, T. (1983) *Living with Loss*. London; Fontana.

Parker, C., & Weiss, R. (1983) *Recovery from Bereavement*. New York: Basic Books.

Parkes, C.M. (1972) *Bereavement*. Harmondsworth: Penguin.

Schneideman, E.S. (ed.) (1984) *Death. Current Perspectives*. Palo Alto, CA: Mayfield.

Stott, M. (1973) *Forgetting's No Excuse*. London: Faber.

Worden, J.W. (1996) *Children and Grief: When a Parent Dies*. New York: Guildford.

Index

abandonment 196–7
abstract ideas: absence from concrete operational thought 157; adolescents' 165; expression in terms of bodily functions 284–5
abuse, childhood 132, 138–9, 225, 238, 254, 256
accommodation 243–4
active 'I' 91
adaptation 57–9, 61
addiction 175
adolescence 104, 162–78, 238–9; and body image 170–1; crisis of 164, 165–6, 169–70, 179; developmental tasks of 162–3; as discontinuity in development 172–6; disturbances of 166–7, 176; 'getting organized' 176–8, 212; ideas on mortality 269; individuation of 196; industriousness of 159–60; necessary immaturity of 211–12; onset 162, 163, 167; parental relationships during 160; peer relations during 177; pubertal and 171–2; rebellion of 161; sexuality 162, 164–5, 167–73, 175, 198; 'storm and stress' conceptualization of 167, 176; termination of 162, 163
'adolescing' 163, 164, 195–6, 200
adult attachment interview 66

adulthood: achieving 163, 165, 177–8; anal fantasies of 102; and play 117–18, 128–9; stages of 266; *see also* marriage; midlife; old age; parents
affective disorders 174–5; *see also specific disorders*
age of majority 180, 181
ageism 272
agency 50
aggression, infantile 43, 54–5
Ainsworth, Mary 65
Aitken, K. 50
Albee, Edward 221
alienation 46
all-or-nothing responses: in babies 60–1; in love 169, 198, 199–200; in three to five year olds 139, 140; in toddlers 77, 84–5
Alzheimer's disease 283–5
ambition 194–5
ambivalence: childhood 84–5, 111–13, 140, 246; marital 214, 223; paternal 17–18
Amish people 174
amodal perception 34–5
anal fantasies 99–101
anal intercourse 204
anal period 96–7; *see also* toddlers, two to three years old
anal personalities 102
anal–sadistic excitation 155
anal–sadistic phase 100